T0262976

Preface

This directory was compiled partly out of a feeling of frustration from coming across an ever-increasing number of unfamiliar acronyms and abbreviations while reading trade journals, manufacturers' documents, and research reports. In an attempt to keep up with trends in the computer and related disciplines, I began writing down unfamiliar terms on scratch pads. Soon the pads became too numerous and too cumbersome to use, and the list was put on line to a computer. Eventually it became evident that a database management system (DBMS) was required to make the accessing, updating, and printing of the list more practical. This book is the result of that effort.

For a work such as this, the primary purpose is to provide a ready reference for readers and writers of technical material to quickly look up unfamiliar acronyms. To this end, it will be of considerable use not only to those in technological fields, especially when they come into contact with fields outside their own area of specialty, but also to executives and managers who are not necessarily directly connected to the technical aspects of their respective fields. A second purpose for such a collection is to provide a means of determining whether a newly proposed acronym is already in common use. By avoiding the adoption of acronyms that are already "taken," it should be possible to prevent ambiguity and confusion.

The database that gave rise to this directory is maintained on line and updated continually. Considerable effort was made to expand the acronyms and credit their sources with a high degree of accuracy. As with any documentation, some errors are bound to have occurred. Corrections and additions will be gratefully received by the editor, provided that the items submitted are accompanied by appropriate source citations.

Reference works are usually the result of the combined efforts of many people. It would be virtually impossible to credit all of the individuals who contributed their expertise. Special thanks go to Mr. George Chastain, who helped me get serious with Waterloo Script coding, and to Mr. Allen Daugherty and to Mr. Jerry Burchard for their invaluable OBS WYLBUR expertise. I will be forever indebted to Mr. Jeffrey Brooks for imparting his wisdom in solving intricate Waterloo Script coding puzzles, and for system-related advice. Special thanks to Mr. Jay Justice for supplying the expansions for a number of acronyms that would otherwise have been eliminated. All of the preceding individuals are associated with WVNET.

Thanks also to Mr. Jeffrey Fritz of West Virginia University for contributions in the communications area, to Dr. W. M. Grant of West Virginia University for invaluable assistance in English mechanics, and to Dr. Carolyn Nelson, also at West Virginia University, for suggestions.

Not to be forgotten are Ms. Ruth Dawe, Mr. Andrew Berin, Mr. Henry Boehm, and other patient and understanding associates of Marcel Dekker, Inc., who contributed significantly in editing the manuscript and who allowed me to extend submission due dates without pressure.

For those who contributed and are not recognized individually, my profound apologies, but many thanks.

David Tavaglione

Explanatory Notes

Scope

The main body of this volume, as the title implies, consists of acronyms and abbreviations, primarily of computer software and hardware, communications devices and systems, and general technological methodology. Some organizational abbreviations have been included because of their unique relationship to these fields (e.g., *FCC, NTIS, ISO*). Also included are some corporate and proprietary acronyms or abbreviations that have become commonplace terminology in one area while remaining unfamiliar in another, for example, *PTAT-1*. Certain abbreviations are based on the same root, distinguished only by a numerical suffix. (Examples are *X.25, V.28,* and *LU6.2*.) The derived abbreviations may be formed by adoption of the parent committee name, recommendation report paragraph number, system description designator, and so forth, and result in a number of related, often sequential, acronyms or abbreviations. The superfluous acronyms were deleted to conserve space. Those appearing in the directory were deemed by the editor as having a particularly influential impact on the field.

Some acronyms are frequently used in more than one form. In the interest of consistency, the most widely accepted form appears as the primary entry, whereas other forms appear as alternate forms or variants. An example is *dB* for *decibel*, as opposed to *db*, which appears frequently in the literature but is not widely accepted as the "standard."

While the original intent of this directory was to contain only terms common to usage in the United States, it has become increasingly clear that some international terms and organizations that are in very common usage in this country should also be included. Indeed, some abbreviations appear to have become accepted as international standards. Special symbols such as Greek or German letters and italic characters (such as are used in mathematical and technological texts) are not included in this work. Some excellent texts that contain these special symbols are listed in Appendix B.

Many acronyms are commonly expanded into more than one form, for example, *System* and *Systems, Communication* and *Communications.* The forms appearing in this handbook are the ones most commonly used. In some cases, two distinct words are used for the same acronym. For example, *System* is used interchangeably with *Server* as the last word in the acronym *NFS.* In such cases, the alternate word is enclosed in parentheses. Where there is some doubt that two acronyms are one and the same, both acronyms are listed separately.

Alphabetization

Sorting was accomplished using a combination of traditional and electronic methods. The IBM Extended Binary Coded Decimal Interchange Code (EBCDIC) places lower-case alphabetic characters before upper-case characters, producing a nontraditional sequence.

Primary sorting strictly by EBCDIC order results in lower-case letters appearing before upper-case letters. For example, *uHz (microhertz)* appears before *A (Ampere)*, a most unsettling and unacceptable situation. Disregarding case altogether, and sorting strictly by EBCDIC order, produces an interlacing of lower- and upper-case acronyms. This results in a less-than-aesthetically-pleasing appearance of the list due to the fact that secondary sorting occurs in the description column. For example, disregarding case altogether produces

F	Farad
f	femto
F	Force
f	Frequency

whereas including case consideration produces

f	femto
f	frequency
F	Farad
F	Force

The order produced by sole employment of either the EBCDIC electronic or totally case-independent sorting technique would undoubtedly be viewed by a lexicographer (and the editor) as inconsistent. For this reason, the decision was made to use special processing of the data in order to produce consistent, aesthetically pleasing lexicographic order. The final result is summarized as follows:

1. Special characters (punctuation and "nationals") are treated as blanks. The result is that the portion of the acronym/abbreviation appearing before the special character sorts as though it were a separate entity. For example, *I/O* precedes *IA*, and *DS-3* precedes *DSA*.
2. Mixed lower- and upper-case characters are alphabetically arranged with lower-case preceding upper-case where both cases of the same letter appear in the same position of the acronym. For example, *Mb (Megabit)* precedes *MB (Megabyte)*, and *mW (milliwatt)* precedes *MW (Megawatt)*.
3. Numerics appear last in the sequence. For example, *ZSL* precedes *10Base-T*.
4. Identical acronyms are ordered according to the description column, to which the foregoing rules of alphabetization also apply.

Implied and Nonrepresented Elements

Occasionally, an acronym implies additional wording whose letters do not appear in the acronym itself, or the description contains clarifying information. These words or elements appear in the description in square brackets. For example,

NTN   Neutralized Twisted Nematic [LCD]

In some terms, the characters do not stand for anything individually although they function collectively as a name. These terms are indicated with a dash (−) in the description column, for example, *−X/Open*.

Cross-Referencing Conventions

Cross-references are used to clarify or expand on the identification of certain acronyms. The following cross-referencing conventions are used:

alternate form A secondary, or variant, form. A "see" reference directs the reader to the primary, or preferred, form. The cross-referenced acronym is italicized but not expanded.

BALUN   Balanced to Unbalanced [adapter/coupler]
Alternate form; see *balun*

compare with   Used for closely related acronyms, often sharing a
               common root or base acronym. The cross-referenced
               acronym is italicized and expanded.

               DRAM   Dynamic Random Access Memory
                            Compare with *SRAM, Static Random
                            Access Memory*

inverse of   Used for acronyms whose relationship is complementary
               or opposite. The cross-referenced acronym is italicized
               and expanded.

               CS   Continue Specific
                            Inverse of *CA, Continue Any*

re   "Refers to" or "in reference to." Clarifies for the reader
               the larger or more general subject or term to which the
               acronym refers.

               SMT   Station Management
                            re: Fiber-distributed data interface
                            (FDDI) standard

sa (see also) Additional information is available or a portion of the
               acronym is included as an entry elsewhere. The cross-
               referenced acronym is italicized and usually expanded.

               AAL   ATM Adaption Layer
                            sa *ATM, Asynchronous Transfer Mode*

see   The acronym is valid, but the reader is directed to a
               preferred or more widely used form. Often used in
               conjunction with such qualifying terms as "alternate
               form," "archaic," "variant," etc. The cross-referenced
               acronym is italicized but not expanded.

               USASCII   USA ASCII
                            Archaic; see *ASCII*

which see   The referenced item is contained elsewhere in more or
               clarifying detail. The referenced item is italicized and is
               usually expanded.

               EC   Echo Cancel
                            re: *ISDN*, which see

Acronyms are often composites of other acronyms, consisting usually of a root or base acronym and a prefix, suffix, or other appropriate modifier acronym. All such acronyms appearing as main entries are expanded in full.

DMOSFET   Double-diffused Metal Oxide
Semiconductor Field-Effect Transistor

Sometimes the *expansion* of an acronym contains other, secondary acronyms. In such cases, the secondary acronyms are not expanded, although they usually appear as main entries elsewhere in the directory.

DCFL   Direct-Coupled FET Logic

Accuracy

Proofreading of this collection has proven to be a real challenge. Some acronyms are commonly used in *both* upper-case and lower-case. The two acronyms can conceivably be sorted in nonadjacent positions, making elimination of duplicates difficult. There are a few acronyms that are used in both cases so universally that they defy editing. These have been included in both forms along with the appropriate cross-references.

Virtually all of the sources indicated are certain. However a few have been entered by a "consensus" of opinion as opposed to absolute certainty. An ellipsis (. . .) indicates sources that are obscure. A question mark is used to indicate unknown or questionable data.

Some of the sources appear in abbreviated form. The fully expanded form of some of the sources has been lost over the years. Information regarding these sources will be gratefully received and entered into future editions.

Contents

Acronyms and Abbreviations

a	atto	. . .
	Prefix for 10^{-18}	
A	A [battery, or supply]	. . .
	Designation given to represent the primary battery or power supply of radios, etc.; usually used to provide power to vacuum tube filaments	
A	Absolute	. . .
	Temperature scale with increments equal in size to the Celsius scale, and in which zero degrees absolute is reached when all molecular motion ceases	
A	Adenosine	. . .
	A compound important in biochemistry; a component of *DNA*, which see	
A	Ampere	. . .
	Unit of current flow	
	Named in honor of French physicist André Marie Ampère (1775–1836)	
A	Angstrom	. . .
	Alternate form; see $\overset{\circ}{A}$	

Å	Angstrom	. . .
	Metric unit of length, $= 10^{-8}$ cm	
	Named in honor of Swedish physicist	
	Anders Jonas Ångström (1814–1874)	
A/D	Analog to Digital	. . .
	Alternate form; see *ADC*	
A/UX	Apple UNIX	Apple
A-V	Audio-Visual	. . .
	Sometimes designated by *AV*	
AA	AA [cell]	. . .
	Voltaic cell, measuring approximately 0.65″	
	diameter by 2″ long	
AA	Arithmetic Average	IEEE
AA	Auto Answer	. . .
AAA	AAA [cell]	. . .
	Voltaic cell, measuring approximately 0.4″	
	diameter by 1.75″ long	
AAcS	Advanced Academic System	IBM
AACS	Airways and Air Communications Service	US Army
	Formerly *Army Airways Communications*	
	Service (prior to 1946)	
AAL	Absolute Assembly Language	. . .
AAL	ATM Adaption Layer	. . .
	sa *ATM, Asynchronous Transfer Mode*	
AAM	Air-to-Air Missile	US Air Force
AAMRS	Automated Ambulatory Medical Record	. . .
	System	
AARP	AppleTalk Address Resolution Protocol	Apple
AAS	Advanced Automation System	FAA
	Continuously updated air traffic tracking	
	display	
AAS	Arithmetic Assignment Statement	. . .
AASF	Advanced Address Space Facility	IBM
AATC	Automatic Air Traffic Control [system]	. . .
AAV	Alternate Access Vendor	. . .
ABBS	Apple-Based Bulletin Board Service	. . .
ABC	Accounting By Computer	Dome
ABC	Advanced Blade Concept	Ames Res. Ctr.
	re: Helicopter rotors	
ABC	Automatic Bandwidth Control	IEEE
ABC	Automatic Brightness Control	IEEE
ABEND	Abnormal Ending	. . .
	re: Computer technology; abnormal	
	termination of a program or other	
	processing sequence	
ABEP	Advanced Burst Error Processor	AMD

ABI	Application Binary Interface	AT&T
ABM	Accunet Bandwidth Manager	AT&T
	sa *Accunet*	
ABM	Anti-Ballistic Missile	DoD
ABM	Asynchronous Balance Mode	IBM
	re: *HDLC, High-Level Data Link Control*	
ABR	Automatic Backup Restore	Innovation
ABRD	Auto Baud Rate Detector	. . .
ABS	Acrylonitrile Butadiene Styrene	. . .
	A polymer widely used in the electronics idustry	
ABT	Automatic Bench Test	. . .
Ac	Actinium	. . .
	Atomic element number 89	
AC	Access Control	IEEE
	Field in IEEE 802.5 token ring data communications specification sa *IEEE, Institute of Electrical and Electronics Engineers*	
AC	Alternating Current	. . .
AC	Analog Computer	. . .
AC&WS	Air Control and Warning System	. . .
ACA	Adjacent Channel Attenuation	IEEE
ACA	Alternating Current Amperes	. . .
ACA	Application Control Architecture	. . .
ACAMI	Alternate Channel/Alternate Mark Inversion	. . .
ACAP	Automatic Circuit Analysis Program	. . .
ACAS	Airborne Collision-Avoidance System	. . .
ACB	Access [method] Control Block	IBM
ACCAP	Autocoder to COBOL Conversion and Program	IBM
	sa *COBOL, Common Business Oriented Language*	
ACCEL	Automated Circuit Card Etching Layout	IEEE
ACCESS	Aircraft Communication Electronic Signalling System	IEEE
ACCESS	Automatic Computer-Controlled Electronic Scanning System	IEEE
Accunet	Accunet	AT&T
	Digital service network	
ACD	Automatic Call Director	AT&T
	(The device)	
ACD	Automatic Call Distribution	AT&T
	(The system)	
ACE	Adapter Communication Executive	TI
ACE	Advanced Computing Environment	. . .

ACE	Adverse Channel Enhancement	Microcom
ACE	Animated Computer Education	. . .
ACE	Application Construction Environment	Computer Associates
ACE	Application Control Environment	Cohen, G., Info. Bldrs.
ACE	Array Contactless EPROM EPROM integrated circuit (IC) structure without metal contacts sa *EPROM, Eraseable Programmable Read Only Memory*	TI
ACE	Automatic Calculating Engine Early (c.1946) electronic computer	. . .
ACE	Automatic Computer Evaluation	IEEE
ACF	Advanced Communication Function Pertains to software for the IBM 3705 Communications Controller	IBM
ACFNET	Advanced Communication Function Network	IBM
ACG	Addressed Command Group re: IEEE Standard 488; sa *IEEE*	IEEE
ACGIH	American Conference of Governmental Industrial Hygienists	ACGIH
ACH	Automated ClearingHouse	. . .
ACI	Advanced Chip Interconnect	S3
ACI	Automatic Card Identification	IEEE
ACID	Accessor Identification	Computer Associates
ACID	Automatic Classification and Identification of Data	IEEE
ACK	Acknowledge Transmission control 6 (TC_6) under CCITT Recommendation V.3 sa *TC_n, Transmission Control$_n$,* and *RFNM, Ready for Next Message*	CCITT
ACL	Access Control Language (for Network/440)	IBM
ACL	Access Control List	. . .
ACL	Advanced CMOS Logic sa *CMOS, Complementary Metal Oxide Semiconductor*	VTC
ACL	Application Control Language	IEEE
ACL	Automatic Cartridge Loader	Memorex Telex
ACLS	All-Weather Carrier Landing System	US Navy
ACM	Association for Computing Machinery	ACM
ACMS	Application Control and Management System	DEC

ACO	Auto Call Originate Pertains to the IBM 3705 Communications Controller	IBM
ACP	Acyl Carrier Protein A compound important in biochemistry	. . .
ACP	Advanced Computational Processor	Sylvania
ACP	Airline Control Program	. . .
ACP	Ancillary Control Process	DEC
ACPS	Attitude Control Propulsion System	NASA
ACR	Airfield Control Radar	IEEE
ACRTC	Advanced Cathode-Ray Tube Controller	. . .
ACRV	Assured Crew Return Vehicle	NASA
ACS	Access Control Set	. . .
ACS	Advanced Communications Service	AT&T
ACS	Advanced Concepts Simulator	NASA
ACS	Alternating Current Synchronous	IEEE
ACS	Assembly Control System	IBM
ACS	Attitude Control System	IEEE
ACS	Automated Cartridge System	STC
ACS	Automatic Call Sequencer	. . .
ACS	Auxilliary Core Storage	. . .
ACSE	Application Common Service Element	. . .
ACSE	Association Control Service Element	. . .
ACSL	Advanced Continuous Simulation Language	MGA
ACSU	Advanced Channel Service Unit	. . .
ACT	Acoustic Charge Transport	. . .
ACT	Advanced Composites Technology	NASA
ACT	Advanced Computing Technology	MC&T
ACT	Algebraic Compiler and Translator	. . .
ACT	Applied Computerized Telephony	H-P
ACT	Automatic Code Translation	IEEE
ACTO	Automatic Computing Transfer Oscillator	IEEE
ACTRAN	Autocoder to COBOL Translator sa COBOL, Common Business Oriented Language	. . .
ACTS	Advanced Communications Technology Satellite	NASA
ACTV	Advanced Compressed Television	. . .
ACU	Address Control Unit	. . .
ACU	Arithmetic and Control Unit	IEEE
ACU	Automatic Calling Unit	. . .
ACUTA	Association of College and University Telecommunications Administrators	ACUTA
ACV	Alternating Current Volts	. . .
AD	Applications Development	IBM
AD/CYCLE	Applications Development/Cycle	IBM

Ada	Ada	DoD
	Programming language developed by the U.S. Department of Defense (DoD). Named in honor of English mathematician Lady Ada Lovelace (1815–1852), who helped complete development of Babbage's *analytical engine* and who is generally acknowledged as "the world's first programmer"	
ADA	Automatic Data Acquisition	IEEE
ADABAS	Adaptable Database	Software AG
	Data base management system	
ADAM	Advanced Direct-Landing Apollo Mission	NASA
ADAM	Automatic Distance and Angle Measurement	IEEE
ADAMS	Automatic Dynamic Analysis of Mechanical Systems	M D
ADAPS	Automatic Display and Plotting System	IEEE
ADaPSO	Association of Data Processing Service Organizations	. . .
ADAR	Advanced Design Array Radar	IEEE
ADARTS	Ada-based Design Approach for Real-Time Systems	SPC
ADARTS	Automated Data Retrieval Technical System	US Army
ADAS	Architecture Design and Assessment System	Cadre
	Disk space allocation system	
ADAS	Automatic Data Acquisition System	IEEE
ADB	Apple Desktop Bus	Apple
ADC	Air Data Computer	. . .
ADC	Airborne Digital Computer	IEEE
ADC	Analog to Digital Converter	. . .
ADC	Automatic Data Collection	IEEE
ADCCP	Advanced Data Communications Control Procedure	ANSI
ADCR	Alternate Destination Call Redirection	AT&T
ADCSP	Advanced Defense Communications Satellite Program	DoD
ADCU	Advanced Data Communications Utility	IBM
ADCU	Association of Data Communications Users	ADCU
ADD	Advanced Digital Diagnosis	Wayne Kerr
ADDAR	Automatic Digital Data Acquisition and Recording	IEEE
ADDAS	Automatic Digital Data Assembly System	IEEE
ADDDS	Automatic Direct Distance Dialing System	AT&T
	Now commonly referred to as *DDD*	
ADE	Applications Development Engineering	. . .
ADE	Applications Development Environment	IBM

ADE	Automated Design Engineering	IEEE
ADE	Automated Drafting Equipment	IEEE
ADES	Automatic Digital Encoding System	IEEE
ADF	Airborne Direction Finder	IEEE
ADF	Application Development Facility For use under IMS/VS sa *IMS, Information Management System* and *VS, Virtual Storage*	IBM
ADF	Automatic Direction Finder	IEEE
ADF	Automatic Document Feeder	. . .
ADI	Attitude Director Indicator	IEEE
ADIF	Analog Data Information Format	Tektronix
ADIOS	Automatic Digital Input-Output System	IEEE
ADIS	Air Defense Integrated System	IEEE
ADIS	Automatic Data Interchange System	IEEE
ADIT	Analog-Digital Integration Translator	IEEE
ADIX	Advanced Digital Information Exchange	Iwatsu America
ADL	Applications Development Language	. . .
ADL	Automated Disk Library	Kodak
ADL	Automatic Data Link	IEEE
ADM	Adaptive Delta Modulation	. . .
ADM	Add-Drop Multiplexer	. . .
ADMA	Advanced Direct Memory Access	. . .
ADMD	Administrative Management Domain	. . .
ADMIRE	Automatic Diagnostic Maintenance Information Retrieval	IEEE
ADMS	Automatic Data Message Switching	IEEE
ADMSC	Automatic Digital Message Switching Center	IEEE
ADN	Advanced Digital Network	Pacific Bell
ADO	Address Only [transfer] re: VME bus data transfer; sa *VME, Virtual* *Memory Extended*	. . .
ADOC	Air Defense Operation Center	US Air Force
ADONIS	Automatic Digital On-Line Instrumentation System	IEEE
ADP	Adenosine 5′-Diphosphate A compound important in biochemistry	. . .
ADP	Airborne Data Processor	. . .
ADP	Automatic Data Processing	IBM
ADPC	Automatic Data Processing Center	. . .
ADPCM	Adaptive Differential Pulse Code Modulation	. . .
ADPE	Auxilliary Data Processing Equipment	. . .
ADPSO	Automatic Data Processing Selection Office	US Navy
ADRAC	Automatic Digital Recording and Control	IEEE
ADRMP	Automatic Dialer Recorded Message Player	. . .
ADRS	Analog-to-Digital Data Recording System	IEEE

ADS	Agency Data System	Amer. Air.
ADS	Application Development System	Computer Associates
ADS	Automated Design System	Microsoft
ADS	Automatic Dependent Surveillance	FAA
	An air traffic monitoring system	
ADS	Avion Development System	Avion
ADSC	Automatic Digital Switching Center	IEEE
ADSS	Accelerated Data Storage Subsystem	Bull HN Info. Sys.
ADT	Address Data Transceiver	. . .
ADT	Automated Data Transfer	. . .
ADTS	Automated Driver License Testing System	Bull HN Info. Sys.
ADU	Asynchronous Data Unit	AT&T
ADU	Automatic Dialing Unit	IBM
ADW	Application Development Workbench	KnowledgeWare
ADX	Automatic Data Exchange	. . .
AE	Application Entity	. . .
AE	Arithmetic Element	. . .
AEA	American Electronics Association	AEA
AEC	Atomic Energy Commission	AEC
	Now the *NRC, Nuclear Regulatory Commission*	
AED	Automated Engineering Design	. . .
AEL	Accessible Emission Limit	. . .
	re: classes of lasers	
AEN	Asynchronous Event Notification	ANSI
	re: ANSI SCSI-2 standard; sa *ANSI, American National Standards Institute* and *SCSI, Small Computer Systems Interface*	
AES	Atomic Emission Spectroscopy	. . .
AESA	Active Electronically Scanned Array	. . .
	re: Radar antenna technology	
AEW	Airborne Early Warning	. . .
AF	Advanced Function	IBM
AF	Audio Frequency	. . .
	20 Hz–20 kHz	
AFATDS	Advanced Field Artillary Tactical Data System	US Army
AFC	Automatic Frequency Control	. . .
AFCAC	Air Force Computer Acquisition Center	US Air Force
AFCC	Air Force Communications Command	US Air Force
AFDAS	Accunet Flexible Digital Access Service	. . .
	sa *Accunet*	
AFE	Aeroassist Flight Experiment	NASA
AFF	Automatic Frequency Follower	. . .

AFG	Advanced Frame Grabber	Imaging Technology
AFIPS	American Federation of Information Processing Societies	AFIPS
AFIS	Automated Fingerprint Identification System	FBI
AFM	Atomic Force Microscope	. . .
AFM	Automated Flexible Manufacturing	. . .
AFN	Advanced Fractional Networking Routing and management services for fractional T1 (FT1) communications	AT&T
AFP	Advanced Function Printing	Intel
AFP	AppleTalk Filing Protocol	Apple
AFPDS	Advanced Function Printing DataStream	IBM
AFRSI	Advanced Flexible Reusable Surface Insulation Thermal protection system for NASA's Space Shuttle	NASA
AFRTS	American Forces Radio and Television Service	AFRTS
AFS	Andrew File System	CMU
AFSCC	Air Force Super Computer Center	US Air Force
AFT	Automated Funds Transfer	. . .
Ag	Argentum Symbol for *silver*, atomic element number 47	. . .
AGC	Automatic Gain Control	. . .
AGHF	Advanced Gradient Heating Facility	Soterem
AGS	Alternating Gradient Synchrotron	. . .
AGV	Automatic Guided Vehicle	. . .
Ah	Ampere-hour Also designated by *AH*	. . .
AH	Ampere-Hours Alternate form; see *Ah*	. . .
AHARS	Altitude Heading and Reference System	Honeywell
AHDL	ABLE Hardware Description Language	Data I/O
AHIP	ARPANET Host Interface Protocol sa *ARPANET, Advanced Research Projects Agency Network*	DoD
AI	Artificial Intelligence	. . .
AIC	Analog Interface Circuit	TI
AIIM	Association for Information and Image Management	AIIM
AIM	Accunet Information Manager sa *Accunet*	AT&T
AIM	Adaptive Inference Machine	. . .
AIM	Astrometric Interferometry Mission Part of NASA's *Great Observatory Program, GOP*, which see	NASA

AIM	Asynchronous Interface Module	AT&T
AIN	Advanced Intelligent Network	Bell Atlantic
AIPC	Army Information Processing Center	US Army
AIPR	Applied Imagery Pattern Recognition	. . .
AIRES	Automated Information Retrieval and Expert System	US Army
AIS	Adaptive Imaging System	Odetics
AIS	Alarm Indication Signal	Tau-Tron
AIT	Advanced Information Technology	UK
AIX	Advanced Interactive Executive	IBM
	UNIX Operating system for IBM's RT PC (RISC) sa *RT, Real-Time, PC, Personal Computer,* and *RISC, Reduced Instruction Set Computer*	
AJTVS	Avalanch Junction Transient Voltage Suppressor	. . .
Al	Aluminum	. . .
	Atomic element number 13	
AL	Analog Loop	. . .
Ala	Alanine	. . .
	A compound important in biochemistry	
ALBO	Automatic Line Build-Out	. . .
	re: T1 communications technology; sa *T1*	
ALC	Air Logistics Center	US Air Force
ALC	Amplitude Limiting Circuit	. . .
ALC	Audio Level Control	. . .
ALC	Automatic Level Control	. . .
ALC	Automatic Light Control	. . .
	re: Operation of video camera devices	
ALD	Automated Logic Diagram	IBM
ALE	Adaptive Line Enhancer	. . .
	re: A mathematical analog elctronic circuit signal filtering technique	
ALGOL	Algorithmic Language	. . .
ALI	Automatic Link Intelligence	Symplex
ALI	Automatic Location Identification	. . .
ALOSH	Appalachian Laboratory for Occupational Safety and Health	CDC
ALS	Advanced Light Source	LBL
	A "third generation" synchrotron	
ALS	Advanced Low-Power Schottky	. . .
	re: High-speed integrated circuit (IC) technology sa *S, Schottky*	
ALT	Accelerated Life Test	. . .
ALT	Alternate [mode]	. . .
ALU	Arithmetic Logic Unit	. . .

ALV	Autonomous Land Vehicle	NASA
Am	Americium	...
	Atomic element number 95	
AM	Algorithm Model	...
AM	Amplitude Modulation	...
AM/FM	Amplitude Modulation/Frequency Modulation	...
AM/FM	Automated Mapping for Facilities Management	...
AMANet	American Medical Association Network	AMA
AMC	Automatic Modulation Control	...
AMDMA	Adaptive Message Division Multiple Access LAN access protocol	Applitek
AME	Angle Measuring Equipment	...
AMHS	Automated Message Handling System	DoD
AMI	Alternate Mark Inversion	...
AMICUS	Automated Management Information Civil User System	US Dept. of Justice
AMIS	Acquisition Management Information System	US Air Force
AMIS	Audio Messaging Interchange Specification Voice messaging standard	AMIS
AMIS	Automated Management Information System	VA
AML	Application Macro Language	...
AMLCD	Active-Matrix Liquid Crystal Display	...
AMM	Analog Measurement Module	...
AMOS	Air Force Maui Optical Station	US Air Force
AMOS	Automated Manpower On-Line Scheduling	IPPG
AMOSLIB	Air Force Maui Optical Station Library	US Air Force
AMP	Adenosine 5'-Monophosphate A compound important in biochemistry	...
AMP	Asymmetrical Multiprocessor(-ing)	DEC
AMPS	Advanced Mobile Phone Service Utilized in cellular radio installations	AT&T
AMR	Automatic Meter Reading	...
AMRF	Automated Manufacturing Research Facility	NIST
AMS	Access Method Services	IBM
AMS	Account Management System	...
AMS	Active Mirror Servo Control system for a telescope secondary mirror	...
AMS	Advanced Memory System	...
AMS	Advanced Monitor System	DEC
AMT	Advanced Manufacturing Technology	...
AMTOR	Amateur Teleprinting Over Radio	IARN
amu	atomic mass unit 1 amu = 1.6600 × 10⁻²⁴ gram	...

ANA	Automated Network Analyzer	. . .
	re: Electronic networks	
ANCOVA	Analysis of Co-Varience	. . .
AND	AND [circuit or logic gate]	. . .
	Electronic circuit which exhibits the Boolean AND logic function	
ANI	Advanced Network Integration	. . .
ANI	Automatic Number Identification	. . .
ANL	American National [Standard] Labels	ASCII
ANL	Automatic Noise Limiter	. . .
ANM	Advanced Network Manager	. . .
ANOVA	Analysis of Variance	. . .
	A statistical package	
ANS	American National Standard	ANSI
ANSI	American National Standards Institute	ANSI
ANT	Alternate Number Translation	AT&T
ANTC	Advanced Networking Test Center	. . .
ANUNEWS	Australian National University News [network]	ANU
AO	Abort Output	DoD
	A TELNET command; sa *TELNET, Telecommunications Network*	
AO	Acousto-Optic	. . .
AOA	Angle of Arrival	. . .
	Radar signal parameter	
AOCS	Attitude and Orbit Control System	. . .
	re: Satellite control	
AOE	Application Operating Environment	AT&T
AOEF	Automated Operations Extension Facility	IBM
AOI	AND OR INVERT [circuit or logic gate]	TI
	Electronic circuit which exhibits a combination of the Boolean AND and OR functions with inverted output	
AOI	Automated Operator Interface	IBM
AOI	Automated Optical Inspection	. . .
AOL	Application Oriented Language	. . .
AOS	Advanced Operating System	Data General
AOS	Alternate Operator Service	. . .
AOS	Automated Operating System	EDS
AOS/VS	Advanced Operating System/Virtual Storage	Data General
AOSO	Advanced Orbiting Solar Observatory	NASA
AOTF	Acousto-Optical Tunable Filter	. . .
AOTV	Aeroassisted Orbital Transfer Vehicle	NASA
AP	Application Process (or Program)	. . .
AP	Application Profile	. . .
AP	Applications Protocol	. . .

APA	All Points Addressable	IBM
APAR	Authorized Program Analysis Report	IBM
APAS	ADABAS Performance Analysis System	Software AG
	sa *ADABAS*; *Adaptable Database*	
APC	Adaptive Predictive Coding	. . .
APC	Automated Production Control	Computer Associates
APC	Automatic Phase Control	. . .
APD	Avalanche Photo Diode	. . .
APDU	Application Protocol Data Unit	. . .
APE	Annealed Proton Exchange	U.T.P.
	re: Optical phase modulation technology United Technologies Photonics	
APF	Authorized Program Facility	IBM
API	Application Program Interface	IBM
APL	A Programming Language	IBM
	"A" sometimes expanded as "Advanced" in IBM literature	
APL2	A Programming Language 2	IBM
	see *APL, A Programming Language*	
APM	Automated Parking Machine	NYNEX
APO	Apochromat(ic)	. . .
	re: Optical devices (such as lenses) with high color correction for red, green, and blue light rays	
APOMA	American Precision Optics Manufacturers Association	APOMA
APP	Application Portability Profile	NBS
APPC	Advanced Peer-to-Peer Communication	. . .
APPC	Advanced Program-to-Program Communication	IBM
APPC	Application Program-to-Program Connectivity	. . .
APPN	Advanced Peer-to-Peer Networking	IBM
APR	Alternate Path Retry	IBM
APS	Advanced Photon Source	ANL
APS	Application Productivity System	Sage Systems
	Batch and on-line prototype development system	
APS	Automated Patent System	PTO
APS	Automatic Protection Switch	. . .
APS	Auxilliary Program Storage	. . .
APSE	Ada Programming Support Environment	DARPA
APT	A Programmer's Tool	Sybase
APT	Asynchronous Performance Tester	Concord Data Systems
APT	Automatic Pattern Translator	IMS

APT	Automatically Programmed Tool	. . .
APU	Adaptive Peripheral Unit	. . .
APU	Auxilliary Power Unit	. . .
APV	Advanced Packetized Voice	. . .
Ar	Argon	. . .
	Atomic element number 18	
AR	Access Register	IBM
AR	Anti-Reflection [coating]	. . .
	re: Fiber-optic communications	
AR	Arithmetic Register	. . .
AR	Autoregression	. . .
	re: Statistical estimation	
ARADS	Army Recruiting and Accounting Data System	US Army
ARAMIS	American Rheumatism Association Medical Information System	. . .
ARAP	AppleTalk Remote Access Protocol	Apple
ARC	Astrophysical Research Consortium	ARC
Ardis	Advanced Radio Data Information Service	IBM/Motorola
	Variant of *ARDIS*	
ARDIS	Advanced Radio Data Information Service	IBM/Motorola
ARDS	Accunet Reserved Digital Service	AT&T
	sa *Accunet*	
Arg	Arginine	. . .
	A compound important in biochemistry	
ARL	Association of Research Libraries	ARL
ARLAN	Advanced Radio Local Area Network	Telesystems SLW
ARM	Acorn RISC Machine	Acorn
ARM	Asynchronous Response Mode	IBM
	re: *HDLC, High-Level Data Link Control*	
ARMA	American Records Management Association	ARMA
ARP	Address Resolution Protocol	Internet
ARP	Advanced (or Automatic) Routing Protocol	. . .
	re: LAN support; sa *LAN, Local Area Network*	
ARPA	Advanced Research Projects Agency	DoD
	Now *DARPA, Defense Advanced Research Projects Administration*	
ARPANET	Advanced Research Projects Agency Network	DoD
ARQ	Automatic Request	. . .
	Request for repeat transmission due to error check, etc.	
ARR	Associated Recovery Routines	IBM
ARRL	American Radio Relay League	ARRL
ARS	Advanced Record System	GSA

ARS	Automatic Route Selection	. . .
	Automatic selection of optimal route; sa	
	LCR, Least Cost Routing	
ART	Access Register Translation	IBM
ART	Automated Reasoning Tool	Ford
ARTB	Advanced Radar Test Bed	. . .
ARTEMIS	Advanced Relay Technological Mission	. . .
	Satellite	
ARTIC	A Real-Time Interface Processor	IBM
ARU	Audio Response Unit	. . .
As	Arsenic	. . .
	Atomic element number 33	
AS	Advanced Schottky	. . .
	re: Electronic integrated circuit (IC) logic	
	family	
ASA	Advanced Software Architecture	Proteon
ASA	American Standards Association	ASA
ASA	Analog Sampling Array	. . .
	A very large scale integrated (VLSI) circuit	
	array used in high-energy physics data	
	collection	
ASAI	Adjunct/Switch Application Interface	AT&T
ASAP	Advanced Symbolic ATE Programming	Schlumberger
	sa *ATE, Automatic Test Equipment*	
ASAS	All Source Analysis System	US Army
ASATE	Application-Specific Automatic Test	Bond, John
	Equipment	
ASB	Analog Source Board	. . .
ASC	Address Space Control	IBM
ASC	American Standards Committee	. . .
ASCII	American Standard Code for Information	. . .
	Interchange	
ASCL	Advanced Scientific Computing Laboratory	NCI/FCRDC
ASCR	Asymmetrical Silicon-Controlled Rectifier	. . .
ASD	Advanced Solution Development	Unisys
ASDE	Airport Surface Detection Equipment	. . .
ASDL	Asymetric Digital Subscriber Line	. . .
	re: Transmission of wide-band information	
	on copper telephone lines	
ASDS	Accunet Spectrum of Digital Services	AT&T
	sa *Accunet*	
ASE	Amplified Spontaneous Emission	. . .
ASET	Adaptive Sub-band Excited Transform	. . .
	Voice encoding and compression technique	
ASFIR	Active Swept Frequency Interferometer Radar	. . .

ASH	Ardire-Stratigakis-Hayduk	Ardire, Stratigakis, Hayduk
	A data compression algorithm	
ASI	American Standards Institute	ASI
ASIC	Analog Semi-Custom Integrated Circuit	. . .
ASIC	Application-Specific Integrated Circuit	. . .
ASID	Address Space Identifier	IBM
ASIMS	Army Standard Information Management System	US Army
ASIP	Application-Specific Image Processor	. . .
ASK	Amplitude Shift Keying	. . .
ASM	Automated Storage Management	CSG
	Disk space management system	
ASM	Auxilliary Storage Manager	IBM
Asn	Asparagine	. . .
	A compound important in biochemistry	
ASN	Abstract Syntax Notation	. . .
ASN	Alabama Supercomputer Network	Alabama
ASN.1	Abstract Syntax Notation One	ANSI
Asp	Aspartic [acid]	. . .
	A compound important in biochemistry	
ASP	Adaptive Signal Processing	. . .
ASPC	Application-Specific Power Conditioning	. . .
ASPI	Advanced SCSI Programming Interface	. . .
	sa *SCSI, Small Computer Systems Interface*	
ASPJ	Airborne Self-Protection Jammer	US Navy
	re: Electronic warfare	
ASR	Automatic Send/Receive	Teletype
ASRF	Automation Sciences Research Facility	NASA
ASRM	Advanced Solid [fuel] Rocket Motor	NASA
ASRS	Automated Storage and Retrieval System	. . .
ASSP	Application-Specific Standard Product	. . .
ASTE	American Society of Test Engineers	ASTE
ASTM	American Society for Testing and Materials	ASTM
ASTN	Automotive Satellite Television Network	. . .
ASTRAL	Analog Schematic Translator to Algebraic Language	. . .
ASTRAM	Advanced Self-Timed Random Access Memory	. . .
ASTTL	Advanced Schottky Transistor-Transistor Logic	. . .
	re: High-speed integrated circuit (IC) technology sa *S, Schottky*	
ASV	Application Source Verifier	AGS/NYNEX
ASW	Accumaster Services Workstation	AT&T

At	Astatine	. . .
	Atomic element number 85	
AT	Address Translation	. . .
AT	Advanced Technology	. . .
ATACS	Automatic Test Access Crosspoint Switch	Crosspoint
ATC	Adaptive Transform Coding	PCSI
	Voice coding algorithm	
ATC	Address Translation Cache	. . .
ATC	Air Traffic Control	. . .
ATCCS	Army Tactical Command and Control System	US Army
ATDM	Analog Time Division Multiplexer	. . .
ATDM	Asynchronous Time Division Multiplexing	. . .
ATDRSS	Advanced Tracking and Data Relay Satellite System	NASA
ATE	Automatic Test Equipment	. . .
ATF	Advanced Tactical Fighter	US Air Force
ATF	Automatic Track Finding	. . .
	Used in digital audio recording, etc.	
ATG	Assistive Technology Group	DEC
	A group involved in assisting the severely handicapped gain accessibility to computers	
ATG	Automatic Test Generator	. . .
ATIS	A Tool Integration Standard	DEC/Atherton
ATL	Automatic Tape Library	. . .
ATM	Asynchronous Transfer Method	NTT
ATM	Asynchronous Transfer Mode	. . .
ATM	Automated(-ic) Teller Machine	. . .
ATMS	Advanced Text Management System	IBM
ATN	Attention	IEEE
	re: IEEE Standard 488; sa *IEEE*	
ATN	Aeronautical Telecommunications Network	FAA
ATOM	Automatic Topographic Mapper	GeoSpectra
ATOS	Automated Technical Order System	US Air Force
ATP	Adenosine 5'-Triphosphate	. . .
	A compound important in biochemistry	
ATP	Air Transportable	. . .
ATPG	Automatic Test Pattern (or Program) Generator	Azix
ATR	Anti-Transmit-Receive [tube]	. . .
	See *T-R, Transmit-Receive* for explanation	
ATR	Automatic Target Recognition	. . .
ATRJ	Advanced Technology Radar Jammer	USA
ATS	Administrative Terminal System	IBM
ATSF	Alert Transport Service Facility	IBM
ATTC	Advanced Television Test Center	ATTC

ATV	Advanced Television	Adv. TV Test Center
ATV	All-Terrain Vehicle	...
ATVG	Automatic Test Vector Generation	...
Au	Aurum	...
	Symbol for *gold*, atomic element number 79	
AU	Arithmetic Unit	...
	re: Computer central processing unit	
AU	Astronomical Unit	...
	Distance equal to the distance from the earth to the sun, 149.5×10^6 meters (m)	
AUI	Access Unit Interface	...
AUI	Attachment Unit Interface	IEEE
AUI	Attachment Universal Interface	...
AURA	Association of Universities for Research in Astronomy	AURA
AURP	AppleTalk Update Routing Protocol	Apple
AUTODIN	Automatic Digital Network	...
AUTOFLOW	Automatic Flowcharting	ADR
	Documentation system for software	
AUX	A UNIX [implementation for the Macintosh II]	Apple
	sa *UNIX*	
AV	Audio-Visual	...
	Sometimes designated by *A-V*	
AVC	Audio-Visual Connection	IBM
AVC	Automatic Volume Control	...
AVC	Auxilliary Video Connector	IBM
AVIRIS	Airborne Visible/Infrared Imaging Spectrometer	NASA
AVIU	Audio-Video Integration Unit	Vidicom
AVL	Automated Vehicle Locator	...
AVLC	Adaptive Variable Length Coder	...
AVLIS	Atomic Vapor Laser Isotope Separation	...
AVLSI	Advanced Very Large Scale Integration	...
AVNL	Automatic Video Noise Limiter	...
AVR	Automatic Volume Recognition	IBM
	re: Recognition of labeled tape volumes	
AVS	Application Visualization Software	Stardent
AVS	Application Visualization Sysem	DEC
AW	Acoustic Wave	...
AWACS	Advanced Warning and Control System	...
AWACS	Airborne Warning and Control System	DoD
AWARS	Airborne Weather and Reconnaissance System	...
AWDS	Automated Weather Distribution System	US Air Force

AWG	American Wire Guage	. . .
	Wire size standard; sa *B&S, Brown and Sharpe*	
AWG	Arbitrary Waveform Generator	. . .
AWIPS	Advanced Weather Interactive Processing System	NOAA
AWS	Air Weather Service	US Air Force
AX	Authorization Index	IBM
AXAF	Advanced X-Ray Astrophysical Facility	NASA
	Part of NASA's *Great Observatory Program, GOP*, which see	
AYT	Are You There?	. . .
	Teletype/Telex inquiry for acknowledgement	
AZTEC	Arizona Telecommunications Educational Cooperative	Westnet

B

B	—Magnetic Flux Density (symbol)	. . .
	Expressed in units of *Teslas*	
	Named in honor of American inventor Nikola Tesla (1857–1943)	
B	—Susceptance (symbol)	. . .
	Expressed in units of *Siemens, S*, which see	
B	B [battery, or supply]	. . .
	Designation given to represent the secondary battery or power supply of radios, etc.; usually used to provide vacuum tube plate power	
B	Bearer [channel]	. . .
	re: 64 kbps communications link used in ISDN service sa *ISDN, Integrated Services Digital Network*	
B	Boron	. . .
	Atomic element number 5	
B-Channel	B-Channel	AT&T
	64-kbps channel in *ISDN*, which see	
B-DCS	Broadband Digital Cross-Connect System	CCITT
B-ISDN	Broadband ISDN	. . .
	sa *ISDN, Integrated Services Digital Network*	
B-MAC	B-version Multiplexed Analog Component	. . .
	Satellite data transmission protocol	
b/s	bits per second	. . .
	Alternate form of *bps*	
B&S	Brown and Sharpe	. . .
	Wire standard; sa *AWG, American Wire Guage*	

B/W	Black and White	...
	Synonym for *monochrome*	
Ba	Barium	...
	Atomic element number 56	
BA	Bus Arbiter	...
BAL	Basic Assembly Language	...
balun	balanced to unbalanced [adapter/coupler]	...
	Now accepted as an English word;	
	previously alternately designated by *BALUN*	
BALUN	Balanced to Unbalanced [adapter/coupler]	...
	Alternate form; see *balun*	
BAR	Base Address Register	...
BARRNet	Bay Area Regional Research Network	BARRNet
BART	Basic Aerodynamic Research Tunnel	NASA
BASIC	Basic Algebraic Symbolic Interpretive	...
	Compiler	
BASIC	Beginner's All-purpose Symbolic Instruction	...
	Code	
BAW	Bulk Acoustic Wave	...
BB	Base Band	...
BB	Broadband	...
BB	Building Block	...
	Designation given to components, systems,	
	or subsystems used in network development	
BB	Bulletin Board	...
	Designation given to public electronically	
	accessible computer data storage	
BBO	Beta Barium Borate	...
	Laser crystal	
BBR	Bad Block Replacement	DEC
	re: Disk memory management	
BBRAM	Battery Backup Random Access Memory	...
BBS	Bulletin Board Service	...
BBS	Bulletin Board Software	...
BBUG	Boole and Babbage User Group	Boole & Babbage
BBXRT	Broad Band X-Ray Telescope	NASA
BC	Bus Controller	...
BCB	Benzocyclobutene	...
	A dielectric substance used in the	
	production of high density microchips	
BCB	Bit Control Block	IBM
BCB	Buffer Control Block	IBM
BCC	Blind Complimentary Copy	...
	re: e-mail duplicate ("carbon copy")	

BCC	Block Check Character	. . .
BCC	Business Card Computer	Motorola
	re: Very small microcomputer	
BCD	Binary-Coded Decimal	. . .
BCDIC	Binary-Coded Decimal Interchange Code	. . .
	Commonly reduced to *BCD*	
BCF	Background Communications Facility	IBM
BCH	Block Control Header	IBM
BCI	Binary-Coded Information	. . .
BCIS	Bank Credit Information System	. . .
BCM	Basic Control Monitor	Xerox
BCM	Bit Compression Multiplexer	AT&T
BCP	Biphase Communications Processor	Nat'l.Semi-conductor
BCRT	Bus Controller/Remote Terminal	. . .
BCRTM	Bus Controller/Remote Terminal/Monitor	UTMC
BCS	Basic Catalog Structure	IBM
	re: IBM's *Integrated Catalog Facility, ICF*	
BCS	Basic Control System	H-P
BCU	Block Control Unit	IBM
BCUG	Bilateral Closed User Group	CCITT
	re: CCITT Recommendation X.87; sa *CCITT*	
BCUGO	Bilateral Closed User Group with Outgoing access	CCITT
	re: CCITT Recommendation X.87; sa *CCITT*	
BCW	Buffer Control Word	. . .
BDAM	Basic Direct Access Method	IBM
BDDF	Bidirectional Diffraction Distribution Function	. . .
BDES	Basic Data Exchange Services	IBM
BDU	Basic Device Unit	IBM
Be	Beryllium	. . .
	Atomic element number 4	
BEC	Bit Error Correction	. . .
BECN	Backward Explicit Congestion Notification	ANSI
	Field used in frame relay data communications protocol	
BEEM	Ballistic Electron Emission Microscope	. . .
BEL	Bell	CCITT
	Control-G on a computer or terminal keyboard; a part of CCITT Recommendation V.3; sa *CCITT* and *V.3*	
Bellcore	Bell Communications Research	Bell Labs
BEM	Basic Editor Monitor	Sperry-Univac
BER	Bit Error Rate	. . .

BERR*	Bus Error [signal] Note: "*" indicates that a signal (called "active high") must be present at the circuit terminal in order for the described function to be activated.	. . .
BERT	Bit Error Rate Test	. . .
BESTNET	Binational English and Spanish Telecommunications Network	Beryl Bellman
BET	Brunauer-Emmett-Teller Name given to a mathematical procedure for surface analysis methodology	Brunauer, et al.
Beta	Beta Video tape recording format	. . .
BETRS	Basic Exchange Telecommunications Radio Service	. . .
BETUS	Barcode Equipment Tracking and Utilization System	JFK Space Ctr.
BeV	Billion electron Volts 10^9 electron volts; also designated by *GeV*, *Giga electron volts*	. . .
BEV	Bird's-Eye-View re: Graphics representation on a work station or other cathode ray tube (CRT) display	. . .
BEX	Broadband Exchange	. . .
BF	Boundary Function Subset of SNA subarea that controls non-subarea resources sa *SNA*, *Systems Network Architecture*	. . .
BFL	Back Focal Length	. . .
BFO	Beat Frequency Oscillator	. . .
BFT	Binary File Transfer	EIA
BGP	Border Gateway Protocol	DEC
BHE	Bus High Enable Pin signal on cpu chip	. . .
Bi	Bismuth Atomic element number 83	. . .
BI	Backplane Interconnect	DEC
BIB	Burn-In Board Life test device for electronic circuits	. . .
BiCMOS	Bi-polar Complementary Metal Oxide Semiconductor Hybrid chip consisting of two dissimilar solid-state (SS) technologies	. . .
BIDFET	Bipolar Diffused Field Effect Transistor	TI
BIF	Benchmark Interchange Format	. . .

BIF	Bus Interface	. . .
BiFIFO	Bidirectional First In First Out	IDT
BIG	Bismuth-Iron-Garnet	. . .
	Faraday-rotating magneto-optic material	
	Also refers to a variety of other bismuth-	
	iron-garnet laser crystals	
BIH	Bureau International de l'Heure	BIH
	(French) International Time Bureau (Paris,	
	France) The central agency which	
	determines world time	
BiMOS	Bipolar Metal Oxide Semiconductor	. . .
Binac	Binary Automatic Computer	. . .
	First U.S. high-speed computer operating on	
	the binary number system	
BINAC	Binary Automatic Computer	Eckert &
		Mauchly
	Successor to the *ENIAC*, which see	
BIND	Berkeley Internet Name Domain	UC-Berkeley
	re: UNIX security services; sa *UNIX*	
BIOP	Buffer Input/Output Processor	Cray Research
BIOS	Basic Input/Output System	. . .
BIPM	Bureau International des Poids et Measures	BIPM
	International Bureau of Weights and	
	Measures	
BISAM	Basic Indexed Sequential Access Method	IBM
BISDN	Broadband Integrated Services Digital	AT&T
	Network	
BIST	Built-In Self-Test	. . .
	Self-testing circuitry on chip level	
Bisync	Binary Synchronous [communication]	IBM
	Preferred designation; alternately designated	
	by *BiSync*; sa *BSC, Binary Synchronous*	
	Communication	
BiSync	Binary Synchronous [communication]	. . .
	Alternate form; see *Bisync*	
bit	binary digit	. . .
BIT	Bipolar Integrated Technology	. . .
BIT	Built-In Test	. . .
BITBLT	Bit Block Transfer	. . .
	Process (in software) of rotating display	
	blocks on graphics terminals	
BITDOC	BITnet Development and Operations Center	EDUCOM
BITE	Built-In Test and Evaluation	. . .
BITnet	Because It's Time network	. . .
	sa *CREN, Corporation for Research and*	
	Educational Networking	

BITNIC	BITnet Network Information Center	EDUCOM
BIU	Basic Information Unit	IBM
BIX	Byte Information Exchange	Byte Magazine
	McGraw-Hill's *Byte Magazine* bulletin board	
BJT	Bipolar Junction Transistor	. . .
Bk	Berkelium	. . .
	Atomic element number 97	
	Named after Berkeley, CA, home of the University of California, where this element was first synthesized	
BLAST	Blocked Asynchronous Transmission	. . .
BLDL	Build List [macro]	IBM
BLERT	Block Error Rate Test	. . .
BLISS	Basic Language for Implementing Systems Software	. . .
BLOB	Binary Large Object	. . .
	A string of bits (ones and zeros) resulting from a scanned and digitized document, drawing, photo, etc.	
BLP	Bypass Label Processing	IBM
BLT	Basic Language Translator	. . .
BLT	Block Transfer	. . .
	re: VME bus data transfer; sa *VME, Virtual Memory Extended*	
BLU	Basic Link Unit	IBM
	re: IBM's *Systems Network Architecture, SNA*	
BMC	Buffer Management Chip	. . .
BMDP	Bio-Medical Data Processor	UCLA
	Statistical package for the medical sciences	
BMIC	Bus-Master Interface Controller	Intel
BMP	Batch Message Processing	IBM
BMS	Bandwidth Management Service	AT&T
BMS	Basic Mapping Support	IBM
BMS	Basic Monitor System	DEC
BMWG	Benchmark Methodology Working Group	Internet
BNA	Burroughs Network Architecture	Burroughs
BNC	Baby N Connector	Neill and Concelman
	A widely used connector for high-frequency signals; also called *Baby Neill-Concelman*, after its inventors	
BNL	Brookhaven National Laboratory	BNL
BNU	Branch Neuron Unit	. . .

BOB	Break-Out Box	. . .
	A device used for indicating the status of communications lines	
BOBCAT	Bobst [Library] Catalog	NYU
BOC	Bell Operating Companies	AT&T
BOMP	Bill of Material Processor	IBM
	Software for IBM System/3	
Boris	Bit-oriented reduced instruction set	Mietec Alcatel
BORSCHT	Battery-feed Overvoltage-protection, Ringing, Supervision, Coding/Decoding, Hybrid Testing	AT&T
	Pertaining to the AT&T *5ESS*, which see	
BOS	Basic Operating System	. . .
BOS	Batch Operating System	Honeywell
BOT	Beginning of Tape	. . .
BOTDA	Brillouin Optical Fiber Time Domain Analysis	. . .
BPAM	Basic Partitioned Access Method	IBM
BPF	Band Pass Filter	. . .
bpi	bits per inch	. . .
	re: Magnetic tape recording density; see *cpi, characters per inch* for hard copy print analog	
BPI	Bytes Per Inch	. . .
	re: Data recording density	
BPON	Broadband over a Passive Optical Network	. . .
bps	bits per second	. . .
BPS	Bytes Per Second	. . .
	re: Data transmission rate	
BPSK	Binary Phase Shift Keying	. . .
	A transmission modulation method	
BPSS	Basic Packet Switching System	AT&T
BPV	Bipolar Violation	. . .
	Digital communications fault	
bR	bacteriorhodopsin	. . .
	A protein currently being researched as a possible ultra-high density data storage medium	
Br	Bromine	. . .
	Atomic element number 35	
BRA	Basic Rate Access	. . .
BRAIN	Belgian Rapid Access to Information	RTT/Alcatel-Bell
BRDF	Bidrectional Reflectance Distribution Function	. . .
BRE	Bridge Relay Encapsulation	Timeplex
BRF	Benchmark Reporting Format	. . .

BRI	Basic Rate Interface	AT&T
	ISDN notation for 144-kbps aggregate data rate; sa *PRI, Primary Rate Interface* and *ISDN, Integrated Services Digital Network*	
BRK	Break	. . .
BRL	Ballistic Research Laboratory	US Army
BRM	Bendix Real Miniature [connector]	Bendix Research Labs
	Precursor to the subminiature A (SMA) connector	
BRS	Business Recovery Service	IBM
	Commercial information retrieval service	
BS	Backspace	CCITT
	Format effector 0 (FE_0); a component of the binary code in CCITT Recommendation V.3; sa *FE_n, Format Effector n, CCITT* and *V.3*	
BSA	Basic Service Element	FCC
	re: *ONA, Open Network Architecture*	
BSAM	Basic Sequential Access Method	IBM
BSC	Binary Synchronous Communication	IBM
	Also designated by *BiSync*	
BSD	Berkeley Software Distribution	UC-Berkeley
BSD	Berkeley System Distribution	UC-Berkeley
	A version of UNIX	
BSD	Boundary Scan Diagnosis	. . .
BSDL	Boundary Scan Description(-ive) Language	H-P
BSE	Basic Service Element	. . .
BSE	Basic Serving Arrangement	FCC
	re: *ONA, Open Network Architecture*	
BSET	Big Set	Stephenson, Brad
	Utility for setting environment strings in excess of 122 characters	
BSI	Boundary Scan Input	. . .
	Input pin on chip with self-scan capability	
BSO	Boundary Scan Output	. . .
	Output pin on chip with self-scan capability	
BSP	Business Systems Planning	IBM
BSR	Boundary Scan Register	. . .
BSRF	Basic Standard Reference Frequency	. . .
	Public network synchronizing clock signal	
BST	Boundary Scan Test	. . .
BSTAT	Basic Status [register]	IBM
BTAM	Basic Telecommunications Access Method	IBM

BTDF	Bidirectional Transmittance Distribution Function	. . .
BTL	Backplane Transistor Logic	IEEE
BTM	Batch Timesharing Monitor	Xerox
BTM	Benchmark Timing Methodology	. . .
BTOS	Burroughs Time-Share Operating System	Burroughs
Btu	British Thermal Unit	. . .
	Quantity of heat, equivalent to approximately 252 calories	
BTU	Basic Transmission Unit	IBM
	re: IBM's *Systems Network Architecture, SNA*	
BTU	British Thermal Unit	. . .
	Alternate form; see *Btu*	
Btuh	British thermal units per hour	. . .
BTV	Broadcast Television	. . .
BVR	Balanced Visual Response	Cambridge Instruments
	re: Stereomicroscope optical design	
BWG	Beam Waveguide	. . .
BX.25	Bell X.25	Bell System
	Bell System version of CCITT X.25; sa *CCITT* and *X.25*	
B28	Binary 2 of 8 [code]	. . .
B8ZS	Binary Eight Zero Substitution (or Suppression)	AT&T
	ISDN protocol for obtaining 24 clear channels on DS-1, which see; sa *ISDN* and *CCC* for related information	

C

c	c (symbol)	. . .
	Speed of light *in vacuo*	
	2.9979246×10^{10} cm/sec	
c	centi	. . .
	Prefix for 10^{-2}	
C	−100	. . .
	Roman numeral designation for 100	
C	C [battery, or supply]	. . .
	Designation given to represent the tertiary battery or power supply for radios, etc.; usually used to provide vacuum tube grid bias	
C	C [cell]	. . .
	Voltaic cell, measuring approximately 1″ diameter by 2″ long	

C	Celsius	...
	Temperature scale based on 100 equal increments between melting ice and boiling water; named in honor of Swedish astronomer Anders Celsius (1701–1744)	
C	Centigrade	...
	Scale of temperature measurement now known as Celsius See *C, Celsius* for further detail	
C	Capacitance	...
	Expressed in units of *Farads*; sa *F, Farad*	
C	Carbon	...
	Atomic element number 6	
C	Constant	...
	re: Mathematics; for example, the partial result of indefinite integration	
C	Coulomb	...
	Unit of electric charge; named in honor of French physicist Charles Augustin de Coulomb (1736–1806)	
C	Cytosine	...
	A compound important in biochemistry; a component of *DNA, Deoxyribonucleic Acid*, which see	
C-Band	C-Band	...
	Microwave frequency allocation of 4.0 to 8.0 GHz	
C/CSI	Commercial/Computer Systems Integration	...
C/I	Command and Indication	...
	Controlling signals for digital signal processing (DSP) chip control	
C/R	Carriage Return	...
	Alternate for *CR*	
C/R	Command/Response	...
	Field in frame relay (FR) data format	
c/s	cycles per second	...
	Alternate form; see *cps*; sa *Hz, Hertz*	
Ca	Calcium	...
	Atomic element number 20	
CA	Closest Approach	...
	re: Astronomy: planets, comets, etc.; satellite tracking	
CA	Collision Avoidance	...
CA	Common Applications	IBM
CA	Construction Analysis	...

CA	Continue Any [mode]	. . .
	Inverse of *CS, Continue Specific* [mode]	
CAAD	Computer-Aided Analysis and Design	. . .
CAAGR	Compounded Average Annual Growth Rate	. . .
CABS	Computer-Assisted Budgeting System	CMD
CACE	Computer-Aided Control Engineering	. . .
CACOP	Computer-Aided Constable on Patrol	Vizard, Michael
CACR	Cache Control Register	. . .
CAD	Computer-Aided Design	. . .
CAD	Computer-Aided Drafting	. . .
CAD/CAM	Computer-Aided Design and Manufacturing	. . .
CADD	Computer-Aided Design and Development	. . .
CAE	Computer-Aided Engineering	. . .
CAE	Common Applications Environment	X/Open
CAE	Computer-Assisted Electrocardiography	. . .
CAEDS	Computer-Aided Engineering Design System	IBM
CAF	Computer-Aided Fixturing	ICT
CAFE	Computer-Aided Facilities Engineering	PlanPrint
CAI	Common Air Interface	. . .
	Wireless telephone standard	
CAI	Computer-Aided Industry	. . .
CAI	Computer-Aided Instruction	. . .
CAIP	Computer Aids for Industrial Productivity	Rutgers Univ.
CAIS	Computer-Aided Intelligent Service	ROSH Intelligent Sys.
CAIS	Customs Artificial Intelligence System	Grumman Data Systems
CALS	Computer-Aided Acquisition and Logistics Support	US Dept. of Commerce
CAM	Computer-Aided Manufacturing	. . .
CAM	Computer-Automated Machining	. . .
CAM	Contact Angle Measurement	. . .
CAM	Content-Addressable Memory	Signetics
CAMAC	Computer-Automated Measurement and Control	IEEE
	IEEE 583 data acquisition and control system; sa *IEEE*	
CAMD	Computer-Aided Molecular Design	. . .
	re: Pharmaceutical synthesis	
CAMMU	Cache And Memory Management Unit	. . .
CAMS	Computerized Automotive Maintenance System	General Motors
CAN	Campus Area Network	. . .
CAN	Cancel	CCITT
	A component of the binary code in CCITT Recommendation V.3 sa *CCITT* and *V.3*	

CAN	Controller Area Network	ISO
CANDE	Command and Edit	Burroughs
	Management control system for Burroughs computers	
CANTO	Caribbean Association of National Telecommunications Organizations	. . .
CAO	Computer-Aided (or -Automated) Office	. . .
CAP	Communications Applications Processor	. . .
CAP	Compiler Assembly Program	. . .
	A programming tool used for teaching compiler development c. 1960	
CAP	Computer-Aided Publishing	. . .
CAPD	Computer-Automated Performance Data	Mini-Circuits
CAPO	Computer Aids in the Physician's Office	. . .
CAPP	Computer-Aided (or -Automated) Process Planning	. . .
CAPS	Computer-Aided Product Selection	C.T.I.S.
CAPTAIN	Character And Pattern Telephone Access Information Network	. . .
CAR	Check Authorization Record	. . .
CAR	Computer-Assisted Retrieval	. . .
CARD	Computer-Aided Remote Driving	NASA
CARE	Clinical Assessment Research and Education	. . .
CARL	Colorado Alliance of Research Libraries	CARL
CARS	Coherent Anti-Stokes Raman Spectroscopy	. . .
CARTS	Capacitor and Resistor Technology Symposium	CARTS
CAS	Cartridge Access Station	Memorex Telex
CAS	Channel-Associated Signalling	CCITT
CAS	Column Address Select (or Strobe)	. . .
	Address selection method in memory controller	
CAS	Communications Applications Specification	Intel
CAS	Computer Access Site	. . .
CASE	Common Application Service Element	ANSI
CASE	Computer-Aided Software Engineering	. . .
CASL	Crosstalk Application Script Language	DCA
CAST	Center for Advanced Studies in Telecommunications	CAST
CAST	Computer-Aided Software Translation	PRC
CAT	Computer-Aided Test	H-P
CAT	Computer Axial Tomography	. . .
CAT	Control and Analysis Tool	Robbins-Gioia
CATD	Computer-Aided Test Development	. . .
CATE	Computer-Aided Test Engineering	. . .

CATI	Computer-Automated Testing and Implementation	Compuware
CATT	Center for Advanced Technology in Telecommunications	Polytechnic Univ.
CATV	Community Antenna Television Also called *Cable Television*	. . .
CAU	Coaxial Access Unit	Joing Electronics
CAU	Control Access Unit re: Token ring physical attachment	IBM
CAV	Constant Angular Velocity	. . .
CAW	Channel Address Word	. . .
CB	Citizens Band [radio] 26.965 to 27.405 MHz, in 10.0 kHz channels	. . .
CB	Common Base Transistor circuit configuration; applied also to integrated circuits, *ICs*, containing microtransistors	. . .
CB	Congestion Backward A bit used in frame relay communications to indicate conditions; sa *CF, Congestion Forward*	. . .
CBC	Cipher Block Chaining re: Data encryption technology	ANSI
CBDS	Circuit Board Design System	IBM
CBE	Computer-Based Education	Box Hill
CBEMA	Computer and Business Equipment Manufacturers of America	CBEMA
CBI	Computer-Based Instruction	. . .
CBI	Computer-Based Instrumentation	. . .
CBIC	Complementary Bipolar Integrated Circuit	. . .
CBLAN	Centralized Bus Local Area Network	AT&T
CBMS	Computer-Based Messaging System (or Service)	. . .
CBR	Constant Bit Rate	. . .
CBT	Computer-Based Training	. . .
CBTA	Canadian Business Telecomm Alliance	CBTA
CBTS	Computer-Based Training System	. . .
CBTS	Computerized Business Telephone System	Rolm
CBWF	Call Back When Free Telephone service in which the call originator is notified when a busy subscriber is free	. . .
CBX	Campus Branch Exchange Computerized business system	Rolm
CC	Condition Code	IBM

CC	Constant Current	. . .
CCA	Circuit Card Assembly	. . .
CCA	Common Cryptographic Architecture	IBM
CCAR	Channel Command Address Register	. . .
CCB	Channel Control Block	DEC
CCBS	Call Completion to Busy Subscriber	CCITT
	Telephone feature whereby a call is	
	automatically attempted repeatedly until it	
	is completed	
CCC	Clear Channel Capability	AT&T/CCITT
	64 kbps channel in *ISDN, Integrated*	
	Services Digital Network	
CCC	Command Control and Communications	DoD
CCC	Constituency Coordination Center	NREN
CCCI	Command, Control, Communications, and	DoD
	Intelligence	
CCCS	Current-Controlled Current Source	. . .
CCD	Charge-Coupled Device	. . .
	Solid-state (SS) array photodetector used as	
	video camera imaging device	
CCDF	Chi-Square Cumulative Distribution Function	. . .
	re: Statistical analysis	
CCDI	Chi-Square Cumulative Distribution Inverse	. . .
	re: Statistical analysis	
CCDS	Center for Commercial Development of Space	NASA
CCE	Call Command Exit	IBM
CCE	Cooperative Computing Environment	Unisys
CCF	Controller Configuration Facility	IBM
CCF	Crystalline Colloidal Filter	. . .
CCFT	Cold Cathode Fluorescent Tube	. . .
CCI	Common Communication Interface	Computer Associates
CCIR	International Radio Consultative Committee	CCIR
CCIS	Common Channel Interoffice Signalling	AT&T
CCITT	Consultative Committee for International	CCITT
	Telephone and Telegraph	
CCK	Clustered Cavity Klystron	. . .
CCMT	Computer-Controlled Microwave Tuner	. . .
CCP	Certified Computer Professional	. . .
CCP	Command Control Program	IBM
CCP	Cooperative Computing Platform	Unisys
CCPD	Charge-Coupled Photodiode	. . .
CCR	Catalog Control Record	IBM
CCR	Customer Controlled Reconfiguration	AT&T
	re: *T1* service, which see	
CCRS	Centrex Customer Rearrangement Service	Bellcore

ccs	Hundred Call Seconds	AT&T
	re: Communications user measurement unit	
CCS	Common-Channel Signalling	CCITT
CCS	Common Command Set	. . .
CCS	Common Communications Support	IBM
CCS	Continuous Composite Servo	ANSI
	5¼″ optical disk format	
CCSA	Common Controlled Switching Arrangement	AT&T
CCSI	Commercial Communications Systems Integration	. . .
CCSS	Common Channel Signalling System	AT&T
CCS7	Common Channel Signalling [system] Seven	AT&T/Sprint
CCT	Comité Consultatif de Thermometrie (French) International Consultative Committee on Thermometry	CCT
CCTA	Central Computer and Communications Agency	UK
CCTV	Closed Circuit Television	. . .
CCU	Camera Control Unit	Focal Point
CCU	Central Control Unit	. . .
CCVS	Current-Controlled Voltage Source	. . .
CCW	Channel Command Word	. . .
CCW	Continuous Composite Write [once] re: Optical disk technology	. . .
CCW	Counterclockwise	. . .
Cd	Cadmium Atomic element number 48	. . .
CD	Carrier Detect	. . .
CD	Circular Dichroism re: Physical optics	. . .
CD	Compact Digital [recording]	. . .
CD	Compact Disk	. . .
CD-I	Compact Disk-Interactive Variant of *CDI*, which see	N.V. Philips
CD-ROM	Compact Disk Read Only Memory	. . .
CDA	Combined Digital Aggregate	. . .
CDA	Compound Document Architecture	DEC
CDA	Customer-Defined Array re: Customer-configurable random access memory (RAM)	Motorola
CDAS	Conceptual Design Analysis and Simulation	. . .
CDB	Command Descriptor Block	ANSI
CDB	Communications Data Base	. . .
CDB	Corporate Data Base	US Coast Guard
CDC	Compression/Decompression	. . .

CDCP	Common Distributed Computing Platform	Sun Microsystems
CDD	Common Data Dictionary	DEC
CDDI	Copper Distributed Data Interface Twisted pair (TP) implementation of the FDDI communications standard; sa *FDDI,* *Fiber-Distributed Data Interface*	ANSI
CDE	Concurrent Design Environment	Mentor Graphics
CDI	Compact Disk-Interactive A data compression/decompression technology	. . .
CDIN	Continental Defense Integrated Network	DoD
CDIP	Ceramic Dual In-Line Package re: Integrated circuit packaging technology sa *PDIP, Plastic Dual In-Line Package*	. . .
CDL	Computer Design Language	Univ. of So. Fla.
CDLA	Computer Dealers and Lessors Association	. . .
CDLC	Cellular Data Link Control Cellular communications protocol	. . .
CDM	Charged Device Model A set of specifications used as test parameters	. . .
CDMA	Code Division Multiple Access *VSAT* access technique, which see	. . .
CDMC	Configurable Dynamic Memory Controller	. . .
CDMP	Compound Document Management Program	DEC
CDO	Controlled Decomposition/Oxidation	IE
CDOS	Customer Data and Operations System	NASA
CDP	Certified Data Professional (or Programmer)	. . .
CDP	Cytidine Diphosphate re: Biophysics	. . .
CDR	Call Detail Recording Time and charges recording of telephone calls	. . .
CDR	Clock and Data Recovery Communications technique for recovering lost signals	. . .
CDR	Compact Disk Recordable	. . .
CDR	Constant Density Recording Commonly used method of recording data on computer disks Compare *ZDR, zoned* *density recording*	. . .
CDRM	Cross-Domain Resource Manager	IBM
CDRS	Computer Disaster Recovery System	. . .

CDRS	Conceptual Design and Rendering System	E & S Computer
	Computer-aided design, graphics, and modelling system	
CDS	Control Data Set	. . .
CDU	Color Difference Unit	. . .
CDV	Compact Disk Video	. . .
	Laser video recording on disk format; sa *LD, Laser Disk*	
Ce	Cerium	. . .
	Atomic element number 58	
CE	Computational Element	. . .
CE	Counterelectrode [layer]	. . .
	re: "Smart window" glass technology, in which transmission of light and heat is directionally controllable	
Ce/NCoReL	Center or Network for Computational Research on Language	. . .
CEAP	Corps of Engineers Automated Processing [network]	DoD
CEBA	Continuous Electron Beam Accelerator	. . .
CEBAF	Continuous Electron Beam Accelerator Facility	DoE
CECOM	Communications and Electronics Command	US Army
CEDAR	Computer Enhanced Digital Audio Restoration	Time-Life
CEG	Continuous Edge Graphics	. . .
CEI	Comparably Efficient Interconnection	FCC
	re: Communications network interface	
CELP	Code-Excited Linear Prediction	JPL (NASA)
	Algorithm used in speech encoding technology	
CELSS	Controlled Ecological Life Support System	NASA
CEM	Command Execution Module	. . .
CEMM	Compaq Expanded Memory Manager	Compaq
CEO	Chief Executive Officer	. . .
CEPT	Conference of European Postal and Telecommunications	CEPT
	A standards organization for telecommunications	
Cer	Ceramide	. . .
	A compound important in biochemistry	
CERDIP	Ceramic Dual In-Line Package (or Plastic)	. . .
	re: An integrated circuit (IC) packaging technology	
CERES	Clouds and Earth's Radiant Energy System	NASA

CERPASS	Center for Experimental Research in Parallel Algorithms, Software and Systems	USC
CERT	Computer Emergency Response Team	CMU
CERT/CC	CERT Coordination Center sa *CERT, Computer Emergency Response Team*	CMU
CES	Coast Earth Station	US Navy
CESD	Composite External Symbol Dictionary	IBM
CETC	Centralized Electrification and Traffic Control sa *CTC, Centralized Traffic Control*	Amtrak
CETI	Continuously Executing Transfer Interface Local area network (LAN) interface	IBM
Cf	Californium Atomic element number 98 Named after the University of California, where this element was first isolated	. . .
CF	Congestion Forward A bit used in frame relay communications to indicate network conditions sa *CB, Congestion Backward*	. . .
CF	Continuous Feed (or Forms) re: Sprocket-feed forms	. . .
CF	Cryptographic Facility	IBM
CFA	Crossed-Field Amplifier	. . .
CFC	Chlorofluorocarbon Any of several refrigerants/solvents	. . .
CFD	Computational Fluid Dynamics	NASA
CFF	Continuous Forms Feed(-er)	. . .
CFG	Color Frame Grabber	Imaging Technology
CFI	CAD Framework Initiative sa *CAD, Computer-Aided Design*	. . .
CFIA	Component Failure Imapct Analysis	. . .
CFM	Continuously Focusable Microscope	Infinity Photo-Opt.
CFM	Cubic Feet per Minute	. . .
CFO	Chief Financial Officer	. . .
CFP	Creation Facilities Program	IBM
CFS	Common File System	AFSCC
CFS	Computerized Forwarding System US Postal Service mail forwarding software	M/A-Com
CFS	Concurrent Filing System	. . .
CFS	Continuous Forms Stacker	. . .
CFT	Cray FORTRAN [compiler] sa *FORTRAN, Formula Translator*	Cray Research

CGA	Color Graphics Adapter	IBM
CGH	Computer Generated Holography	. . .
CGI	Computer Graphics Interface	. . .
CGM	Color Graphics Metafile	. . .
CGM	Computer Graphics Metafile	. . .
	ANSI standard device-independent graphics file sa *ANSI, American National Standards Institute*	
cgs	centimeter-gram-seconds [system of units]	. . .
	Fundamental units of physical measurement	
CHAP	Channel Processor	Pixar
CHC	Chlorinated Hydrocarbon	. . .
CHC	Color Hard Copy	. . .
	re: Color printer	
CHCAT	Clearing House Catalogue	DEC
CHDB	Congressional Hearings Data Base	DoE
CHESS	Cornell [University] High-Energy Synchrotron Source	Cornell Univ.
	A "third generation" synchrotron	
CHIO	Channel Input/Output	IBM
CHPC	Center for High-Performance Computing	Univ. of Texas
CHS	Common Hardware and Software [system]	US Army
CHS	Corporate Hub Station	AT&T
	A private central network switch for very small aperture terminal (VSAT) networks	
CI	Calling Indicator	. . .
CI	Computer Interconnect	DEC
CIAC	Computer Incident Advisory Committee	DoE
CICA	Chicago Industrial Communications Association	CICA
CICC	Custom Integrated Circuits Conference	CICC
CICS	Computerized Information Control System	. . .
CICS	Customer Information Control System	IBM
CID	Connection Identifier	. . .
CID	Charge Injection Device	. . .
	re: Photosensitive detector; sa *CCD, Charge-Coupled Device*	
CIDF	Control Interval Definition Field	IBM
CIDS	Customer-Integrated Development System	. . .
CIF	Common Intermediate Format	CCITT
	re: Videophone image pixel representation (352 × 288 pixels); sa *QCIF, Quarter Common Intermediate Format*	
CIF	Control Information File System	NCR
CIK	Crypto[graphic] Ignition Key	AT&T

CIM	Computer-Integrated Manufacturing	Silicon Graphics
CIM	Corporate Information Management	DoD
CIMS	Computer Information Management System	BMS
CINIT	Control Initiate Request unit for IBM's *Systems Network Architecture, SNA*	IBM
CIO	Chief Information Officer	. . .
CIOUT	Cache Inhibit Out	. . .
CIP	Carbonyl Iron Powder Substance used in making magnetic recording devices (such as tapes, memory cards, and disks) and other ferrite devices	. . .
CIP	Connectionless Internet Protocol	. . .
CIPM	Comité International des Poids et Mesures (French) International Committee of Weights and Measures	CIPM
CIR	Committed Information Rate re: Bandwidth allocation on dynamic bandwidth communications circuits	. . .
CIR	Connect Initiate Received DNA message	DEC
CIS	Connect Initiate Sent DNA message	DEC
CIS	Customer Information System	NPR
CISC	Complex Instruction Set Computer sa *MISC*—two definitions: *Minimum* and *Minuscule Instruction Set Computer* and *RISC, Reduced Instruction Set Computer* for more information	UC-Berkeley
CIT	Computer-Integrated Telephony	DEC
CITIS	Contractor-Integrated Technical Information Service	DoD
CIX	Commercial Internet Exchange	Pansophic
CI2	Computer Inquiry 2 Federal Communications Commission (FCC) ruling concerning operation of public telephone businesses	FCC
CJS	Chained Job Scheduling	IBM
CKDS	Cryptographic Key Data Sets	IBM
Ckt	Circuit	. . .
Cl	Chlorine Atomic element number 17	. . .
CLASS	Custom Local Area Signalling Services	GTE
CLB	Configurable Logic Block re: Integrated circuit (IC) layout design	. . .

CLC	Color Laser Copier	Canon
CLCC	Ceramic Leaded Chip Carrier	. . .
CLEO	Conference on Lasers and Electro-Optics	CLEO
CLG	Compile, Link-Edit, Go	IBM
CLI*	Cache Load Inhibit [signal]	. . .
	Note: "*" indicates that a signal (called "active high") must be present at the circuit terminal in order for the described function to be activated.	
CLIP	Coded Language Information Processing	. . .
CLIPS	C Language Integrated Production System	Riley, Culbert, Lopez
	A forward-chaining, rules-based language intended for expert system development	
CLIST	Command List	. . .
Clk	Clock	. . .
	Ususally refers to a timing signal; a synchronous pulse	
CLLM	Consolidated Link Layer Management	ANSI
	re: Frame relay data communications management software; an ANSI standard specification; sa *ANSI, American National Standards Institute*	
CLNP	Connectionless [mode] Network Protocol	OSI
CLNS	Connectionless [mode] Network Service	. . .
CLOS	Common LISP Object System	DEC
	sa *LISP, List Processor*	
CLR	Clear [virtual call]	CCITT
	X.25 protocol packet assembly/disassembly (PAD) command sa *X.25*	
CLS	Clear Screen	. . .
CLUT	Color LookUp Table	. . .
CLV	Constant Linear Velocity	. . .
	re: Disk access technology	
cm	centimeter	. . .
	Metric unit of length; 10^{-2} meter (m)	
Cm	Curium	. . .
	Atomic element number 96 Named in honor of Marie Sklodowska Curie (1867–1934), and Pierre Curie (1859–1906), for their discovery of radioctive elements	
CM	Common Mode	. . .
	Refers to a signal appearing on a lead with reference to a common (or ground)	
CM	Control Module	. . .
CMA	Communications Managers Association	. . .

CMA	Concert Multithread Architecture	DEC
CMA	Configuration Management Application	CACI
CMAS	Cambridge Multiple Operating System	Univ. of Cambridge
CMAS	Construction Management Accounting System	IBM
CMAU	Coaxial Multi-Station Access Unit	Ericsson
CMC	Certified Management Consultant	. . .
CMC	Communications Management Configuration	IBM
CMC	Computer Mediated Conferencing	. . .
CMDR	Command Reject X.25 protocol command response; sa *X.25*	CCITT
CMF	Comprehensive Management Facility	B&B
CMG	Computer Measurement Group	BBUG
CMI	Computer Memory Interconnect	DEC
CMIP	Common Management Information Protocol	OSI
CMIS	Common Mnangement Information Service	OSI
CML	Computer-Managed Learning	DEC
CML	Current Mode Logic	. . .
CMM	Coordinate Measuring Machine	. . .
CMMS	Computer Maintenance Management System	. . .
CMMU	Cache/Memory Management Unit	. . .
CMOE	Cross Machine Object Execution	Cohen, G., Info. Bldrs.
CMOL	CMIP Over [logical] Link [control] sa *CMIP, Common Management Information Protocol*	. . .
CMOS	Complementary Metal Oxide Semiconductor	. . .
CMOT	CMIP Over TCP/IP sa *CMIP, Common Management Information Protocol* and *TCP/IP, Transmission Control Protocol/Internet Protocol*	. . .
CMP	Cooperative Marketing Program	DEC
CMP	Cytidine Monophosphate A compound important in biochemistry	. . .
CMR	Cellular Mobile Radio	. . .
CMR	Commercial Mail Relay A mail relay service between Internet and other networks	. . .
CMRR	Common Mode Rejection Ratio	. . .
CMS	Code Management System	DEC
CMS	Communications Management Series	Racal-Milgo
CMS	Computer Management System	Burroughs
CMS	Conversational Monitor System	IBM
CMS	Crossatron Modulator Switch	. . .

CMT	Connection Management re: Fiber-distributed data interface (FDDI) specification	. . .
CMY	Cyan-Magenta-Yellow Color standard components	. . .
CMYB	Cyan-Magenta-Yellow-Black Standard used in color printers	. . .
CMYK	Cyan-Magenta-Yellow-Black Color standard for printers (alternate form)	. . .
CN	Customer Node	. . .
CNAR	Computer Network Augmented Research	. . .
CNC	Computer Numeric Control	. . .
CNCP	Canadian National/Canadian Pacific Telecomm	Canada
CNET	Centre Nationale d'Etudes des Télécommunications (French) National Center for Telecommunications Studies	. . .
CNM	Communication Network Management	IBM
CNMS	Common Network Management System	Unisys
CNR	Carrier-to-Noise [ratio] re: electronic circuit characteristic	. . .
CNS	Communications Networking System	. . .
CNS-A	Communications Network Service A	SBS
CNS-B	Communications Network Service B Full-time T1 communications service; sa *T1*	SBS
CNSF	Cornell National Supercomputer Facility	Cornell Univ.
Co	Cobalt Atomic element number 27	. . .
CO	Central Office	AT&T
CO-LAN	Central Office Local Area Network	. . .
CoA	Coenzyme A re: A compound important in physiology and biophysics	. . .
COAM	Customer Owned and Maintained	. . .
COAST	Cambridge Optical Aperture Synthesis Telescope	Cambridge Univ.
COB	Chip-On-Board re: Integrated circuit (IC) surface mount technology (SMT)	. . .
COBE	Cosmic Background Explorer Spacecraft designed to collect data on cosmic radiation Part of NASA's *Great Observatory Program, GOP*, which see	NASA
COBIT	Control-Office Based Intelligence	. . .
COBOL	Common Business Oriented Language	IBM

COC	Central Office Connection	. . .
COCOT	Customer-Owned Coin-Operated Telephone	. . .
CODASYL	Conference On Data Systems Languages	. . .
codec	code(er)—decode(er)	. . .
	Now widely accepted as an English word	
CODEC	Code(-er)—Decode(-er)	. . .
	Alternate form; see *codec*	
COGO	Coordinate Geometry	. . .
COHO	Coherent Oscillator	. . .
COIN	Corporate Office Interconnectivity Network	Grumman
COLAN	Central Office Local Area Network	. . .
	Alternate form: *CO-LAN*	
COM	Computer Output Microform (Microfiche, Microfilm,. . .)	. . .
	Any of *microfiche, microfilm,* . . ., generated by computer	
COMAN	Central Office Metropolitan Area Network	Fritz, J., WVU
COMC	Communications Controller	IBM
COMCAL	Computerized Calendar	DEC
ComNet	Communications Network Conference	. . .
COMPAKTOR	—Disk Compactor	Innovation Software
	Computer operating system (OS) disk management system	
CON	Concentrator	. . .
	A form of multiplexer	
CONCERT	Communications for North Carolina Education, Research, and Technology [network]	CONCERT
CONS	Connection-Oriented Network Service	. . .
COP	Common On-Chip Processor	IBM
CoQ	Coenzyme Q	. . .
	re: Biophysics; ubiquinone	
COR	Class of Restriction	AT&T
CORBA	Common Object Request Broker Architecture	OMG
	An emerging technology (1992) integrating multiple-vendor communications software	
CORN	Computer Resources Nucleus	FAA
CORNAP	Cornell Network Analysis Program	Cornell Univ.
cos	cosine	. . .
	Trigonometric function	
COS	Cassette Operating System	Computer Automation
COS	Class of Service	AT&T
COS	Commercial Operating System	DEC
COS	Concurrent Operating System	Sperry-Univac

COS	Corporation for Open Systems	. . .
COS	Cray Operating System	Cray Research
cos⁻¹	—arc cosine Trigonometric function; inverse cosine: "angle whose cosine is . . ."	. . .
cosh	cosine, hyperbolic Trigonometric function	. . .
cosh⁻¹	cosine, inverse hyperbolic Trigonometric function; "angle whose hyperbolic cosine is . . ."	. . .
COSI	Center of Science and Industry	COSI
COSINE	Cooperation for OSI Networking sa *OSI, Open Systems Interconnection* and *OSINet, Open Systems Interconnection Network*	CCITT
COSMIC	Computer Software Management and Information Center	NASA
COSNAME	Class of Service Name	IBM
COST	Cooperation for Scientific and Technological Research	. . .
COSTAB	Class of Service Table SNA table in ACF/VTAM environment sa *SNA, Systems Network Architecture, ACF, Advanced Communication Function* and *VTAM, Virtual Telecommunications Access Method*	IBM
COSTAR	Computer-Stored Ambulatory Medical Record System	. . .
COSTAR	Corrective Optics Space Telescope Axial Replacement	NASA
COSY	Compact Synchrotron	. . .
cot	cotangent Trigonometric function	. . .
cot⁻¹	—arc cotangent Trigonometric function; inverse cotangent: "angle whose cotangent is . . ."	. . .
coth	cotangent, hyperbolic Trigonometric function	. . .
coth⁻¹	cotangent, inverse hyperbolic Trigonometric function; inverse cotangent: "angle whose hyperbolic cotangent is . . ."	. . .
CoTRA	Computer Threat Research Organization Organization aimed at identifying, analyzing, and destroying computer viruses	CoTRA
cp	centipoise Unit of coefficient of viscosity (tens)	. . .

cp	chemically pure	. . .
CP	Central Processor	. . .
CP	Check Point	. . .
CP	Communications Processor	. . .
CP	Co-Processor	. . .
CP	Connection Processor	. . .
CP	Control Program (or Point)	IBM
CP/M	Control Program/Micro	DR
	Disk operating system for microcomputers	
CP/M-86	Control Program/Micro 8086	. . .
CPC	Card-Programmed Calculator	IBM
	Forerunner of stored-program computer	
CPCS	Comprehensive Planning and Control System	Cincom Systems
CPE	Customer Premises Equipment	AT&T
	re: Communications circuits and devices	
CPEM	Conference on Precision Electromagnetic Measurements	CPEM
CPF	CICS Print Facility	. . .
	sa *CICS*, *Customer Information Control System*	
CPF	Command Propagation Facility	Computer Associates
CPF	Common Purpose Field	IBM
CPF	Cryptographic Programmed Facility	IBM
CPF	Crystal Pulling Furnace	Soterem
cpi	characters per inch	. . .
	re: Density of hard copy print; see *bpi*, *bits per inch* for magnetic recording analog	
CPI	Common Programming Interface	IBM
CPI	Computer-to-PBX Interface	. . .
	sa *PBX*, *Private Branch Exchange*	
CPI	Cycles (or Clock [ticks]) Per Instruction	. . .
	Number of hardware cycles required to complete processing of a computer instruction	
CPI-C	Common Programming Interface for Communications	IBM
CPL	Capillary Pumped Loop	Goddard Space Flt. Ctr.
	re: Thermal transport technology	
CPM	Charged Plate Monitor	. . .
CPM	Colliding Pulse Mode-Lock	. . .
	re: Semiconductor laser technology	
CPM	Control Program Micro	. . .
	Disk operating system for Intel 8086 chip	

CPMS	Control Point Management Services	IBM
	SNA management component	
	sa *SNA, Systems Network Architecture*	
CPN	Control Packet Network	. . .
CPO	Catalog Performance Optimizer	Duquesne
		Systems
CPPC	Circular Performance Profile Charts	Borland
CPR	Cardio-Pulmonary Resuscitation	. . .
cps	characters per second	. . .
cps	cycles per second	. . .
	Now referred to as *Hertz*, which see	
CPS	Conversational Programming System	IBM
CPSR	Computer Professionals for Social	CPSR
	Responsibility	
CPU	Central Processing Unit	. . .
	re: Computer arithmetic and logic device	
	Alternately designated in lowercase: *cpu*	
CPU	Communications Processing Unit	. . .
	re: Message (telephone) switching system	
CPUAX	Central Processing Unit Arithmetic Extended	TRW
CPW	Co-Planar Waveguide	. . .
CQFP	Ceramic Quad Flat Pack	. . .
	re: An integrated circuit (IC) packaging	
	technology	
Cr	Chromium	. . .
	Atomic element number 24	
CR	Carriage Return	CCITT
	Format effector 5 (FE_5) under the CCITT	
	Recommendation V.3; sa *CCITT*	
CR	Compressive Receiver	. . .
	Radio/radar receiver with superior signal	
	resolution capability	
CR	Computed Radiography	. . .
	re: Computer image analysis	
CR	Condition Register	IBM
CRA	Catalog Recovery Area	IBM
	re: IBM's *Integrated Catalog Facility, ICF*	
CRAF	Comet Rendezvous and Asteroid Flyby	NASA
CRB	Cache Reload Buffer	IBM
CRB	Channel Request Block	DEC
CRC	Cyclic Redundancy Check	. . .
	A method of checking received data for	
	accuracy sa *LRC, Longitudinal Redundancy*	
	Check and *VRC, Vertical Redundancy Check*	
CRE	Certified Reliability Engineer	. . .

CREN	Corporation for Research and Educational Networking Union of BITnet and CSNET, August, 1989 sa *BITnet, "Because It's Time Network"* and *CSNET, Computer Science Network*	. . .
CREOL	Center for Research in Electro-Optics and Lasers	Univ. of Central Fla.
CRJE	Conversational Remote Job Entry	IBM
CRLF	Carriage Return, Line Feed	. . .
CRMA	Cyclic Reservation Multiple Access Fiber-based metropolitan area network (MAN)	IBM
CRMS	Communications Resource Management System	CHI/COR
CRO	Cathode Ray Oscilloscope	. . .
CRP	Channel Request Priority	IBM
CRRES	Combined Release and Radiation Effects Satellite	NASA
CRS	Color Recognition Sensor	. . .
CRS	Computerized Reservation System	. . .
CRS	Configuration Report Server Part of IBM's local area network (LAN) manager that runs as a NetView/PC application	IBM
CRT	Cathode Ray Tube	. . .
CRTC	Cathode Ray Tube Controller re: Solid-state (SS) circuit chip	. . .
CRV	Code Rule Violation re: CSMA/CD network; sa *CSMA/CD, Carrier Sense Multiple Access/Collision Detect*	IEEE
CRV	Cryptography Verification [request]	. . .
Cs	Caesium Atomic element number 55	. . .
CS	Chip Select re: Computer memory selection circuits	. . .
CS	Communications Server	. . .
CS	Continue Specific [mode] Inverse of *CA, Continue Any* [mode]	. . .
CS	Control Signal	. . .
CSA	Carrier-Serving Area	. . .
CSA	Client Service Agent	. . .
CSA	COBOL Structuring Aid sa *COBOL, Common Business-Oriented Language*	Marble Computer

CSA	Common Storage (or System) Area	IBM
CSA	Communication Subsystem Architecture	IBM
csc	cosecant	. . .
	Trigonometric function	
csc^{-1}	—arc cosecant	. . .
	Trigonometric function; inverse cosecant: "angle whose cosecant is . . ."	
csch	cosecant, hyperbolic	. . .
	Trigonometric function	
$csch^{-1}$	cosecant, inverse hyperbolic	. . .
	Trigonometric function; "angle whose hyperbolic cosecant is. . ."	
CSDB	Common Source Data Base	DoD
CSDC	Circuit-Switched Digital Capability	AT&T
CSECT	Control Section	IBM
CSEM	Current-Sheet Equivalence Material	. . .
	re: A permanent magnet in synchrotron technology	
CSENET	Child Support Enforcement Network	. . .
CSF	Course Structuring Facility	CSR
CSF	Critical Success Factor	. . .
	re: structural analysis	
CSG	Constructive Solids Geometry	Cadkey
	re: Computer-aided design (CAD) algorithm	
CSH	Complementary Software House	DEC
CSI	Client-Server Interface	Sybase
CSI	Computer Systems Integration	. . .
CSIC	Customer Specified Integrated Circuit	Motorola
CSIF	Communications Services Industrial Fund	DARPA
CSIR	Classified Search Image Retrieval [system]	PTO
CSL	Computer Security Laboratory	NIST
CSLM	Confocal Scanning Laser Microscope	SiScan Systems
CSM	Central System Manager	ISI
CSM	Communications Server Module	. . .
CSMA/CA	Carrier Sense Multiple Access/Collision Avoidance	Braegen
CSMA/CD	Carrier Sense Multiple Access/Collision Detect	. . .
CSMC	Communications Services Management Council	CSMC
CSMP	Continuous Systems Modeling Program	IBM
CSNET	Computer Science Network	. . .
	A network organized to promote research in computer science sa *CREN, Corporation for Research and Educational Networking*	
CSP	Certified Systems Professional	. . .
CSP	Communicating Sequential Process	. . .

CSP	Cross-System Product	IBM
CSPP	Computer Systems Policy Project US legislative lobbying group	. . .
CSR	Control and Status Register	DEC
CSS	CALS Software Submission sa *CALS, Computer-Aided Acquisition and* *Logistics* System	DoD
CSS	Center for Seismic Studies	. . .
CSS	Complete Statistical System	StatSoft
CSSCS	Combat Service Support Control System	US Army
CSSF	Customer Software Support Facility	IBM
CST	Central Standard Time	. . .
CSU	Cartridge Storage Unit	Memorex Telex
CSU	Channel Service Unit	. . .
CSVR	Common Signal-to-Voltage Ratio	. . .
CSW	Channel Status Word	IBM
CT	Cellular Telephone	. . .
CT	Computerized Tomography	. . .
CT *nnn*	Circuit *nnn*, *nnn* = three digit number Used in CCITT Recomm. V.25; sa *CCITT*	CCITT
CTA	Constant Temperature Anemometer	. . .
CTB	Concentrator Terminal Buffer	. . .
CTC	Centralized Traffic Control sa *CETC, Centralized Electrification and* *Traffic Control*	. . .
CTC	Channel-To-Channel [adapter]	IBM
CTC	Coaxial Token-Ring Connector	Ericsson
CTCA	Canadian Telecommunications Carrier Association	. . .
CTCA	Channel to Channel Adapter	IBM
CTE	Charge Transfer Efficiency re: Charge-coupled devices (CCDs), image intensifiers, etc.	. . .
CTE	Coefficient of Thermal Expansion	. . .
CTIA	Cellular Telecommunications Industry Association	CTIA
CTN	Compensated Twisted Nematic [display] A flat display panel technology	CTN
CTOD	Crack-Tip-Opening-Displacement	Langley Research Ctr.
CTORS	Conformance Testing Operational Requirement	ETCOM
CTOS	Concurrent Technologies Operating System	Concurrent Technologies
CTP	Cytidine Triphosphate A compound important in biochemistry	. . .

CTR	Count Register	IBM
CTR	Current Transfer Ratio re: Optoisolators, relays, solid-state (SS) switches	. . .
CTRL	Control Key on computer/terminal keyboard	. . .
CTS	Carpal Tunnel Syndrome A painful malady of the wrist, common in the data entry field sa *RSI, Repetitive Strain Injury*	. . .
CTS	Clear to Send Modem control signal; sa *RS-232-C*	. . .
CTS	Commercial Transaction System	. . .
CTS	Computer Technical Specialist	USFS
CTS	Conversational Terminal System	IBM
CTS	Conversational Time Sharing	. . .
CTSS	Compatible Time-Sharing System	MIT
CTSS	Cray Time Sharing System	Cray Research
CTVPT	Color Television Picture Telephone	Nippon Tel. & Tel.
CTX	Cosine Transform Exchange (or Extended) Video coder/decoder (codec) with data compression	CLI
CT2	Cordless Telephone, 2nd generation Cordless telephone standard	. . .
CT3	Cordless Telephone, 3rd generation Cordless telephone standard	. . .
Cu	Cuprum Symbol for *copper*, atomic element number 29	. . .
CUA	Common User Access	IBM
CUFS	College and University Financial System	AMS
CUFT	Center for the Utilization of Federal Technology	NTIS
CUG	Closed User Group	CCITT
CUI	Character-Based User Interface Inverse of *GUI, Graphical User Interface*	. . .
CUI	Common User Interface	IBM
CUPS	Connection Updates per Second re: Performance of neural nets	. . .
CUT	Control Unit Terminal	. . .
CV	Constant Velocity	. . .
CV	Constant Voltage	. . .
CVD	Chemical Vapor Deposition	. . .
CVG	Constructive Variational Geometry	Tektronix
CVGA	Color Video Graphics Adapter	. . .
CVL	Copper Vapor Laser	. . .

CVR	Crystal Video Receiver	. . .
CVSD	Continuously Variable Slope Delta [modulation]	. . .
	Algorithm commonly used for voice digitization	
CVSDM	Continuously Variable Slope Delta Modulation Variant; see *CVSD*	. . .
CVT	Constant Voltage Transformer	. . .
CVTS	Compressed Video Transmission Service	. . .
CW	Carrier Wave	. . .
CW	Clockwise	. . .
CW	Continuous Wave	. . .
Cx-Band	—Cx-Band	. . .
	Designation given to radar frequencies of 5.2 to 10.9 GHz (wavelength of 3 cm); also called *X-Band*	
cXDMS	Cell-Controller Database Management System	Computer-X
CXI	Common X Interface	H-P
cXOS	cX Operating System	Computer-X
Cys	Cysteine	. . .
	A compound important in biochemistry	
C^2I	Command, Control and Intelligence	US Army
C3	Command, Control, and Communications Variant; see C^3	DoD
C^3	Command, Control, and Communications	DoD
C^3I	Command, Control, Communications and Intelligence	DoD
C3I	Command, Control, Communications and Intelligence Variant; see *C^3I*	. . .
C^4I	Command, Control, Communications, Computer and Intelligence	DoD

D

d	deci	. . .
	Prefix for 10^{-1}	
D	—500	. . .
	Roman numeral designation	
D	—Electric Displacement (symbol)	. . .
	(Usually printed in boldface type: **D**)	
	Expressed in units of *Maxwells* Units	
	named in honor of Scottish physicist James Clerk Maxwell (1831–1879)	
D	D [Cell]	. . .
	Voltaic cell, measuring approximately 1.3″ diameter by 2.4″ long	

D	D [channel]	. . .
	16 kbps data channel used in ISDN communications sa *ISDN*, *Integrated Services Digital Network*	
D	Delivery	CCITT
	Confirmation bit in *X.25* protocol, which see	
D	Delta [channel]	AT&T
	re: Integrated Services Digital Network (ISDN) "out-of-band" communications channel	
D	Density (electric flux)	. . .
	Expressed in units of *Coulombs per square meter*, *C/m²* sa *C*, *Coulomb*	
D	Deuterium	. . .
	Hydrogen isotope, with one extra neutron	
D/A	Digital to Analog [converter, or conversion]	. . .
	Alternate form; see *DAC*	
D-RAM	Dynamic Random Access Memory	. . .
	Alternate form; see *DRAM*, *Dynamic Random Access Memory*	
da	deka	. . .
	Prefix for 10	
DA	Demand Assignment	. . .
DA	Destination Address	IEEE
	Field in IEEE 802.5 token ring data communications specification sa *IEEE*, *Institute of Electrical and Electronics Engineers*	
DAA	Data Access Arrangement	. . .
DAA	Distributed Application Architecture	Data General
DAB	Digital Audio Broadcasting	. . .
DAC	Data Acquisition Controller	. . .
DAC	Design Automation Conference	DAC
DAC	Digital-to-Analog Converter	. . .
DAC	Discretionary Access Control	. . .
	re: UNIX file access control per Department of Defense (DoD) criteria; sa *UNIX*	
DAC	Dynamic Astigmatism Control	Toshiba
	Compensation of electron beam focus at corners of a cathode ray tube display	
DACA	Demand Assigned Circuit Access	. . .
DaCK	Data Communications Kit	USFS
DACS	Data Access Control System	. . .
DACS	Data Acquisition and Capture Subsystem	NASA
DACS	Digital Access and Cross-Connect Switch (or System)	. . .

DAD	Digital Authentication Device	Digital Pathways
DADiSP	Data Analysis Digital Signal Processing	DSP Development
DAF	Dedicated Access Facility	. . .
DAF	Destination Address Field	IBM
	re: *SNA, Systems Network Architecture,* which see	
DAI	Data Acquisition Instrument	. . .
DAIS	Database Access Integration Services	EPRI
DAL	Data Access Language	Apple
	Structured query language (SQL) equivalent	
DAL	Digital Authoring Language	DEC
DAM/QAM	Dynamically Allocated Multicarrier-Quadrature Amplitude Modulation	. . .
DAMA	Dynamic (or Demand) Assignment Multiple Access	. . .
DAP	Data Access Protocol	DEC
DAP	Data Acquisition Processor	Microstar Labs
DAPA	Demand-Assigned Packet Access	. . .
DAR	Digital Acquire RAM	. . .
	sa *RAM, Random Access Memory*	
DAR	Digital Audio Recording	. . .
DARPA	Defense Advanced Research Projects Administration	DoD
DARS	Document Archival Retrieval System	. . .
DAS	Data Acquisition System	Analogic
DAS	Direct Analog Storage	ISD
DAS	Dual Attachment Station	. . .
DASD	Direct Access Secondary Storage	. . .
DASD	Direct Access Storage Device	IBM
DASE	Directory Access Protocol	. . .
DASP	Digital Array Signal Processor	. . .
DASS	Design Automation Standards Subcommittee	IEEE
DASS	Direct Access Secondary Storage	. . .
DAT	Date [of status]	IBM
DAT	Digital Audio Tape (or Technology)	. . .
DAT	Disk Allocation Table	IBM
DAT	Dynamic Address Translation	IBM
DATACOM/DB	Data Communications Database	. . .
DAU	Data Acquisition Unit	. . .
DAU	Distributed Access Unit	Bytex
DAV	Data Valid	IEEE
	re: IEEE Standard 488; sa *IEEE*	
DAVID	Distributed Access View Integrated Database	NASA

DAVSAT	Data-Audio-Voice Small Aperture Terminal	. . .
DAX	Digital Access Cross-Connect	. . .
db	decibel	. . .
	Variant; see *dB*	
dB	decibel	. . .
	Unit of relative power level	
DB	Data Base	. . .
	Usually written as *Database*	
DB/DC	Data Base/Data Communications	. . .
DBA	Data Base Administration(-or)	. . .
DBCS	Double-Byte Character Set	IBM
DBD	Data Base Definition	. . .
dBf	decibels [referred to one] femtowatt	. . .
DBF	Data Base Facility	. . .
DBF	Data Base Format	. . .
DBF	Dynamic Beam Focus	Mitsubishi
dBm	decibels [referred to one] milliwatt	. . .
DBM	Data Buffer Memory	. . .
DBMS	Data Base Management System	. . .
DBMS-10	Data Base Management System [for DEC System]-10	DEC
DBMS-20	Data Base Management System [for DEC System]-20	DEC
DBOMP	Data Base Organization and Maintenance Processor	IBM
dBr	decibels Relative	. . .
DBR	Distributed Bragg Reflector	. . .
	re: Semiconductor laser technology	
DBR	Disaster Backup and Recovery	. . .
DBRAD	Data Base Relational Application Dictionary	IBM
dBrn	decibels [above] reference noise	. . .
	A reference level commonly used in audio circuit literature	
DBRT	Delay Before Repeat Time	. . .
	re: Auto-repeat key circuitry on personal computers (PCs), terminals and other keyboard devices	
DBS	Direct Broadcast Satellite	
dBu	decibels [referenced to 0.775V RMS]	. . .
	A reference level commonly used in audio circuit literature sa *RMS, Root Mean Square*	
dBV	decibels [referenced to one] Volt (RMS)	. . .
	A reference level commonly used in audio circuit literature sa *RMS, Root Mean Square*	
dBW	decibels [referenced to one] Watt	. . .
	A reference level commonly used in audio circuit literature	

DB2	Database 2	IBM
DB2PM	Database 2 Performance Monitor	IBM
DB9	DB9	. . .
	Designation given to nine-conductor connector commonly used for inter-connection of computers with printers, etc.	
DB15	DB15	. . .
	Designation given to 15-conductor connector commonly used in computer data communications circuits	
DB25	DB25	. . .
	Designation given to 25-conductor connector commonly used in data communications circuits conforming to the *RS-232-C* standard, which see	
DB37	DB37	. . .
	Designation given to 37-conductor connector commonly used in computer data communications circuits	
DB50	DB50	. . .
	Designation given to 50-conductor connector commonly used in computer data communications circuits	
DC	Direct Current	. . .
DC	Double Channel	. . .
	re: Laser construction	
DC-PBH	Double-Channel-Planar Buried Heterostructure	NEC
	Manufacturing method of producing highly reliable laser diodes	
DCA	Data Center Administration	Computer Associates
DCA	Defense Communications Agency Systems	DoD
	Now *DISA*, *Defense Information Systems Agency*	
DCA	Dewar-Cooled Assembly	. . .
	re: Chilled radiation detector	
DCA	Direct Current Amperes	. . .
DCA	Distributed Communications Architecture	. . .
DCA	Document Content Architecture	IBM
DCAA	Defense Contract Audit Agency	DARPA
DCB	Data Control Block	IBM
DCB	Device Control Block	IBM
DCB	Disk Co-processor Board	. . .
DCC	Double-Coax Conversion	CCITT
DCD	Data Carrier Detect	. . .
DCD	Data Correlation and Documentation	IBM

DCD	Digital Clock Distributor	. . .
DCE	Data Circuit-terminating Equipment	. . .
DCE	Data Communications Equipment	. . .
DCE	Distributed Computing Environment	OSF
DCEA	Distributed Computing Environment Architecture	OSF
DCF	Data Communication Facility	IBM
DCF	Data Count Field	IBM
DCF	Document Composition Facility	IBM
DCFL	Direct-Coupled FET Logic sa *FET, Field Effect Transistor*	. . .
DCG	Dichromated Gelatin Substance used in laser phase grating production	. . .
DCL	Digital Command Language	DEC
DCL	Devices Clear IEEE Standard 488 bus command; sa *IEEE*	IEEE
DCL	Digital Control Logic	. . .
DCLZ	Data Compression Lempel-Ziv Proprietary data compression technology	H-P
DCM	Device Communications Manager	Cabletron Systems
DCM	Digital Circuit Multiplexing	. . .
DCM	Distributed Computing Model	. . .
DCME	Digital Circuit Multiplication Equipment	ANSI
DCMF	Distribution Change Management Facility	IBM
DCMP	Distributed Cooperative Marketing Program	DEC
DCMS	Device Control Management System	Electronic Data Sys.
DC_n	Device Control n (n=1,2,3,4) Generic description of certain keys on a computer or terminal keyboard; a part of the CCITT Recommendation V.3 These keys have no fixed assignment in the CCITT recommendation. sa *CCITT* and *V.3*	CCITT
DCO	Digitally Controlled Oscillator	. . .
DCOM	Data Center Operations Manager	. . .
DCP	Digital Communications Protocol	AT&T
DCP	Distributed Communications Processor	. . .
DCPSK	Differentially Coherent Phase Shift Keyed	. . .
DCPTF	Digitally Controlled Programmable Transversal Filter	TI
DCR	Diffraction-Coupled Resonator	. . .
DCS	Data Communication Standard	. . .
DCS	Dealer Communications System	BMW

DCS	Digital Classified Software	DEC
DCS	Digital Cross-Connect Switch	. . .
DCS	Digitizing Camera System	Tektronix
DCS	Distributed Communications System	AT&T
DCS	Distributed Control System	. . .
DCSP	Defense Communications Satellite Program	DoD
DCSS	Digital Conferencing and Switching System	AT&T
DCSS	Discontiguous Shared Segment	IBM
DCT	Destination Control Table	IBM
DCT	Device Characteristics Table	IBM
DCT	Digital Communications Terminal	US Marine Corps
DCT	Discrete Cosine Transform Algorithm useful in image compression techniques	. . .
DCT	Dispatcher Control Table	IBM
DCTN	Defense Commercial Telecommunications Network	DoD
DCU	Data Cache Unit	IBM
DCU	Data Control Unit	. . .
DCV	Direct Current Volts	. . .
DCW	Digital Chart of the World	DMA
DCWS	Debris Collision Warning Sensor	NASA
DD	Data Definition	IBM
DD	Data Dictionary	. . .
DD	Direct Detection re: Optical communication	. . .
DD/D	Data Dictionary/Directory	. . .
DDA	Digital Differential Analyzer	. . .
DDB	Device Data Block	. . .
DDB	Device Descriptor Block	IBM
DDB	Digital Data Bank	. . .
DDB	Distributed Data Base	Computer Associates
DDBM	Distributed Data Base Manager	. . .
DDBMS	Distributed Data Base Management Systems	. . .
DDCMP	Digital Data Communication Message Protocol	DEC
DDD	Direct Distance Dialing	AT&T
DDE	Dynamic Data Exchange	Microsoft
DDF	Dump Display Facility	. . .
DDGL	Device-Dependent Graphics Layer	. . .
DDHI	Direct Digital Holographic Imaging	ADH
DDI	Device Driver Interface	AT&T
DDIF	Digital Document Interchange Format	DEC
DDL	Data Definition (or Description) Language	. . .

DDL	Device Descriptor Language	IBM
DDL	Dispersive Delay Line	. . .
	An electronic device that resolves closely spaced radio frequency (RF) signals into time-separated signals	
DDM	Desktop Document Manager	Alacrity Systems
DDM	Device Descriptor Module	IBM
DDM	Distributed Data Management	IBM
DDMS	Design Data Management System	Mentor Graphics
DDN	Defense Data Network	DoD
DDNAME	Data Definition Name	IBM
DDNS	Demand Digital Network Service	Williams Telecomm
	Video teleconferencing service	
DDP	Distributed Data Processing	. . .
DDPM	Distributed Data Processing Management	. . .
DDR	DASD Dump Restore	IBM
	sa *DASD, Direct Access Storage Device*	
DDR	Dynamic Device Reconfiguration	IBM
DDRS	Defense Data Repository System	DoD
DDS	Data Description Specification	IBM
DDS	Data Dictionary System	. . .
DDS	Dataphone Digital Service	AT&T
DDS	Difference Detection System	Computer Associates
DDS	Digital Data Service	AT&T
DDS	Digital Data Storage	H-P/Sony
DDS	Digital Data System	ANSI
	Digital data recording format standard	
DDS	Digital-Distributed Software	DEC
DDS	Direct Digital Synthesis	. . .
DDSA	Digital Data Service Adapter	. . .
DDSA-SC	Dataphone Digital Service—Secondary Channel	AT&T
DDSN	Digital Derived Services Network	Telecom
DDT	Dichloro-diphenyl-trichloroethane	. . .
DDT	Driver Dispatch Table	DEC
DDT	Dynamic Debugging Technique	DEC
DE	Discard Eligibility	ANSI
	Field used in frame relay data communications protocol	
DEA	Data Encryption Algorithm	. . .
DEB	Data Extent Block	IBM
DECCO	Defense Commercial Communications Office	DARPA

DECmcc	Digital Equipment Corporation Management Control Center	DEC
DECnet	Digital Equipment Corporation Network	DEC
DECT	Digital European Cordless Telephone	. . .
DECUS	Digital Equipment Computer Users' Society	DEC
DEDB	Data Entry Data Base	IBM
DEDFA	Distributed Erbium-Doped Fiber Amplifier re: Laser technology	. . .
DEF	Data Encryption Facility	. . .
DEF	Destination Element Field	IBM
deg	degree Unit of heat, expressed in terms of degrees Celsius, C, Centigrade, C, or Farenheit, F; or unit of angular measurement, indicated in both cases by °	. . .
DEL	Delete ASCII standard specification; sa *ASCII*	CCITT
DEL	Delete Key on computer/terminal keyboard	. . .
DELNI	Digital Ethernet Local Network Interface	DEC
DEMPR	Digital Ethernet Multi-Portable Repeater	DEC
DEMS	Digital Electronic Message Service	. . .
DES	Data Encryption Standard	NBS
DES	Digital Encryption Standard	. . .
DES	Document Exchange System	SCC
DESC	Defense Electronics Supply Center	DoD
DevHlp	Device Driver Helper	IBM
DF/DM	Dedicated Function Database Machine	. . .
DFA	Design For Accessability	. . .
DFA	Design for Assembly	. . .
DFB	Distributed Feedback Generally used to describe a type of laser technology	. . .
DFC	Data Flow Control	IBM
DFD	Data Flow Diagram	. . .
DFD	Digital Frequency Discriminator	. . .
DFDL	Distributed-Feedback Dye Laser	. . .
DFDSS	Data Facility Data Set Services	IBM
DFE	Decision Feedback Equalizer re: *ISDN, Integrated Services Digital Network*	. . .
DFFT	Discrete Fast Fourier Transform	. . .
DFHSM	Data Facility Hierarchical Storage Manager	IBM
DFLD	Device Field	IBM
DFM	Design For Manufacturability	. . .

DFMS	Digital Facilities Management System	Northern Telecom
DFP	Data Facility Product	IBM
DFP	Diisopropylphosphofluoride A compound important in biochemistry	. . .
DFR	Dynamic Flexible Routing	AT&T
DFS	Distributed File Service (or System, or Server)	DEC
DFS	Distributed Function Support A communications satellite	IBM
DFSMS	Data Facility System-Managed Storage re: *DFP, Data Facility Product*	IBM
DFT	Design For Testability	. . .
DFT	Diagnostic Function Test	IBM
DFT	Discrete Fourier Transform re: Mathematical analysis of waveforms sa *FT, Fourier Transform* and *FFT, Fast Fourier Transform*	. . .
DFT	Distributed Function Terminal	IBM
DFU	Data File Utility	IBM
DG	Datagram [service]	AT&T
DGIS	Direct Graphics Interface Standard	GSS
DGS	Data Generation System	BitWise Designs
DHCF	Distributed Host Command Facility	IBM
DHM	Dexterous Hand Master re: Robotic hand development technology	EXOS
DI	Device Interconnect	DEC
DI	Dielectric Isolated (or Isolation)	. . .
DIA	Document Interchange Architecture	IBM
DIAG	Diagnostic Packet in *X.25* protocol, which see	CCITT
DIAL	Differential Absorption Lidar	. . .
DIB	Data Integrity Block	IBM
DIB	Directory Information Base	. . .
DIBOL	Digital Business-Oriented Language	DEC
DIC	Differential Interference Contrast re: Photomicrography after Nomarski illumination method	. . .
DICE	DARPA Initiative on Concurrent Engineering sa *DARPA, Defense Advanced Research Projects Administration*	DARPA
DICEP	Document Image Compression and Expansion Processor	. . .
DID	Direct Inward Dialing re: Communications circuits	AT&T
DIF	Data Interchange Format	. . .

DIF	Device Input Format	IBM
DIGL	Device-Independent Graphics Layer	. . .
DIGS	Device-Independent Graphics Services	. . .
DILUT	Double Input Look-Up Table	. . .
DIMES	Departmental Information Management Exchange System	US Dept. of H & HS
DIN	Deutches Institut für Normung Official standards-making body of German standards commonly encountered in electronic devices	DIN
DIOCB	Device Input/Output Control Block	IBM
DIOP	Disk Input/Output Processor	Cray Research
DIOP	Distributed Input/Output Processor	Parallel
DIP	Digital Image Printer	. . .
DIP	Dual In-line Package (or Plastic) Description of integrated circuit packaging sa *SIP, Single In-line Packaging*	. . .
DIPP	Document Image Pre-Processor	. . .
DIRMAINT	Directory Maintenance	IBM
DIS	Data Interpretation System	IBM
DIS	Disconnect Initiate Sent DNA message	DEC
DIS	Draft International Standard Standards defined by ISO. (Viz., FORTRAN, Pascal and others) sa *ISO, International Standards Organization*	ISO
DISA	Defense Information Systems Agency Formerly the *Defense Communications Agency, DCA*	US Army
DISA	Direct Inward System Access	AT&T
DISASM	Disassembler	IBM
DISC	Disconnect X.25 protocol command; sa *X.25*	CCITT
DISCO	Distributed Switching with Centralized Optics	AT&T
DISN	Defense Information Systems Network	DoD
DISNET	Defense Integrated Secure Network A component of the Department of Defense's *Defense Data Network, DDN*	DoD
DISOSS	Distributed Office Support System	IBM
DISSPLA	Display Integrated Software System and Plotting Language	. . .
DITTO	Data Interfile Transfer Testing and Options [utility] File copy and management software under IBM *DOS*, which see	IBM
DIU	Display Interface Unit	. . .

DIW	D-Inside Wire (or Wiring)	. . .
	re: Commonly used interior telephone wiring	
DKI	Driver Kernel Interface	AT&T
DL	Diode Laser	. . .
	A solid-state (SS) coherent light source	
DL/I	Data Language I	IBM
	re: A transaction processing (TP) service program	
DL/1	Data Language 1	IBM
	re: A data manipulation language	
DLA	Data Link Adapter	IBM
DLA	Defense Logistics Agency [network]	DoD
DLC	Data Link Connection	. . .
	re: *LAPD* implementation, which see	
DLC	Data Link Control	. . .
DLC	Direct Linear Conversion	. . .
	A digital-to-analog conversion (DAC) technology used in digital audio recording and reproduction	
DLCI	Data Link Connection (or Circuit) Identifier	. . .
	Field used in frame relay data communications protocol, *DCP* in *LAPD* implementation sa *DCP, Distributed Communications Protocol* and *LAPD, Link Access Protocol D*	
DLE	Data Link Escape	CCITT
	Transmission control 7 (TC₇) under CCITT Recommendation V.3; sa *CCITT, V.3* and *TCn*	
DLE	Differential Linearity Error	. . .
DLI	Data Link Interface	Schneider & Koch
	Protocol handler for interfacing the fiber distributed data interface (FDDI)	
DLL	Data Link Layer	. . .
DLL	Dynamically Linked Library(-ies)	. . .
DLM	Data Link Mapping	. . .
DLM	Data Line Monitor	. . .
DLM	Distributed Lock Manager	DEC
DLN	Digital Lightwave Network	DEC
DLPI	Data Link Provider Interface	. . .
DLR	DOS LAN Requester	IBM
	sa *DOS, Disk Operating System,* and *LAN, Local Area Network*	
DLS	Distributed Load Sharing	Vitalink

DLT	Data Loop Transceiver	IBM
dm	decimeter	. . .
	Metric unit of linear measure; 10^{-1} meter (m)	
dkm	dekameter (or decameter)	. . .
	Metric unit of length; 10 meters (m)	
DM	Data Mark	DoD
DM	Disconnect Mode	CCITT
DM	Distribution Manager	IBM
DMA	Defense Mapping Agency	DMA
DMA	Direct Memory Access	. . .
DMA	Distributed Management Architecture	IBM
DMAC	Direct Memory Access Controller	. . .
DMATS	Defense Metropolitan Area Telephone System	. . .
DMC	Differential Mode Coupling	. . .
DME	Distributed Management Environment	OSF
DMERT	Duplex Multi-Environment Real-Time	AT&T
DMF	Dual Tone Multifrequency	AT&T
DMH	Device Message Handler	IBM
DMI	Digital Multiplexed Interface	. . .
DML	Data Management Language	Software Publishing
DML	Data Manipulation Language	DEC
DML	Database Management Language	. . .
DMM	Digital Multi-Meter	. . .
DMOS	[Double] Diffused Metal Oxide Semiconductor	Signetics
DMOSFET	Diffused Metal Oxide Semiconductor Field-Effect Transistor	. . .
DMS	Data Management Software	3M
DMS	Data Management System	Sperry-Univac
DMS	Database Management System	Burroughs
DMS	Defense Message System	DoD
DMS	Design Management System	Sherpa
DMS	Display Management System	IBM
DMS	Distribution Management Syatem	Computer Associates
DMS	Document Management Software	3M
DMS	Document Management System	Univ. of MD
DMSP	Defense Meteorological Satellite Program	DoD
DMT	Design Maturity Test	DEC
DMT	Development Management Tool	. . .
DMTF	Diffraction Modulation Transfer Function	. . .
DNA	Defense Nuclear Agency	DNA
DNA	Deoxyribonucleic Acid	. . .
	The "double-helix" of genetic information transmittance fame	

DNA	Digital Network Architechture	DEC
DNA	Distributed Network Architecture	Sperry
DNAU	Distributed Network Access Unit	Bytex
DNC	Direct Numeric Control	. . .
DNCMS	Distributed Network Control and Management System	NEC
DNFB	Dinitrofluorobenzene A compound important in biochemistry sa *FDNB*	. . .
DNI	Desktop Network Interface	Cabletron Systems
DNI	Dialed Number Identification	. . .
DNIS	Dialed (or Direct) Number Identification Service	. . .
DNL	Differential Non-Linearity	. . .
DNMS	Dial-Up Network Management	. . .
DNP	2,4-Dinitrophenol A compound important in biochemistry	. . .
DNQS	Distributed Network Queueing System	. . .
DNS	Distributed Name Service	DEC
DNS	Domain Naming System re: Naming convention on the Internet	. . .
DOC	Department of Commerce	US Dept. of Commerce
DOC	Department of Communications	Canada
DOCS	Display Operator Console Support	CFS
DoD	Department of Defense	. . .
DOE	Diffractive Optical Element	. . .
DOE*	Data Output Enable [signal] Note: "*" indicates that a signal (called "active high") must be present at the circuit terminal in order for the described function to be activated.	. . .
DOF	Device Output Format	IBM
DOJ	Department of Justice	US Dept. of Justice
DOMF	Distributed Object Management Facility	H-P/Sun Microsystems
DOMSAT	Domestic Satellite	NASA
DOPA	Dihydroxyphenylalanine A compound important in biochemistry	. . .
DOS	Disk Operating System	IBM
DOSTN	Department of State Telecommunications Network	US Dept. of State
DOTS	Digital Optical Tape System	. . .

DOTTS	Department of Treasury Telecommunications Systems	US Treasury Dept.
DOV	Data Over Voice	. . .
DP	Data Processing	. . .
DP	Display Processor	. . .
DP	Double Pole [switch]	. . .
DPA	Demand Protocol Architecture	3Com
DPA	Destructive Physical Analysis	. . .
DPAGE	Device Page	IBM
DPCM	Differential Pulse Code Modulation	. . .
DPCX	Data Processing Control Executive Word processing operating system for IBM 8100	IBM
DPDT	Double-Pole Double-Throw [switch] A switch to select two of four circuits simultaneously	. . .
dpi	dots per [linear] inch Measure of printer density	. . .
dpi	dots per [square] inch Measure of photo density	. . .
DPL	Diode-Pumped Laser	. . .
DPL	Distributed Program Link re: Multi-platform CICS management sa *CICS, Customer Information Control System* and *ESA, Enterprise Systems Architecture*	IBM
DPLL	Digital Phase Locked Loop	. . .
DPLS	Digital Private Line Service	MCI
DPM	Digital Panel Meter	. . .
DPM	Distributed Plant Management	DEC
DPM	Distributed Presentation Management	IBM
DPMA	Data Porcessing Management Association	. . .
DPMI	DOS Protected Mode Interface sa *DOS, Disk Operating System*	Intel
DPNSS	Digital Private Network Signalling System	British Telecom
DPnT	Double-Pole *n*-Throw [switch] Two-circuit switch with *n* circuit positions	. . .
DPP	Digital Patch Panel	. . .
DPP	Disposable Plotter Pen	Koh-I-Noor
DPPX	Distributed Processing Programming Executive Operating system for the IBM 8100	IBM
DPS	Distributed Presentation Services	IBM
DPS	Document Processing System	Univ. of MD
DPSK	Differential Phase Shift Keying	. . .
DPSS	Diode-Pumped Solid-State [laser]	. . .

DPST	Double-Pole Single-Throw [switch]	. . .
	An on/off switch for controlling two circuits simultaneously	
DPT	Driver Prolog Table	DEC
DPU	Data Path Unit	TI
DPU	Data Processing Unit	. . .
DQCB	Disk Queue Control Block	IBM
DQDB	Distributed Queue Dual Bus	. . .
	Open ring network using dual contradirectional busses	
DQL	DataEase Query Language	DataEase Int'l
DQM	Dual Quadrature Mixer	. . .
	re: Radio frequency (RF) electronic circuits	
DQS	Distributed Queuing Services (or System)	DEC
DR	Dielectric Resonator	. . .
DRAM	Dynamic Random Access Memory	. . .
	Memory chip that must be refreshed periodically Compare with the electronic converse, *SRAM, Static Random Access Memory* Alternately designated by *D-RAM*	
DRAW	Direct Read After Write	. . .
DRC	Data Recording Control	IBM
DRC	Design Rule Check	. . .
DRCS	Dynamically Redifinable Character Sets	. . .
DRD	Data Recording Device	IBM
DRDA	Distributed Relational Database Architecture	IBM
DRDS	Dynamic Reconfiguration Data Set	IBM
DRDW	Direct Read During Write	Optotech
DRFM	Digital Radio Frequency Memory	. . .
DRI	Defense Research Internet	DoD
DRIS	Diagnostic Radiology Information System	. . .
DRO	Dielectric Resonator Oscillator	. . .
DRO	Digital Recording Oscilloscope	Gould Elect.
DRP	Distributed Resource Planning	. . .
DRQ	Data Ready Queue	IBM
DRS	Data Reconfiguration Service	. . .
DRS	Data Recovery System	Sterling Softw
DRT	Diffuse Reflectance and Transmittance	Optronic Laboratories
DS	Data Set	. . .
DS	Datagram Service	. . .
DS	Development System	IBM
DS-SSS	Direct-Sequence Spread-Spectrum System	. . .
	re: Interference suppression of spread-spectrum signals	

DS-0	Digital Signal Level 0 64 kbits/s data channel on T1 facility; equiv. to D4 sa *D4* and *T1*	AT&T
DS-1	Digital Signal [rate] 1 1.544 Mbit/s data channel on T1 facility sa *T1*	. . .
DS-1C	Digital Signal Level 1C 3.152 Mbit/s data channel on T1 facility sa *T1*	AT&T
DS-3	Digital Signal Level 3 44.736 Mbit/s data channel; equiv to T-3 (28 T1 channels) sa *T1*	CCITT
DSA	DASD Space Accounting sa *DASD, Direct Access Storage Device*	Computer Associates
DSA	Digital Storage Architecture	DEC
DSA	Digital Subtraction Angiography re: Computer image analysis	. . .
DSA	Digitizing Signal Analyzer	. . .
DSA	Directory Service Agent	. . .
DSA	Directory System Agent	. . .
DSAB	Data Set Access Block	. . .
DSACK*	Data and Size Acknowledge [signal] Note: "*" indicates that a signal (called "active high") must be present at the circuit terminal in order for the described function to be activated.	. . .
DSAF	Destination Subarea Field re: IBM's *Systems Network Architecture, SNA*	IBM
DSB	Defense Science Board	DSB
DSC	Digital Scanning Calorimeter(-try)	NASA
DSCB	Data Set Control Block	IBM
DSD	Data Set Definition	IBM
DSDF	DSA Standard Disk Format sa *DSA, Direct Storage Architecture*	DEC
DSDT	Data Set Definition Table	IBM
DSE	Data Set Extension	IBM
DSE	Data Switching Exchange	IBM
DSF	Data Set Functions	IBM
DSF	Device Support Facility	IBM
DSI	Data Stream Interface	IBM
DSI	Digital Speech Interpolation	. . .
DSIN	Digital Software Information Network	DEC
DSL	Data Set Label	IBM
DSL	Digital Subscriber Line	AT&T

DSLO	Distributed Systems License Option	IBM
DSM	Data Services Manager	IBM
DSM	Digital Standard MUMPS	DEC
	sa *MUMPS, Massachusetts [General Hospital] Utility Multi-Programming System*	
DSM	Digitizing Scope Module	Tektronix
DSM	Distributed Systems Management	. . .
DSMO	Data Site Management Officer	AT&T
DSMS	Distributed Systems Management Solutions	. . .
DSN	Data Set Name	IBM
DSN	Deep Space Network	NASA
DSN	Defense Switched Network	DoD
DSN	Digital Service Node	. . .
	Interface between analog (or linear) and digital communications	
DSO	Dielectric-Resonator Stabilized Oscillator	. . .
DSO	Digital Sampling Oscilloscope	. . .
DSO	Digital Storage Oscilloscope	. . .
DSP	Digital Signal Processing	. . .
DSP	Directory Service Protocol	. . .
DSP	Directory System Protocol	. . .
DSP	Domain Specific Part	. . .
DSPT	Display Station Pass-Through	. . .
DSPU	Downstream Physical Unit	IBM
	re: IBM's *Systems Network Architecture, SNA*	
DSR	Detector Spectral Analysis	Optronic Laboratories
DSR	Digital Standard Runoff	DEC
	Text-formatting program for the DEC VAX Operating System sa *VAX, Virtual Address Extension*	
DSR	Document Structure Recognition	. . .
DSRB	Data Services Request Block	IBM
DSRI	Digital Standard Relational Interface	DEC
DSRR	Digital Short-Range Radio	CEC
DSS	Decision Support System	. . .
DSS	DECnet System Service	DEC
DSS	Differential Systems Simulation	Schiesser, W.E.
DSS	Digital Simulation System	. . .
DSS	Distributed Software Services	. . .
DSSA	Distributed System Security Architecture	DEC
DSSE	Directory System Service Element	. . .
DSSI	Digital Storage System Interconnect	DEC
DSST	Digital Spread Spectrum Technology	Cylink
DST	Data Services Task	IBM

DST	Daylight Saving Time	. . .
	Archaic; now *DT*, *Daylight Time*	
DSTN	Double Supertwisted Nematic [display]	. . .
	Color liquid crystal display (LCD)	
	technology	
DSU	Data Service Unit	. . .
DSU	Digital Service Unit	. . .
DSX	Digital Signal Cross-Connect	. . .
	re: T1 communications; sa *T1*	
DSX	Distributed Systems Executive	IBM
DSX-1	Digital Signal Cross-Connect Level 1	. . .
	Cross connection of DS1 signals; sa *DS1*	
DS0	Data Service 0 (64 kbps)	. . .
DS0	Digital Signal 0	. . .
DS1	Data Service 1	. . .
	1.544 Mbps communications service;	
	equivalent to *T1*, which see	
DS2	Data Service 2	. . .
	6.312 Mbps communications service;	
	equivalent to *T2*, which see	
DS3	Data Service 3	. . .
	44.736 Mbps communications service;	
	equivalent to *T2*, which see	
DT	Daylight Time	. . .
	Sometimes referred to as *DST*, *Daylight Saving Time*	
DT	Digital Terminal	. . .
DTB	Dynamic Transaction Backout	IBM
DTCU	Dynamic Torque Calibration Unit	Agronin, M.L., JPL
DTE	Data Terminal Equipment [clear]	CCITT
	X.25 protocol packet assembly/disassembly (PAD) service signal to clear a remote call; sa *X.25*, *PAD*	
DTED	Digital Terrain Evaluation Data	NASA
DTF	Data Transfer Facility	DEC
DTF	Diagnostics Testbed Facility	. . .
DTGS	Deuterated Triglycine Sulfate	. . .
	Pyroelectric detector material	
DTIC	Defense Technical Information Center	US Government
DTIF	Digital Tabular Interchange Format	DEC
DTL	Diode-Transistor Logic	. . .
	Early integrate circuit (IC) technology, c. 1960	

DTMF	Dual Tone Multiple Frequency	AT&T
	Button phone dialing system; also known as Touch Tone	
DTO	Digitally Tuned Oscillator	. . .
DTP	Desk Top Publishing	. . .
DTP	Distributed Transaction Processing	IBM
DTR	Data Terminal Ready	. . .
	re: RS-232-C standard, pin 20; sa *RS-232-C*	
DTR	Data Transfer Rate	. . .
DTS	Dedicated Transmission Service	AT&T
DTS	Digital Termination Service	AT&T
DTS	Digital Termination System	. . .
DTSS	Dartmouth Timesharing System	Dartmouth Univ.
DTW	Dynamic Time Warping	. . .
	re: Voice recording in a time-compressed or time-expanded format	
DUA	Directory User Agent	. . .
DUAL	Dispatchable Unit Access List	IBM
DUART	Dual Universal Asynchronous Receiver/ Transmitter	. . .
DUAT	Dual User Access Terminal	FAA
DUT	Device Under Test	. . .
	sa *UUT, Unit Under Test* and *LUT, Logic Under Test*	
DUV	Data Under Voice	. . .
DVHSP	Digital Video High-Speed Processor	. . .
DVI	Digital Video Interactive [technology]	. . .
	A digital compression/decompression technology	
DVI	Digital Video Interface	. . .
	re: Compression/decompression video standard interfacing	
DVM	Data/Voice Module	AT&T
DVM	Data/Voice Multiplexer	AT&T
DVM	Digital Voice Multiplexer	AT&T
DVM	Digital Voltmeter	. . .
DVN	Digital Video Network	DEC
DVNS	Data/Voice Network Server	Micom
DVOM	Digital Volt-Ohm-Milliameter	. . .
DVT	Device Vector Table	IBM
	re: IBM's Series 1 System	
DVT	Digital Video Teleconferencing	Intel
DVT	Dynamic Velocity Taper	. . .
	Used in design of traveling wave tubes	
DVX	Digital Voice Exchange	Wang

DWB	Direct Wafer Bonding	. . .
DWL	Design Waveform Language	Genrad
DWS	Diskless Work Station	. . .
	Personal computer (PC) with solid-state (SS) storage but no disk storage	
DWSS	DPPX Work Station Support	IBM
	sa *DPPX, Distributed Processing Program Executive*	
DX	Directory Exchange	. . .
	re: Electronic mail in X.400 systems	
DX	Distance	. . .
	Abbreviation commonly used in communications	
DX	Dual Attach	Sun Microsystems
DXAM	Distributed Indexed Access Method	IBM
DXC	Digital Cross-Connect System	. . .
DXF	Data Exchange Format	. . .
	Computer-aided design (CAD) data format	
DXI	Data Exchange Interface	. . .
Dy	Dysprosium	. . .
	Atomic element number 66	
D2T2	Dye Diffusion Thermal Transfer	. . .
D4	Digital [frame format] 4	CCITT
	64 kbits/s data channel; sa *DS-0*	

E

e	electron charge	. . .
	1.60206×10^{-19} Coulomb	
E	Electric [field strength vector]	. . .
	Expressed in units of *Volts per meter, V/m* Usually denoted by boldface type: **E**	
E	Exa	. . .
	Prefix for 10^{18}	
E/D	Enhancement/Depletion	. . .
E-LPA	Enhanced Line-Powered Amplifier	Tollgrade
e⁻ Mail	electronic Mail	. . .
	Alternate form; sa *e-mail*	
E&M	Ear and Mouth	. . .
	Receive and transmit leads of a signalling system, generally voice circuits	
e-mail	electronic mail	. . .
	Variously indicated as *e⁻* Mail, using the electronic negative charge symbol, or *E-Mail*	

E-R	Entity-Relationship	. . .
	Alternate form; see *E/R*	
E/R	Entity/Relationship	. . .
	Analytical modelling technique for databases	
EA	Extended Address	. . .
	Field used in frame relay data communications protocol	
EADS	Engineering and Analysis Data System	NASA
EAM	Electrical Accounting Machine	ANDIF
EAR	Electronically Agile Radar	. . .
EARN	European Academic Research Network	. . .
EAROM	Electrically Alterable Read Only Memory	. . .
EASL	External Applications Software Library	DEC
EAX	Electronic Automatic Exchange	General Telephone
EBCDIC	Extended Binary-Coded Decimal Interchange Code	ANDIP
EBIC	Electron Beam Induced Current	. . .
EBR	Electron Beam Recording	ANDIP
EBR	Employee Badge Reader	AT&T
EBRS	Electronic Batch Records System	DEC
EBT	Electronic Benefits Transfer	US Treasury Dept.
	An electronic funds transfer (EFT) system for dispersing government benefits	
EBT	Equipment-Based Training	. . .
EC	Echo Cancel	. . .
	re: *ISDN*, which see	
EC	Electrochromic [layer]	. . .
	re: "Smart window" glass technology, in which transmission of light and heat is directionally controllable	
EC	Engineering Change	IBM
EC	Erase Character	DoD
	TELNET command	
EC[n]	Enzyme Commission [n]	Enzyme Commission
	A formal classification of enzymes	
ECA	Extended Contingent Allegiance	ANSI
	re: Error recovery in SCSI-2 implementation; sa *SCSI, Small Computer Systems Interface*	
ECAD	Enhanced Computer-Aided Design	. . .
ECAN	Electro-Cardiographic Analysis	. . .
ECAP	Electronic Circuit Analysis Program	. . .
ECB	Ethernet Control Board	Equinox

ECB	Event Control Block	
ECC	Error Checking and Correcting	IBM
ECC	Error Correcting Code	DEC
ECC	Error Correction Circuit	Ampex
ECCM	Electronic Counter-Countermeasures	. . .
ECD	Envelope-to-Cycle Difference	. . .
	re: Loran-C navigational and time/frequency standard broadcasts; sa *Loran-C, Long range navigation-C*	
ECF	Enhanced Connectivity Facilities	IBM
ECG	Electrocardiogram	. . .
	Alternate; see *EKG*, international and preferred form	
ECH	Echo-Cancelling Hybrid	. . .
ECL	Emitter-Coupled Logic	. . .
	Integrated circuit (IC) technology developed c 1960	
ECLSS	Environmental Control and Life Support System	NASA
ECM	Electrochemical Machining	. . .
ECM	Electronic Counter Measure	US Air Force
	re: Countermeasures against enemy radar	
ECMA	European Computer Manufacturers Association	. . .
ECMA-nn	—ECMA-nn	ECMA
	re: Standards published by *ECMA*, which see	
ECN	Executive Computer Network	US Army
ECO	Electron-Coupled Oscillator	. . .
ECO	Engineering Change Order	. . .
ECP	Embedded Control Processor	Intel
ECPI	Elastomeric Conductive-Polymer Interconnect	. . .
	A flexible contact medium	
ECPS	Extended Control Program Support	IBM
ECR	Electron Cyclotron Resonance [effect]	. . .
	re: Plasma source technology	
ECS	Extended Channel Support	Amdahl
ECS	Extended Character Set	. . .
ECSA	Extended Common Storage (or System) Area	IBM
ECU	Electronic Control Unit	. . .
ECW	Equivalent Concentration of Water	. . .
ED	End Delimiter	IEEE
	Field in IEEE 802.5 token ring data communications specification sa *IEEE, Institute of Electrical and Electronics Engineers*	

ED	Extra Density	IBM
	re: Very high density 5¼″ diskettes—4 megabyte (MB) capacity	
ED	Extra-Low Dispersion	Nikon
	Designation given to Nikon optical glass	
ED-*n*	Exposure Dosage (or Density)—*n*	. . .
	where *n* is equal to percentage of tissue damage expectancy i.e., ED-50 implies tissue damage in 50% of the exposures at ED-50	
EDA	Electronic Design Automation	. . .
EDA	Exploratory Data Analysis	Tukey, John W.
EDA	Enterprise Data Access	IBM
EDAC	Error Detection and Correction	. . .
EDBMF	Extended Data Base Management Facility	IBM
EDC	Error Detection Code	. . .
EDC	Error Detection and Correction	. . .
EDCS	Electronic Data Control System	DEC
EDF	Execution Diagnostic Facility	IBM
EDFA	Erbium-Doped-Fiber Amplifier	. . .
EDGAR	Electronic Data Gathering, Analysis and Retrieval [system]	SEC
EDGE	Extensible Display Geometry [machine] Proprietary graphics-processor chip set	Intergraph
EDI	Electronic Data Interchange	CCITT
EDIF	Electronic Design Interchange Format	. . .
EDIFACT	Electronic Data Interchange for Administration, Commerce and Transport sa *EDI, Electronic Data Interchange*	DEC
EDIMS	EDI Messaging Service sa *EDI, Electronic Data Interchange*	CCITT
EDIMS	EDI Messaging System sa *EDI, Electronic Data Interchange*	CCITT
EDIRF	EDI Responsibility and Forwarding sa *EDI, Electronic Data Interchange*	CCITT
EDL	Engineering Data Library	CDC
EDM	Electrical Discharge Machining	Wells, D., JSC
EDM	Environment Description Manager	IBM
EDM	External Data Manager	. . .
EDMICS	Engineering Data Management Information and Control System	DoD
EDN	Enhanced Digital Networking	. . .
EDNA	Event-Driven Numerical Acquisition	Bio-Optronics
EDNS	Enterprise-Defined Network Services	Infonet
EDOS	Extended Disk Operating System	CSC
EDP	Electronic Data Processing	. . .

EDP	Extended Density Platform	NEC
EDRAM	Enhanced Dynamic Random Access Memory	. . .
EDSL	Enhanced Digital Subscriber Line	AT&T
EDSX	Electronic Digital Signal Cross-Connect	CCITT
EDTA	Ethylenediaminetetraacetic Acid	. . .
	A compound important in biochemistry	
EDTV	Extended Definition Television	. . .
	Television with resolution between standard and high definition television (HDTV)	
EDVAC	Electronic Discrete Variable Calculator	Eckert & Mauchly
	Eckert and Mauchly's second machine	
EDX	Energy Dispersive X-Ray [spectroscopy]	. . .
EDX/CF	Event-Driven Executive/Communications Facility	IBM
EE	Extended Edition	IBM
	re: *OS/2*, which see	
EECL	Enhanced Emitter Coupled Logic	John Price
EEG	Electroencephalogram	. . .
	Recording of brain electrical activity	
EEL	Edge-Emitting Laser	. . .
EEM	Electronic Engineer's Master	Hearst
EEMC	Electronics Equipment Manufacturers Committee	EMPF
EEMS	Enhanced Expanded Memory Specification	. . .
EEPLD	Electronically Eraseable Programmable Logic Device	Adv. Micro Dev.
	An integrated circuit (IC) which is user-programmable into a wide variety of logical configurations For other programmable logic devices (PLDs) see *EPLD, FPGA, FPLA, PAL, PEEL, PGA, PIC, PLA* and *PLD*	
EET	Edge Enhancement Technique	Destiny Technology
	Technique for improving dot matrix printer quality	
EF/DM	Extracted Function Database Machine	. . .
EFDMIM	Ethernet-to-FDDI-Distributed Media Interface Module	Cabletron
	sa *FDDI, Fiber Distributed Data Interface* and *Ethernet*	
EFL	Effective (or Equivalent) Focal Length	. . .
EFMS	Environmental and Facilities Management System	NASA
EFS	End-of-Frame Sequence	FDDI
EFS	Error-Free Seconds	. . .

EFS	Extended Frame Superformat	AT&T
EFT	Electrical Fast Transient	. . .
EFT	Electronic Funds Transfer	. . .
EGA	Enhanced Graphics Adapter	. . .
EGC	Enhanced Group Call	INMARSAT
EGP	Extended Gateway Protocol	. . .
EGP	Exterior Gateway Protocol	DoD
EGRET	Energetic Gamma Ray Experiment Telescope	NASA
EHF	Extremely High Frequency 30 to 300 GHz	. . .
EHLLAPI	Emulator High-Level Language Application Program Interface	IBM
EIA	Electronics Industry Association	. . .
EIAJ	Electronic Industry Association of Japan	EIAJ
EIB	Execute Interface Block	IBM
EIC	Ethernet Interface Coupler	NCR Comten
EIES	Electronic Information Exchange System	EPA
EII	Electronically Invisible Interconnect	Augat
EIN	Equivalent Input Noise A measurement commonly used in audio literature	. . .
EIS	Engineering Information System	US Air Force
EIS	Enterprise Integration Services	DEC
EIS	Executive Information System	Timeline
EISA	Extended Industry Standard Architecture	. . .
EISPACK	Eigensystem Package A collection of mathematical routines	Smith, Boyle, et al.
EIT	Engineer In Training	. . .
EKG	Electrokardiogram (German) Preferred international abbreviation; sa *ECG*	. . .
EL	Electroluminescent (-ence)	. . .
EL	Erase Line TELNET command; sa *TELNET*, *Telecommunications Network*	DoD
ELAN	Enhanced Local Area Network	. . .
ELAS	Earth Resources Laboratory Applications Software	NASA
ELCA	Excimer Laser Coronary Angioplasty	. . .
ELD	Electroluminescent Display	. . .
ELEAT	Entry Level Enhanced Advanced Technology	Chips & Technologies
ELED	Edge-Emitting Light-Emitting Diode A solid-state (SS) non-coherent light source	. . .

ELF	Extremely Low Frequency 30 to 300 Hz	. . .
Elint	Electronic Intelligence Complex electronic processing of radar signals	. . .
ELL	Excimer Laser Lithography	. . .
ELS	Entry Level System	Novell
ELT	Emergency Locator Transmitter	FCC
EM	Electromagnetic	. . .
EM	Electronic Mail Alternate form; see e- Mail	. . .
EM	End of Medium A key on a computer or terminal keyboard; a part of CCITT V.3; sa *CCITT* and *V.3*	CCITT
EM	Expandable(-ed) Memory	. . .
EMA	Enterprise Management Architecture	DEC
EMAT	Electro-Optical Model for Aerial Targeting	DNA
EMC	Electromagnetic Compatibility	. . .
EMC	Electromagnetic Coupling	. . .
EMD	Equilibrium Mode Distribution re: Fiber-optic communications	. . .
emf	electromotive force Also designated by *EMF*	. . .
EMG	Electromyogram(-graph) Recording of muscle electrical activity	. . .
EMI	Electromagnetic Interference	. . .
EML	Established Measured Loss	. . .
EMM	Ethernet Management Module	Chipcom
EMMA	Electronic Morphometry Mapping Analysis	Bloom, F., & Young, W.
EMP	Electromagnetic Pulse	. . .
EMPF	Electronics Manufacturing Productivity Facility	US Navy
EMR	Electromagnetic Radiation	. . .
EMS	Electromagnetic Susceptibility	. . .
EMS	Electronic Messaging System	. . .
EMS	Electronic Mail Service	DEC
EMS	Element Management Service	Timeplex
EMS	Energy Management System	. . .
EMS	Enterprise Management Station	DEC
EMS	Expanded Memory Specification	Lotus/Intel/ Microsoft
EMS	Extended Memory Specification	AST Research
EMV	Effective Mode Volume re: Fiber-optic communications	. . .

endec	encoder/decoder Variant; see *codec*	. . .
ENET	Enhanced Network	Northern Telecom
ENIAC	Electronic Numerical Integrater And Calculator Eckert and Mauchly's first digital computer (early 1940s) Sometimes designated by *Eniac* in the literature	Eckert & Mauchly
ENOB	Effective Number of Bits A measure of analog-to-digital conversion (ADC), and digital-to-analog conversion (DAC) performance	. . .
ENQ	Enquiry aracter] Transmission control 5 (TC_5) under CCITT Recommendation V.3; sa *CCITT*, *V.3* and *TCn*	CCITT
ENS	Enterprise Network Switch	. . .
ENTELEC	Energy Telecommunications and Electrical Association	ENTELEC
Envoy1	Envoy 1 Electronic mail system based on *Telemail*, which see	TCTS
EO	Electro Optic(-al, -s)	. . .
EOA	End Of Address	. . .
EOB	End Of Block	. . .
EOC	End Of Chain	IBM
EOD	End Of Data	. . .
EOE	End Of Extent	IBM
EOF	End Of File	IBM
EOI	End Or Identify re: IEEE Standard 488; sa *IEEE*	IEEE
EOL	End Of Line	. . .
EOL	End Of List	. . .
EOM	End Of Message	. . .
EOM	Eraseable Optical Memory	. . .
EON	End of Number [control character] CCITT Recomm. V.24; sa *CCITT* and *V.24*	CCITT
EOPM	Electro Optic Phase Modulation	. . .
EOPP	Earth-Orbiting Polar Platform	. . .
EOS	Earth-Observing System	NASA
EOS	Earth-Orbiting Satellite	. . .
EOS	Electrical Overstress Stress testing of electronic components	. . .
EOS	End Of String	. . .

EOSDIS	Earth-Observing System Data and Information System	NASA
EOT	End Of Tape	. . .
EOT	End Of Transmission	CCITT
	Transmission control 4 (TC₄) under CCITT Recommendation V.3; sa *CCITT*, *V.3* and *TC*n	
EOV	End Of Volume	IBM
EP	Emulation Program	IBM
	Pertains to software for IBM the 3705 Communications Controller	
EP	Environmentally Protected	. . .
EP	Extended Platform	DCA
	A personal computer (PC) to local area network (LAN) gateway device	
EPA	Environmental Protection Agency	US
EPA	Event Processor Array	. . .
EPCAD	Electronics Packaging Computer-Aided Design	NEPCON
EPDM	Ethylene-Propylene-Diene [co-polymer]	. . .
EPIRB	Emergency Position Indicating Radio Beacon	FCC
EPLD	Eraseable Programmable Logic Device	. . .
	An integrated circuit (IC) which is user-programmable into a wide variety of logical configurations For other programmable logic devices (PLDs) see *EEPLD*, *FPGA*, *FPLA*, *PAL*, *PEEL*, *PGA*, *PIC* and *PLA*	
EPN	Expansion Port Network	AT&T
	Element of Generic 3 telephone switching system	
EPR	Electron Paramagnetic Resonance	. . .
EPRI	Electric Power Research Institute	EPRI
EPROM	Eraseable Programmable Read Only Memory	. . .
	sa *EEPROM* and *UVEPROM* for specific EPROM devices	
EPS	Electrophysiological Study	. . .
EPS	European Physical Society	EPS
EPS	Extended Protocol Specification	. . .
	A graphics standard	
EPSCS	Enhanced Private Switched Communications System	. . .
EPSF	Encapsulated PostScript File	Page Studio Graphics
EPSS	Experimental Packet-Switched Service	UK
EQL	English Query Language	Info. Bldrs.

Er	Erbium	. . .
	Atomic element number 68	
	Named after Ytterby, Sweden, site of a quarry from which the ore was first obtained	
ER	Explicit Route	IBM
	In SNA: simplex physical path between subarea nodes sa *SNA, Systems Network Architecture*	
Er:YAG	Erbium-Yttrium-Aluminum-Garnet	. . .
	A type of laser crystal	
ERA	Electrically Reconfigurable Array	. . .
	re: Solid-state (SS) logic device	
ERATO	Exploratory Research in Advanced Technologies	Japan
ERC	Engineering Research Center	NSF
ERC	Engineering Rule Check	. . .
ERD	Entity Relationship Diagram	. . .
EREP	Environmental Recording, Editing, and Printing	IBM
ERICA	Eyegaze Response Interface Computer Aid	Hutchinson, T.
ERMA	Electronic Recording Method of Accounting	General Electric
	Name of General Electric's first commercial computer (c. 1950)	
ERP	Error Recovery Program	IBM
	Pertains to software for the IBM 3705 Communications Controller	
ERP	Extended Research Program	DEC
ERR	Error [in local procedure]	CCITT
	X.25 protocol packet assembly/disassembly (PAD) service signal sa *X.25*	
ERS	Earth Resources Satellite	. . .
ERS	ESA Remote-Sensing Satellite	ESA
	sa *ESA, European Space Agency*	
ERS	Emergency Reporting System	. . .
Es	Einsteinium	. . .
	Atomic element number 99	
	Named in honor of American theoretical physicist and mathematician Albert Einstein (1879–1955)	
ES	End System	. . .
ES	Errored Second	Tau-Tron
ES-IS	End System-to-Intermediate System	OSI
ESA	Enterprise Systems Architecture	IBM
ESA	European Space Agency	ESA
ESC	Enhanced Services Complex	AT&T

ESC	Escape	CCITT
	A key on a computer or terminal keyboard; a part of CCITT Recommendation V.3; sa *CCITT* and *V.3*	
ESCA	Electron Spectroscopy for Chemical Analysis	. . .
ESCON	Enterprise Systems Connection [architecture] re: Dense electronic circuit interconnection technology	IBM
ESD	Electronic Software Distribution	. . .
ESD	Electrostatic Discharge	. . .
ESD	External Symbol Dictionary	IBM
ESDI	Enhanced Small Device (or Disk) Interface	. . .
ESDS	Electrostatic Discharge Sensitivity	. . .
ESDS	Entry Sequenced Data Set	. . .
ESE	Electronic Storage Element Solid-state (SS) disk storage	. . .
ESE	Expert System Environment	IBM
ESF	Extended Superframe Format	. . .
ESF	External Source Format	IBM
ESFMU	Extended Superframe Monitoring Unit	. . .
ESI	Enhanced Serial Interface	Hayes
ESL	Equivalent Series Inductance Parasitic inductance present in capacitors	. . .
ESML	Extended Software Modeling Language	Bruyn-Ward
ESN	Emergency Service Network	. . .
ESnet	Energy Services Network	ESnet
ESNIB	European Science News Information Bulletin	ESNIB
ESO	European Southern Observatory	ESO
ESP	Econometrics Software Package	Synergy
ESP	Engineering Support Processor re: Reduced instruction set computer (RISC) hardware design	IBM
ESP	Enhanced Serial Port	Hayes
ESP	Enhanced Service Package	MCI
ESP	Enhanced Service Provider	. . .
ESR	Electron Spin Resonance	. . .
ESR	Equivalent Series Resistance re: Low resistance in high-discharge-rate capacitors	. . .
ESRF	European Synchrotron Radiation Facility	. . .
ESS	Electronic Switching System	AT&T
ESS	Environmental Stress Screening	. . .
ESS	Executive Support System	. . .
EST	Eastern Standard Time	. . .
ESTSC	Energy Science and Technology Software Center	DoE

ESU	Electrostatic Unit	. . .
	Unit of electrical charge	
ESU	Electro-Surgery Unit	. . .
	A device which separates tissue by means of pulsed high voltage (HV) at high frequency (HF)	
ESVM	Electrostatic Voltmeter	. . .
ET	Electronic Typewriter	. . .
ET	Exchange Termination	. . .
ETB	End of Transmission Block	CCITT
	Transmission control 10 (TC_{10}) under CCITT Recommendation V.3; sa *CCITT, V.3* and *TCn*	
ETC	ECL, TTL, CMOS	. . .
	sa *ECL, Emitter-Coupled Logic, TTL, Transistor-Transistor Logic* and *CMOS, Complementary Metal Oxide Semiconductor*	
ETCOM	European Testing for Certification of Office and Manufacture	ETCOM
ETDEF	Entry Table Descriptor Definition	IBM
ETDL	Electronics Technology and Device Laboratory	US Army
ETFE	Ethylenetetrafluoroethylene	. . .
	A material used for fiber-optic cables	
Ethernet	—Ethernet	. . .
	re: Communications network protocol	
EtherNIM	Ethernet Network Integrity Monitor	. . .
ETL	ECL and TTL Logic	. . .
	Combined form of *ECL, Emitter-Coupled Logic* and *TTL, Transistor-Transistor Logic*	
ETM	Element Test and Maintenance	. . .
ETN	Electronic Tandem Networks	AT&T
ETNC	E-Threaded Neill-Concelman	. . .
	Electronics connector used chiefly in microwave applications	
ETOM	Electron-Trapping Optical Memory	. . .
ETP	Electron Transfer Particle	. . .
	re: Biochemical membrane activity	
ETR	Early Token Release	. . .
	A token released immediately following a data frame on a token ring network	
ETR	External Throughput Rate	IBM
ETRR	External Throughput Rate Ratio	IBM
ETS	Electronic Tandem Switching	. . .
ETS	Experimental Technologies Satellite	. . .
ETSI	European Telecommunication Standards Institute	ETSI

ETSS	Entry Time-Sharing System	IBM
ETTM	Electronic Tolls and Traffic Management	. . .
ETU	Emulator Transfer Utility	Softw. Sys.
ETX	End of Text	CCITT
	Transmission control 3 (TC_3) under CCITT Recommendation V.3; sa *CCITT*, *V.3* and TC_n	
Eu	Europium	. . .
	Atomic element number 63	
EUIT	Educational Uses of Information Technology	EDUCOM
EUV	Extreme Ultraviolet	. . .
	10^{17} to 10^{18} Hertz; wavelength of 30 cm to 3 $\times$ 10^{-8} cm	
eV	electron Volt	. . .
	Energy of one eV is equivalent to 1.602×10^{-19} Joule	
EVA	Extra Vehicular Activity	NASA
	re: Space exploration	
EVE	European Videoconference Experiment	. . .
EVE	Extensible VAX Editor	DEC
	sa *VAX*, *Virtual Address Extension*	
EVIS	Electronic Vibration Isolation System	. . .
EW	Electronic Warfare	. . .
EWAN	Enterprise Wide Area Network	. . .
EWC	Electrode Width Control	. . .
	re: Surface acoustic wave (SAW) device fabrication	
EWI	Electronic Work Instruction	Palette
EWI	Engineering Work Instructions	TechView
EWOS	European Workshop for Open Systems	EWOS
Ex	Exciter	. . .
	re: Radio-electronics and power generation	
EXCP	Execute Channel Program	IBM
EXEC	Execute	. . .
	Used in verb form to designate execution of a series of system commands; also used as a noun to designate the name of such a series of commands	
EXIP	Execute In Place	. . .
	IEEE memory card specification in which the entire card can be mapped into main memory sa *XIP*, *LXIP* and *IEEE*	

F

f	frequency	. . .
	Expressed in units of *Hertz*, *Hz*, which see	

f	femto	...
	Prefix for 10^{-15}	
F	Fahrenheit	...
	Scale of temperature measurement; named in honor of German physicist Gabriel Daniel Fahrenheit (1686–1736)	
F	Farad	...
	Unit of electric charge Named in honor of English physicist Michael Faraday (1791–1867)	
F	Faraday [constant]	...
	9.648×10^4 C/mol Named in honor of English physicist Michael Faraday (1791–1867)	
F	Fast	Motorola
	re: A high-speed Schottky-TTL integrated circuit (IC) logic family; sa *TTL, Transistor-Transistor Logic*	
F	Flag	IBM
	re: *Synchronous Data Link Control, SDLC*	
F	Fluorine	...
	Atomic element number 9	
F	Force	...
	Expressed in units of *Newtons, N*, which see	
F/B	Foreground/Background	...
F-Band	F-Band	...
	Microwave frequency allocation of 3 to 4 GHz	
F/O	Fiber-Optic	...
	Also designated by *FO*	
F-T1	Fractional T1	...
	Alternate form; see *FT1*	
fA	femtoampere	...
	10^{-15} Ampere	
FA	Failure Analysis	...
FA	Fatty Acid	...
	Chemical structure important in biochemistry	
FAA	Federal Aviation Administration	FAA
FAAR	Forward Area Alerting Radar	....
FAB	File Access Block	DEC
FAC	Function Authority Credential	IBM
FACETS	Factory Automation Control Environment Tool Set	CTS
FACT	Fairchild Advanced CMOS Technology sa *CMOS, Complementary Metal Oxide Semiconductor*	Fairchild

FACT	Fast-Action Computer Terminal	Land Rover Parts
FACT	Federation of Automated Coding Technologies	FACT
FACT	Flexible Automatic Circuit Tester	Hughes
FACT	FOCUS Application Creation Tool	Information Bldrs
	sa *FOCUS*	
FAD	Flavin Adenine Dinucleotide	. . .
	A compound important in biochemistry	
FAM	File Access Manager	. . .
FAMOS	Floating-Gate Avalanche Metal Oxide Semiconductor	. . .
FAPL	Formats and Protocols Language	IBM
FAQS	Financial Analysis and Query System	Goal
	Partition balancer	
FARMS	Flexible Agricultural Robotics Manipulator System	NASA
FARNET	Federation of American Research Networks	FARNET
FAS	Flexible Access System	. . .
FASIC	Function and Algorithm-Specific Integrated Circuit	. . .
FASS	Frequency Agile Signal Simulator	H-P
FAST	Failure Analysis and Support Technology	IBM
FAST	Fairchild Advanced Schottky TTL	Fairchild
	re: High-speed integrated circuit (IC) technology sa *S*, *Schottky* and *TTL*, *Transistor-Transistor Logic*	
FAST	First Application System Testing	Northern Telecom
FAST	Flow Analysis Software Toolkit	NASA
FAST	Functional At-Speed Test	Outlook Technology
FASTBOL	Fast COBOL [maintenance facility]	. . .
	sa *COBOL*, *Common Business-Oriented Language*	
FAT	File Allocation Table	. . .
FATAR	Fast Analysis Tape and Recovery	IDP
	Tape surface verification facility	
FATS	Fast Analysis of Tape Surface	. . .
	Required for *FATAR*, which see	
FAUST	Far Ultraviolet Shuttle Telescope	UC-Berkeley
fax	facsimile	
	Gaining acceptance as an English word, both as a noun and as a verb	
FAX	Facsimile	. . .
	Alternate form; see *fax*	
FBA	Fixed-Block Architecture	IBM

FBL	Fly By Light	NASA
FBT	Fused Biconic Taper re: Fiberoptic coupler technology	. . .
FC	Frame Control Field in IEEE 802.5 token ring data communications specification sa *IEEE, Institute of Electrical and* *Electronics Engineers*	IEEE
FCB	File Control Block	DEC
FCB	Forms Control Buffer	. . .
FCC	Federal Communications Commission	. . .
FCC	Flight Control Computer	NASA
FCDF	F Cumulative Distribution Function re: Statistical analysis	. . .
FCDI	F Cumulative Distribution, Inverse re: Statistical analysis	. . .
fci	flux changes per inch Alternate form; see *fcpi*	. . .
FCLA	Florida Center for Library Automation	FCLA
FCM	Field Coupling Mode Electromagnetic interference caused by field coupling into ground loops	. . .
FCMS	Factory Control and Management System	Dun & Bradstreet
fcpi	flux changes per inch A measure of linear recording density of magnetic media sa *FTPI, Flux Transitions* *Per Inch*	. . .
FCPI	Flux Changes Per Inch Alternate form; see *fcpi*	. . .
FCPSI	Flux Changes Per Square Inch A measure of surface recording density of magnetic media	. . .
FCS	File Control System	DEC
FCS	Financial Control System Financial information storage and retrieval system	UCC
FCS	Fluorescent Color Standard	. . .
FCS	Frame Check Sequence Field in IEEE 802.5 token ring data communications specification sa *IEEE, Institute of Electrical and* *Electronics Engineers*	IEEE
FCT	Fast CMOS TTL-Compatible sa *CMOS, Complementary Metal Oxide* *Semiconductor* and *TTL, Transistor-* *Transistor Logic*	. . .

FCT	File Control Table	IBM
Fd	Ferredoxin	. . .
	A compound important in biochemistry	
FD	Full Duplex	. . .
	Data communications in two directions simultaneously Also designated by *FDX*	
FDAS	Flight Dynamics Analysis System	Goddard Space Flt. Ctr.
FDC	Floppy Disk Controller	. . .
FDD	Flexible Disk Drive	. . .
FDDI	Fiber-Distributed Data Interface	IBM
	100 Mbit/s fiber optic communications standard	
FDDI-II	Fiber-Distributed Data Interface II	. . .
	16 separate and equal channels of 98.304 Mbits/s each	
FDHD	Floppy Drive High Density	Apple
FDHM	Full Duration at Half Maximum	. . .
FDL	Facility(-ies) Data Link	. . .
FDL	File Definition Language	DEC
FDM	Frequency-Division Multiplexing	. . .
FDMA	Frequency-Division Multiple Access	. . .
FDNB	1-Fluoro-2,4-Dinitrobenzene	. . .
	A compound important in biochemistry sa *DNFB*	
FDP	Fructose 1,6-Diphosphate	. . .
	A compound important in biochemistry	
FDR	Fast Dump and Restore	IDP
	Disk-to-tape software	
FDRB	Fully Distributed Redundant Bridging	Xyplex
	re: Communications between a local area network (LAN) and a remote network	
FDRS	Field Device Replacement System	US Postal Service
FDT	Formal Description Technique	CCITT
FDX	Full Duplex	. . .
	Communications circuit capable of handling data traffic in both directions (transmission and reception) simultaneously; dual extension of *half duplex*, *HDX*, in which transmission and reception are accomplished seperately; converse of *simplex* communications in which only transmission or only reception is possible	
Fe	Ferrum	. . .
	Symbol for *iron*, atomic element number 26	

FE	Front End	. . .
	Generally refers to a pre-processor computer in large scale computing systems (usually "supercomputers"), but also applied to any device that interfaces a larger system	
FEA	Finite Element Analysis	. . .
	re: Mathematical procedure	
FEBE	Far End Block Error	. . .
FEC	Forward Error Correction	. . .
	Error correction without resorting to retransmission of the original message	
FECN	Forward Explicit Congestion Notification	ANSI
	Field used in frame relay (FR) data communications protocol	
FED-STD	Federal Standard	. . .
FEFO	First Ended/First Out	. . .
FEG	Field Emission Gradient	
	re: Scanning electron microscope (SEM)	
FEI	Front End Interface	Cray Research
	See *FE, Front End* for additional information	
FEL	Free Electron Laser	. . .
FELT	Full Etchstop Layer Transfer	TI
	An improved method of manufacturing silicon-on-insulator (SOI) integrated circuits (ICs)	
FE_n	Format Effector n (n=0, 1, 2, 3, 4, 5)	ISO
	Generic designation for ISO seven-bit code positions X08 through X0B; see FE_0 through FE_5	
FE_0	Format Effector 0	ISO
	Backspace (BS); sa FE_n	
FE_1	Format Effector 1	
	Horizontal tab (HT); sa FE_n	
FE_2	Format Effector 2	ISO
	Line feed (LF); sa FE_n	
FE_3	Format Effector 3	ISO
	Vertical tab (VT); sa FE_n	
FE_4	Format Effector 4	ISO
	Form feed (FF); sa FE_n	
FE_5	Format Effector 5	ISO
	Carriage return (CR); sa FE_n	
FEP	Fluorinated Ethylenepropylene	. . .
	A material used for fiber-optic cables	
FEP	Front End Processor	. . .

FERS	Facility Error Recognition System	IBM
FET	Field-Effect Transistor	. . .
fF	femtofarad	. . .
	Unit of capacitance; 10^{-15} farad	
	sa *Farad, F*	
FF	Flip-Flop	. . .
	Electronic multivibrator (MV) circuit	
FF	Form Feed	CCITT
	Format effector 4 (FE_4); a component of the	
	binary code in CCITT Recommendation	
	V.3; sa *FE$_n$, CCITT* and *V.3*	
FFMS	Factory Floor Management Software	. . .
FFS	Flash File System	Microsoft
FFT	Fast Fourier Transform	. . .
	re: Mathematical analysis of waveforms	
	sa *FT, Fourier Transform*	
FGA	Font Graphics Accelerator	Toshiba
FGD	Flue Gas Desulfurization	. . .
	re: Coal fuel exhaust cleaning technology	
FH	Frequency-Hopped	. . .
	Re: Covert message detection; sa *TH, Time-*	
	Hopped, and *PN, Pseudonoise* for related	
	acronyms	
FHG	Fourth Harmonic Generation	. . .
FHP	Fractional Horsepower	. . .
FH_2	dihydrofolic acid	. . .
	A compound important in biochemistry	
FH_4	tetrahydrofolic acid	. . .
	A compound important in biochemistry	
FIA	Field Image Alignment	Nikon
	re: Precision integrated circuit (IC) wafer	
	overlay alignment	
FIB	Focused Ion Beam	. . .
FICS	Financial Control System	UCC
FID	File Identifier	DEC
FID	Format Identification	IBM
	re: *SNA, Systems Network Architecture*	
FIDL	Flat Image Display List	VITec
FIE	File Interface Extension	. . .
FIFO	First In/First Out	. . .
FILO	First In/Last Out	. . .
FIMS	Forms Interface Management System	. . .
FINAC	Fast Interline Non-active Automatic Control	AT&T
FIPS	Federal Information Processing Standard	FCC
FIR	Far Infrared	. . .

FIR	Finite Impulse Response	. . .
	A filtering process for digital signal	
	processing	
FIRMR	Federal Information Resources Management	GSA
	Regulations	
FIRST	Frequency Domain Resonant Superconducting	. . .
	Transmission	
	re: Superconducting infrared detector	
FISO	Fast In/Slow Out	. . .
	A very large scale integrated circuit (VLSIC)	
	technology used in high-speed collection of	
	large amounts of data	
FISP	Fuzzy Inference Step Processor	. . .
	An electronic processing element using fuzzy	
	logic	
FISSS	Frequency-Independent Strong Signal	. . .
	Suppressor	
FIST	Flight Information System Testbed	NASA
FIT	Frame-Interline-Transfer	. . .
	re: Image sensor device, especially as used	
	for high-definition television (HDTV)	
fL	foot-Lambert	. . .
	Unit of luminance	
FLC	Ferroelectric Liquid Crystal	. . .
FLIPS	Forest Level Information Processing System	USFS
FLL	Frequency-Locked Loop	. . .
FLM	Fiber Loop Multiplexer	. . .
FLOPS	Floating Point Operations Per Second	. . .
FLS	Floating License Server	Frame
		Technology
FLSF	Font Library Service Facility	IBM
Fm	Fermium	. . .
	Atomic element number 100	
	Named in honor of Italian physicist Enrico	
	Fermi (1901–1954)	
FM	Facilities Management	. . .
FM	Frequency Modulation	. . .
FM	Function Management	IBM
FMB	FORCE Message Broadcast	. . .
FMBS	Frame Mode Bearer Services	CCITT
	Service provided by the frame relay protocol	
FMID	Function Modification Identification	IBM
FMIS	FTS2100 Management Information System	AT&T
	sa *FTS2100*	
FMN	Flavin Mononucleotide	. . .
	A compound important in biochemistry	

FMS	Flexible Manufacturing System	. . .
FMS	Forms Management System	DEC
FMS	FORTRAN Monitor System	NAA
	sa *FORTRAN, Formula Translator*	
FMVFT	Frequency Modulation Voice Frequency Transmission	. . .
FN	Feature Node	CCITT
FN/SI	Feature Node/Service Interface	Ameritech/ Bellcore
FNMS	FTS2000 Network Management System	AT&T
	sa *FTS2000*	
FO	Fiber-Optic	. . .
	Also designated by *F/O*	
FOA	First Office Application	AT&T
	Field verification of systems and their interfaces	
FOC	Faint Object Camera	ESA
	Specialized camera originally installed on the *Hubble Space Telescope, HST*, which see	
FOCAL	Formula Calculator	DEC
FOCUS	—FOCUS	. . .
	4th generation language	
FOG	Fiber-Optic Gyroscope	. . .
FOGM	Fiber-Optic Guided Missile	DoD
FOIRL	Fiber-Optic Inter-Repeater Link	Micro Linear
FOL	Fiber-Optic Link	. . .
FOLAN	Fiber-Optic Local Area Network	. . .
FOM	Fiber-Optic Modem	. . .
FOMAU	Fiber-Optic Medium Attachment Unit	. . .
FOME	Fiber-Optic Mesh Extender	Honeywell/Intel
	Technology for interconnection of multiple supercomputer systems	
FOPP	Fiber-Optic Patch Panel	. . .
Foresight	—Foresight	Orbit Semi-
	Integrated circuit (IC) prototyping service	conductor
FORTRAN	Formula Translator	IBM
FOS	Fiber-Optic Sensor	. . .
FOTLAN	Fiber-Optic Tactical Local Area Network	JPL
FOTS	Fiber Office Telecommunications System	. . .
FOTS	Fiber-Optic Transmission System	. . .
FOV	Field Of View	. . .
	re: Optical instruments; stated in degrees of angle, or linear measurement	
FOX	Fiber-Optic Extender	. . .

FP	Fabry-Perot	. . .
	re: Interferometer, light interaction	
	Named in honor of the collaborators,	
	French physicists Charles Fabry (1867–1945)	
	and Jean-Baptiste Perot (1863–1925)	
FP	Flat Panel	. . .
FP	Flavoprotein	. . .
	re: Biochemistry	
FP	Frame Pointer	DEC
FPA	Floating Point Accelerator	DEC
FPA	Focal Plane Array	. . .
	re: Image detector construction	
FPC	Floating-Point Coprocessor	. . .
	An add-in chip for microprocessor	
	enhancement	
FPD	Fine Pitch Device	. . .
	Electronic circuit chip with dense pin	
	spacing (0.025″)	
FPD	First Part Done	DEC
	A bit indicating instruction completion used	
	in multiprogramming systems	
FPD	Flat Panel Display	. . .
FPE	Floating Point Engine	. . .
FPE	Fluorinated ethylpropylene	. . .
	Teflon	
FPGA	Field Programmable Gate Array	. . .
	An integrated circuit (IC) which is user-	
	programmable into a wide variety of logical	
	configurations For other programmable logic	
	devices (PLDs) see *EEPLD, EPLD, FPLA,*	
	PAL, PEEL, PGA, PIC and *PLA*	
FPGAs	Flexible Programmable Gallium Arsenide	. . .
	re: Electronic integrated circuit (IC) logic	
	device	
FPI	Fabry-Perot Interferometer	. . .
	Optical interference measuring device	
	See *FP, Fabry-Perot*	
FPIC	Field-Programmable Interconnect Component	Aptix
FPLA	Field-Programmable Logic Array	. . .
	An integrated circuit (IC) which is user-	
	programmable into a wide variety of logical	
	configurations For other programmable logic	
	devices (PLDs) see *EEPLD, EPLD, FPGA,*	
	PAL, PEEL, PGA, PIC and *PLA*	
FPM	Fast Packet Multiplexing	. . .
	High speed data transmission technology	

FPP	Floating Point Processor	. . .
FPR	Floating Point Register	IBM
fps	feet per second	. . .
fps	frames per second	. . .
	re: Cathode ray tube (CRT) display refresh	
	rate, communications data packet rate	
FPS	Fast Packet Switching	. . .
	A technology for utilizing all available	
	bandwidth in a communications network	
	through high-speed time-sharing	
FPT	Fine Pitch Technology	. . .
	Method of producing very dense integrated	
	circuits (ICs) with high lead count	
FPU	Floating Point Unit	IBM
FQDN	Fully Qualified Domain Name	Internet
	re: Electronic mail addresses	
Fr	Francium	. . .
	Atomic element number 87	
FR	Frame Relay	. . .
	re: Digital telecommunications technology	
FRACAS	Failure-Reporting and Corrective-Action	. . .
	System	
FRAD	Frame Relay Access Device	. . .
FRAD	Frame Relay Assembler/Disassembler	. . .
FRAM	Ferroelectric Random Access Memory	Ramtron
FRISC	Fast Reduced Instruction Set Computer	Rensselear P.I.
FRL	Financial Reporting Language	. . .
FRMR	Frame Reject	CCITT
	X.25 protocol command response; sa X.25	
FRP	Fiberglass-Reinforced Plastic	. . .
FRS	Fiber-Reinforced Superalloy	Rockwell
	Composite material used in rocket engines	
FRS	Financial Reporting System	P-W
FRS	Friction Reduction System	. . .
FRU	Field Replaceable Unit	IBM
fs	femtosecond	. . .
	10^{-15} second	
FS	File Separator (IS$_4$)	CCITT
FS	Finite State	. . .
FS	Frame Status	IEEE
	Field in IEEE 802.5 token ring data	
	communications specification	
	sa IEEE, Institute of Electrical and	
	Electronics Engineers	
FS	Frame Sync	. . .
	re: Integrated services digital network	
	(ISDN) message synchronization	

FSA	Flexible System Architecture	. . .
FSA	Future Systems Architecture	IBM
FSD	Fixed Shroud Duplex	. . .
	A data connector construction	
fsec	femtosecond	. . .
	10^{-15} second; also designated by *fs*	
FSK	Frequency Shift Keying	. . .
FSM	Finite State Machine	IBM
FSM	Frequency Shift Modulation	. . .
	sa *FM, Frequency Modulation*	
FSP	Full Screen Product	SAS
FSR	Free Spectral Range	. . .
FSS	Flight Service Station	FAA
FSU	Facsimile Server Unit	. . .
FSU	File Support Utility	. . .
FT	Fault Tolerant	. . .
FT	Fourier Transform	. . .
	re: Mathematical analysis of waveforms	
	Named in honor of its discoverer, French	
	mathematician Jean Baptiste Fourier (1768–	
	1830)	
FTAM	File Transfer Access and Management	OSI
	A data communications protocol	
ftc	footcandle	. . .
	Unit of illumination measurement	
FTE	Fiberoptic Test Equipment	. . .
FTF	Fiber-To-Fiber	. . .
FTIR	Fourier Transform Infrared	. . .
	Designation used in spectrometry	
	sa *FT, Fourier Transform*	
FTP	File Transfer Protocol	. . .
FTPI	Flux Transitions Per Inch	. . .
	Alternate form; see *fcpi, flux changes per inch*	
FTS	Federal Telecommunications System	GSA
FTS	Flight Telerobotic Servicer	NASA
FTS2000	Federal Telecommunications System 2000	GSA
FTS2100	Federal Telecommunications System 2100	GSA
FTTC	Fiber To The Curb	. . .
	re: Future fiber service to businesses and private homes	
FTTH	Fiber To The Home	. . .
	re: Future fiber service to private homes	
FT1	Fractional T1	. . .
	A portion of the T1 bandwidth; sa *T1*	

FT3	Fractional T3	. . .
	A portion of the T3 bandwidth; sa *T3*	
FU	Floating Underflow	. . .
	A condition brought about in a computer when the result is too small to be represented by the machine code	
FUSE	Far Ultraviolet Spectroscopy Explorer	NASA
	Part of NASA's *Great Observatory Program, GOP*, which see	
FUV	Far Ultraviolet	. . .
FVC	Frequency to Voltage Converter	. . .
FWHM	Full Width Half Maximum	. . .
	Bandwidth at 3 dB down from the peak (of amplifier response, communications system response, scintillation counters, etc.) sa *FWTM, Full Width Tenth Maximum*	
FWTM	Full Width Tenth Maximum	. . .
	Bandwidth at one-tenth maximum response sa *FWHM, Full Width Half Maximum*	
FX	Foreign Exchange [service]	AT&T
	Switched communications service	
FXM	Fiber Expansion Module	AT&T
FXP	Full Throughput [architecture]	. . .
FXU	Fixed Point Unit	IBM

G

g	gram	. . .
	Fundamental unit of mass in the cgs system sa *cgs, centimeter-gram-second* [system of units]	
G	Gauss	. . .
	Unit of magnetic flux Named in honor of German mathematician Karl Friedrich Gauss (1777–1855)	
G	Giga	. . .
	Prefix for 10^9	
G	—Conductance (symbol)	. . .
	Reciprocal of resistance; expressed in units of *mhos*	
G	Guanine	. . .
	A compound important in biochemistry; a component of *DNA*, which see	
G-Band	G-Band	. . .
	Microwave frequency allocation of 4 to 6 GHz	

G-P-T	Guam and Philippines to Taiwan Name of a fiberoptic (FO) cable connecting these areas	. . .
G/T	Gain/Temperature Figure of merit for electronic devices	. . .
Ga	Gallium Atomic element number 31	. . .
GA	Go Ahead	. . .
GAA	General Applications Architecture	HNC
GaAs	Gallium Arsenide Semiconductor material	. . .
GAIA	Graphics Access Information and Analysis	Podolsky/ Morehouse
Gal	D-Galactose A compound important in biochemistry	. . .
GALA	Galium Aluminum Arsenide Material used in solid-state (SS) lasers	D.O. Industries
GALOP	General Optical Layout Program	Breault Research Org.
GAM	Graphical Access Method	IBM
GAMS	General Algebraic Modeling System	World Bank
GAN	Global Area Network	. . .
GASP	General Analog Simulation Program	. . .
GATT	General Agreement on Tariffs and Trade	WATTC
Gb	Gigabit 10^9 bits; sometimes "per second" is implied (Gbps)	. . .
GB	Giga Byte 10^9 bytes; sometimes "per second" is implied (GBps)	. . .
GBP	Gain Bandwidth Product re: Operational amplifier (OA) and radio frequency (RF) device specifications	. . .
GBRAM	Group Broadcast Recognizing Access Method	. . .
GBVS	Global Business Videoconferencing Service	AT&T
GBW	Gain Bandwidth A measure of transistor or integrated circuit (IC) behavior sa GBP, Gain Bandwidth Product	. . .
GC	Gas Chromatography	. . .
GC	Generic Controller	. . .
GCA	Ground-Controlled Approach [radar]	. . .
GCC	Graphics Control Center	. . .
GCDF	Gaussian Cumulative Distribution Function re: Statistical analysis	. . .

GCDI	Gaussian Cumulative Distribution, Inverse	. . .
	re: Statistical analysis	
GCI	General Component Interface	. . .
	Electronic circuit chip interface standard	
GCI	Global Climate Initiative	NASA
GCM	Ground Common Mode	. . .
	Common mode impedance coupling	
GCOS	General Comprehensive Operating System	Honeywell
	Based on *GECOS*, which see	
GCPIC	General Concurrent Particle-In-Cell	. . .
	Mathematical algorithm	
GCR	Gaussian-Coupled Resonator	. . .
GCR	Ground-Controlled Radar	. . .
GCR	Group Code Recording	Telex
GCS	Global Communications Subsystem	IBM
GCT	Geometric Control Theory	. . .
	Mathematical theory	
GCT	Generalized Chen Transform	Chen
	A variant of the discrete cosine transform	
	used in image data compression techniques	
Gd	Gadolinium	. . .
	Atomic element number 64	
GDDM	Graphical Data Display Manager	IBM
GDF	Group Distribution Frame	. . .
	re: Frequency-division multiplexing (FDM)	
	equipment	
GDG	Generation Data Group	. . .
GDH	Glutamate Dehydrogenase	. . .
	A compound important in biochemistry	
GDMO	General Definition of Managed Objects	ISO
GDN	Government Data Network	UK
GDP	Generation Data Group	IBM
GDP	Guanosine Diphosphate	. . .
	A compound important in biochemistry	
GDS	Generic Digital Services	. . .
GDSS	Global Decision Support System	US Air Force
GDT	Gas Discharge Tube	. . .
GDT	Global Descriptor Table	Intel
Ge	Germanium	. . .
	Atomic element number 32	
GECOS	General Comprehensive Operating System	GE/Honeywell
GEM	Generic Emulation Module	General Radio
GEMCOS	Generalized Message Control System	IBM
GEMMS	Global Enterprise Manufacturing Management	Datalogix
	System	
GENESIS	General Network Simulation System	Bower, J.

GENIO	General Input/Output	. . .
GEO	Geophysical Earth Orbit	. . .
GEODSS	Ground-Based Electro-Optical Deep Space Surveillance	. . .
GEOS	Graphics Environment Operation System A "windows" environment software for older personal computers (PCs)	Geoworks
GET	Group Execute Trigger IEEE Standard 488 bus command; sa *IEEE*	IEEE
GeV	Giga electron Volts 10^9 electron volts; sometimes designated by *BeV, Billion electron Volts*	. . .
GFA	Gas Fusion Analysis	. . .
GFI	Ground Fault Interrupter	. . .
GFLOPS	Giga Floating Point Operations Per Second 10^9 floating operations per second (FLOPS)	. . .
GFRE	Graphite-Fiber-Reinforced Epoxy	. . .
GFRP	Graphite-Fiber-Reinforced Plastic	. . .
GGG	Gadolinium Gallium Garnet A laser lens material	. . .
GGP	Gateway-to-Gateway Protocol	DoD
GH	Growth Hormone re: Biochemistry	. . .
GHz	Giga Hertz Billions (10^9) of cycles per second sa *Hz, Hertz*	. . .
GI	Gastrointestinal	. . .
GIDEP	Government-Industry Data Exchange Program	. . .
GIF	Graphic Interchange Format	. . .
GIP	Graphics and Image Processing	DuPont Pixel Systems
GIPSY	General Information Processing System	Univ. of Okla.
GIS	Geographic Information Systems	. . .
GIS	General Information System Information inquiry and retrieval system	IBM
GIS	Guidance Information System	IBM,TSC
GISMO	Graphical Interactive Screen Management Object	SL
GIST	Gateway to Information Services and Transport	NYNEX
GJU	Group Junction Unit	Ericsson
GKE	Generic Key Element re: Broadband network technology	. . .
GKS	Graphical Kernel System Two-dimensional graphics software standard	ANSI

Glc	D-Glucose	. . .
	A compound important in biochemistry	
GLC	Gas-Liquid Chromatography	. . .
GLC	Ground Loop Coupling	. . .
GLIM	Generalized Linear Interactive Modelling [system]	NAG
GLIPS	Giga Logical Inferences Per Second 10^9 LIPS Speed rating for artificial intelligence (AI) systems sa *LIPS, Logical Inferences Per Second*	. . .
Gln	Glutamine	. . .
	A compound important in biochemistry	
Gly	Glycene	. . .
	A compound important in biochemistry	
GMAIL	Gateway Mail	. . .
GMF	Graphic Monitor Facility	IBM
GMIS	Government Management Information Sciences A national user group of information systems professionals	GMIS
GML	Generalized Mark-up Language	. . .
GMP	Guanosine Monophosphate	. . .
	A compound important in biochemistry	
GMS	Geometric Modeling Software	Unisys
GMSK	Gaussian-filtered Minimum Shift Keying A radio frequency (RF) communications technology	. . .
GMT	Greenwich Mean Time Time as reckoned at Greenwich, England	. . .
GMTF	Geometric Modulation Transfer Function	. . .
GNS	Global Network Services	British Telecom
GOES	Geosynchronous Orbiting Earth Satellite	. . .
GOP	Great Observatory Program sa *ACE, AIM, COBE, FUSE, SOFIA, SWAS, XTE*	NASA
GOPS	Giga Operations Per Second 10^{12} operations per second	. . .
GOSIP	Government Open Systems Interconnect Protocol (or Profile)	NBS
GP	Graphics Protocol (or Processor)	. . .
GPa	Giga Pascals	. . .
GPC	Gas Phase Chromatography	. . .
GPC	General Precision Connector	. . .
GPC	Graphics Performance Characterization A graphics benchmarking technology sa *GPCmark*	GPCC

GPCmark	Graphics Performance Characterization mark A number quoted by the Graphics Characterization Committee	GPCC
GPDA	General Purpose Data Acquisition	. . .
GPH	Gallons Per Hour	. . .
GPI	Graphical Programming Interface	Microsoft
GPIB	General Purpose Interface Bus	. . .
GPM	Gallons Per Minute	. . .
GPO	Government Printing Office	GPO
GPP	General Purpose Processor	Colorado Data Sys.
GPR	General Purpose Register	IBM
GPS	Global Positioning Satellite (or Service, or System) A multisatellite navagational system	DoD
GPSS	General Purpose Simulation System	. . .
GPTF	General Purpose Transaction Facility	NCR
GP1	Get Password 1 A network virus that collects passwords on NetWare local area networks (*LANs*)	. . .
GQL	Graphical Query Language	Andyne Computing
GQL	Guided Query Language	SMS
GR	General [purpose] Register	IBM
GRAM	Global Reference Atmosphere Model	NASA
GRASS	Geographic Resources Analysis Support System	USDA
GRG	Generalized Reduced Gradient	. . .
GRI	Group Repetition Interval re: *Loran-C* reception, which see	. . .
GRIN	Gradient Refractive Index	. . .
GRINSCH	Graded Index Seperate Carrier Heterostructure re: A laser structure	. . .
GRO	Gamma Ray Observatory	NASA
GRO	Graphics Reporting Option	. . .
GS	Group Separator Information separator 3 (IS$_3$); a component of the binary code in CCITT Recommendation V.3 sa *CCITT* and *V.3*	CCITT
GS	Group Switch Space division multiplexer	Ericsson
GSAM	Generalized Sequential Access Method	IBM
GSD	General Services Division	IBM
GSDN	Global Software-Defined Network	AT&T
GSE	Grating Surface-Emitting [array]	David Sarnoff Res.
	re: Laser technology	

GSFC	Goddard Space Flight Center	NASA
GSG	Ground-Signal-Ground	...
	re: Test lead arrangement in testing	
	microelectronic devices	
GSH	Glutathione	...
	A compound important in biochemistry	
GSM	Groupe Speciale Mobile	...
	(French) Digital cellular phone standard	
GSMBE	Gas Source Molecular Beam Epitaxy	...
	Method of precisely controlling transistor	
	properties during manufacture	
GSP	Graphics Shading Processor	Toshiba
GSP	Graphics System Processor	Tektronix
GSPC	Graphics Standards Planning Committee	ACM
GST	Global Symbol Table	DEC
GSTN	General Switched Telephone Network	CCITT
GTA	Gas-Tungsten-Arc [welding]	...
GTEM	Gigahertz Transversal Electromagnetic [field]	...
GTF	Generalized Trace Facility	IBM
GTL	Go To Local	IEEE
	IEEE Standard 488 bus command; sa *IEEE*	
GTL	Gunning Transceiver Logic	...
GTO	Gate Turn-Off	...
GTO	Graduated Turn-On	...
	re: Thyristor technology	
	A method of reducing overshoot and ringing	
	in solid-state (SS) circuitry	
GTP	Guanosine Triphosphate	...
	A compound important in biochemistry	
GUI	Graphical User Interface	OSF
GVD	Group Velocity Dispersion	...
	Term used to describe behavior of light	
	pulses in optical cavities, waveguides, etc.	
GW	GigaWatt	...
	10^9 watts (W)	
G3P	Glyceraldehyde 3-Phosphate	...
G6P	Glucose 6-Phosphate	...

H

h	—Planck constant (symbol)	Planck, Max
	6.6256×10^{-27} erg sec	
	Named in honor of German physicist Max	
	Planck (1858–1947)	

h	hecto	. . .
	Prefix for 100	
h	hour	. . .
H	—Magnetic Field Strength (symbol)	. . .
	Expressed in units of *Amperes per meter, A/ m*	
H	Henry	. . .
	Unit of inductance	
	Named in honor of American physicist Joseph Henry (1797–1878)	
H	Hexadecimal	. . .
	A suffix indicating that the two preceding characters are in hexadecimal notation; for example, 4DH is the hexadecimal notation for Z (capital Z) sa *X, Hexadecimal*	
H	Hydrogen	. . .
	Atomic element number 1	
H-Band	H-Band	. . .
H-J-K100	Hong Kong to Japan to South Korea [fiber-optic cable]	. . .
HADA	High Availability Disk Array	Data General
HALT	Highly Accelerated Life Test	. . .
HALT*	Halt (signal)	. . .
	Note: "*" indicates that a signal (called "active high") must be present at the circuit terminal in order for the described function to be activated.	
HANDS	Healthcare Application Network Delivery System	US Sprint
HAP	Host Access Protocol	. . .
HARM	High-Speed Anti-Radiation Missile	DoD
HASP	Houston Automatic Spooling Program	. . .
HASS	Highly Accelerated Stress Screening	. . .
HAST	Highly Accelerated Stress Test	. . .
	Method of shortening environmental test time sa *HASS, Highly Accelerated Stress Screening*	
HAW	Hawaiian [fiber-optic cable]	. . .
Hb	Hemoglobin	. . .
	A compound important in biochemistry	
HBA	Host Bus Adapter	. . .
HBM	Human Body Model	. . .
	A set of specifications used as test parameters	
HBS	Holographic Beam Splitter	. . .
HBT	Heterojunction Bipolar Transistor	. . .

HBW	Half Bandwidth	. . .
HC	High-speed Complementary	. . .
	re: A high-speed complementary metal oxide semiconductor (HCMOS) integrated circuit (IC)	
HCD	Hot Carrier Diode	. . .
HCF	Host Command Facility	IBM
HCHP	Harvard Community Health Plan	. . .
HCMOS	High-speed Complementary [Logic] Metal Oxide Semiconductor	Signetics
HCP	Host Communications Processor	. . .
HCS	Hazard Communications Standard	. . .
HCS	Health Care System	IBM
HCT	High-power CMOS Transistor	. . .
	re: A high-power complementary metal oxide semiconductor (HCMOS) transistor-transistor logic (TTL) integrated circuit (IC) logic family	
HCTL	High-power CMOS TTL Logic	H-P
	re: A high-power integrated circuit (IC) used in high-speed servo control applications sa *CMOS, Complementary Metal Oxide Semiconductor* and *TTL, Transistor-Transistor Logic*	
HD	Half Duplex	. . .
HDA	Head/Disk Assembly	. . .
HDAM	Hierarchical Direct Access Method	IBM
HDAS	High-Speed Data Acquisition System	Analogic
HDBV	Host Data Base View	IBM
HDD	High-Density Disk	. . .
HDDR	High-Density Digital Recording	. . .
	Digital data recording in excess of 40 kbpi	
HDI	High-Density Interconnect	General Electric
HDL	Hardware Description Language	. . .
HDLC	Hierarchical Data Link Control	. . .
HDLC	High-Level Data Link Control	IBM
HDMS	High-Density Modem System	Microcom
HDPE	High-Density Polyethylene	. . .
	A plastic material widely used in electronics devices	
HDS	Holographic-Diffractive Structure	. . .
HDSC	High-Density Signal Carrier	DEC
	re: Electronic circuit chip interconnection technology	
HDSL	High-Rate Subscriber Line	. . .
HDTV	High-Definition Television	. . .

HDX	Half Duplex Data communications circuit capable of handling traffic in both directions (transmission and reception) but only one way at a time; see *FDX, Full Duplex* for related information	. . .
He	Helium Atomic element number 2	. . .
HEAT	Helpdesk Expert Automation Tool	Bendata
HECS	Higher Education Calling Service	AT&T
HEDI	High Endoatmospheric Defense Interceptor	US Army
HEMP	High-Altitude Electromagnetic Pulse	. . .
HEMT	High Electron-Mobility Transistor	. . .
HEO	High Earth Orbit	NASA
HEP	High-Energy Physics	. . .
HEPNET	High Energy Physics Network	DoE
Hex	Hexadecimal Number system with base of 16; represented by the numeric digits 1 through 9, and the letters A through F; sa *H, X*	. . .
HEX	Hexadecimal Alternate form; see *Hex*	. . .
Hf	Hafnium Atomic element number 72	. . .
HF	High Frequency 3 to 30 MHz	. . .
HFC	Halogenated Fluorocarbon	. . .
HFD	Hot Fix Device re: Disk storage devices which can be exchanged without the necessity of system down time	. . .
HFDF	High-Frequency Distribution Frame re: Telecommunications technology in the range 12 kHz to 2540 kHz	. . .
HFET	Heterostructure Field Effect Transistor	. . .
HFMS	Hospital Financial Management System	IBM
HFS	Hierarchical File Structure	. . .
Hg	Hydrargyrum Symbol for *mercury*, atomic element number 80	. . .
HH	Horizontal-Horizontal re: Imaging data from transmitted and received radar signals sa *VH, Vertical-Horizontal* and *VV, Vertical-Vertical*	Held, D.N., JPL
HHLS	Hand-Held Laser Scanner	. . .

HHT	Hand-Held Terminal	. . .
Hi-Z	High Impedance	..
HIC	High Information Content	. . .
	re: Advanced liquid crystal display (LCD) panels	
HIC	Highest Incoming Channel	CCITT
HIC	Hybrid Integrated Circuit	Fujitsu
	A combination of analog and digital circuitry on a single integrated circuit (IC) chip	
HICAP	High Capacity	AT&T
	A high-capacity telephone response service	
HIDAM	Hierarchical Indexed Direct Access Method	IBM
HiFI	High-Performance Fiber-Optic Interface	. . .
HILAC	Heavy-Ion Linear Accelerator	UC-Berkeley
HIMOS	High-Injection Metal Oxide Semiconductor	. . .
HIP	Heterojunction Internal Photoemission	NASA
HIPIC	High-Performance Integrated Circuit	. . .
HIPO	Hierarchy: Input, Process, Output	IBM
Hipot	High Potential	. . .
	Variant of *HIPOT*, which see	
HIPOT	High Potential	. . .
	re: Testing for leakage by means of high voltage	
HiPPI	High-Performance Parallel Interface	IBM
	Formerly *HPPI*, which see	
HIPS	HRPT Image Processing Subsystem	NOAA
	sa *HRPT, High Resolution Picture Transmission*	
HIRET	High-Resolution [graphics] Transmission [system]	TSI-Horsham
His	Histidine	. . .
	A compound important in biochemistry	
HIS	Hospital Information System	. . .
HISAM	Hierarchical Indexed Sequential Access Method	IBM
HIT	High-Isolation Transformer	. . .
Hi8ME	High-Density 8-mm Metal Evaporated [tape]	. . .
HLC	Host Language Call	. . .
HLC	Host Local [network] Controller	. . .
HLI	Host Language Interface	Information Bldrs.
HLL	High-Level Language (or Logic)	. . .
HLLAPI	High-Level Language Application Program Interface	IBM

HLM	Heterogeneous LAN Management	IBM/3Com
	sa *LAN, Local Area Network*	
HMAC	High-Performance Memory Array Controller	NCR
HMD	Helmet-Mounted Display	. . .
HMFG	Heavy Metal Fluoride Glass	. . .
	Fiber-optic material	
HMI	Hub Management Interface	Novell
	re: Local area network (LAN) wiring hub	
HMO	Health Maintenance Organization	. . .
HMOS	High-performance Metal Oxide Semiconductor	Intel
	re: A family of high-performance intgrated	
	circuits (ICs)	
HMW	High Molecular Weight	. . .
HNDT	Holographic Non-Destructive Test(-ing)	. . .
Ho	Holmium	. . .
	Atomic element number 67	
Ho:YAG	Holmium-Yttrium-Aluminum-Garnet	. . .
	A type of laser crystal frequently used in	
	medical applications	
HOC	Highest Outgoing Channel	CCITT
HOE	Holographic Optical Element	. . .
HOS	Higher Order Software	. . .
HOSDTN	High-Speed Optical Data Transfer Network	US Navy
HOST	Hawaii Ocean Science and Technology [Park]	Hawaii
HOV	High-Occupancy Vehicle	. . .
hp	Horsepower	. . .
	Alternate; see *HP*	
HP	Horsepower	. . .
	Also designated by h.p. or hp in some	
	reference literature	
HP-UX	Hewlett-Packard UNIX	H-P
	sa *UNIX*	
HPCC	High-Performance Computing and	. . .
	Communications	
HPCPC	High-Performance Centrifugal Partition	US
	Chromatography	Government
HPFS	High-Performance File System	. . .
HPFTP	High-Pressure Fuel Turbopump	Bently Nevada
HPGL	Hewlett Packard Graphics Language	H-P
HPLC	High-Performance (or -Pressure) Liquid	. . .
	Chromotography	
HPO	High-Performance Option	IBM
HPO	Host Processing Option	IBM
HPPI	High-Performance Parallel Interface	ANSI
	ANSI standard for high-speed	
	communications; sa *ANSI* and *HiPPI*	

HPT	Heterojunction Phototransistor	. . .
HRC	Horizontal Redundancy Check	. . .
HRC	Hybrid Ring Control	. . .
HRIN	Human Resources Information Network	. . .
HRMS	Human Resource Management System	. . .
HRPD	High-Repetition-Rate Pulse Doppler	. . .
HRPT	High-Resolution Picture Transmission	NOAA
HRS	High-Resolution System	. . .
	re: High-definition television (HDTV) and	
	similar video systems	
HRS	Human Resources [management] System	Computer
		Associates
HRV	Heat Recovery Ventilator	. . .
HRV	High-Resolution Video	. . .
HSAM	Hierarchic Sequential Access Method	IBM
HSC	Hierarchical Storage Controller	DEC
HSC	High-Speed Channel	. . .
HSC	High-Speed Controller	DEC
HSCT	High-Speed Civil Transport	NASA
HSM	Hierarchical Storage Manager	. . .
	sa *DFHSM, Data Facility Hierarchical*	
	Storage Manager	
HSP	High-Speed Shading Processor	Toshiba
	re: graphics display shading	
HSSI	High-Speed Serial Interface	. . .
	re: Data speeds in excess of 1.2 Mbps	
HSSP	High-Speed Serial Processor	. . .
HST	Hubble Space Telescope	NASA
	Named in honor of American astronomer	
	Edwin Powell Hubble (1889–1953) Part of	
	NASA's *Great Observatory Program, GOP,*	
	which see	
HT	High-Tension	. . .
	British equivalent for US *HV—High Voltage*	
HT	Horizontal Tabulation	CCITT
	Format effector 1 (FE_1); a component of the	
	binary code in CCITT Recommendation	
	V.3; sa *FE_n, CCITT,* and *V.3*	
HTBB	High-Temperature Black Body	. . .
HTGR	High-Temperature Gas-Cooled Reactor	. . .
HTS	Hadamard-Transform Spectrometry	. . .
HTSC	High-Temperature Superconductor	. . .
HTSSE	High-Temperature Superconductivity Space	US Navy
	Experiment	
HTT	High-Temperature [wind] Tunnel	Langley
		Research Ctr.

HUD   Head-Up Display   . . .
            A miniature display for headset mounting,
            especially as used for "virtual reality"
            experiments sa *VR, Virtual Reality*
HUP   Host User Profile   . . .
HV   High Voltage   . . .
HV   Horizontal-Vertical   Held, D.N.,
                                                         JPL

            re: Imaging data from transmitted and
            received radar signals
HVIC   High-Voltage Integrated Circuit   . . .
HVLP   High-Velocity Low-Pressure   . . .
HVQ   Hierarchical Vector Quantization   PictureTel
            Video data compression technology
HWM   High Water Mark   . . .
            A term used to indicate maximum storage
            used during execution of a computer
            program
Hyp   Hydroxyproline   . . .
            A compound important in biochemistry
Hz   Hertz   . . .
            Cycles per second; named in honor of
            German physicist Heinrich Hertz (1857–
            1894) Note: "Hertz" generally refers to the
            repetitive rate of an electronic signal or the
            frequency of a sound source, but it is also
            used to indicate the repetition rate of any
            event.

I

I   —Electric Current (symbol)   . . .
            Expressed in units of *Amperes, A*
I   Information   IBM
            re: *SDLC, Synchronous Data Link Control,*
            which see
I   Intensity   . . .
            Luminous intensity (*illumination*); expressed
            in units of *lux, lx* Sound intensity expressed
            in units of *ergs per cubic centimeter, ergs/*
            cm³
I   Iodine   . . .
            Atomic element number 53
I-AMAP   Integrated Adaptive Multiple-Access Protocol   JPL
I-CASE   Integrated Computer-Aided Software   . . .
            Engineering

I/O	Input/Output	. . .
I/OLM	Input/Output Logic Macrocells	Adv. Micro Dev.
I.122	—I.122 A frame relay standard	CCITT
I-4	International Information Integrity Institute A clearinghouse for network security option decisions	SRI
IA	Incoming Access Refers to public data network call routing	CCITT
IAB	Internet Activities Board	Internet
IAB	Internet Advisory Board	Internet
IAC	Instrument on a Card	IEEE
IAC	Inter-Application Communication	. . .
IAC	Interpret As Command TELNET command; sa *TELNET*	DoD
IAC/IRM	Interagency Committee on Information Resources Management	DoE
IACS	Integrated Access and Cross-Connect System	AT&T
IAD	Interactive Debugging	. . .
IAD	Ion-Assisted Deposition re: Ultra-high vacuum metal deposition	. . .
IALU	Integer and Arithmetic Logical Unit	Multiflow
IAM	Indexed Access Method	IBM
IAM	Innovation Access Method	IDP
IAPS	International Accunet Packet Service	AT&T
IAR	Instruction Address Register	. . .
IARN	International Amateur Radio Network	IARN
IAS	Institute of Advanced Study Site of original John von Neumann automatic computer; also the name of that machine sa *MANIAC, Mechanical And Numerical Integrator And Computer*	IAS
IAS	Interactive Application System	DEC
IAS	ISDN Applications and Services sa *ISDN, Integrated Services Digital Network*	Tel Plus Comm.
IASPM	Infrared Atmospherics and Signatures Prediction Model	. . .
IATA	International Air Transport Association	. . .
IB	Integrated Broadband	. . .
IB	Internetwork Bridge	3Com
IBC	Integrated Broadband Communications	. . .
IBG	Inter-Block Gap	. . .
IBIS	Interagency Border Inspection System	US Customs
IBN	Interim Broadband Network	. . .

IBS	INTELSAT Business Service	AT&T
	sa *INTELSAT, International Telecommunications Satellite*	
IBSYS	IBM System	IBM
	Operating system (OS) for the IBM 709x series of computers	
IBT	Integrated Broadband Termination	. . .
IBX	Integrated Business Exchange	. . .
IC	Image Capture	. . .
IC	Integrated Circuit	Noyce & Kilby
IC	Interlook Code	CCITT
	Refers to public data network call routing	
ICA	Integrated Communications Adapter	. . .
ICA	Interapplication Communication Architecture	Apple
ICA	International Communications Association	ICA
ICAM	Integrated Computer-Aided Manufacturing	. . .
ICASS	Integrated Component Automation Subsystem	. . .
ICAT	Intelligent Computer-Aided Training	. . .
ICB	Incoming Calls Barred	CCITT
	Refers to public data network call routing	
ICC	Image Computer Controller	VITec
ICC	Intelligent Communications Controller	. . .
ICC	Intermediate Cross-Connect	. . .
ICCF	Interactive Computing and Control Facility	IBM
ICCF	Interexchange Carrier Compatibility Forum	. . .
ICCS	Integrated Communications Cabling System	Siemens
ICD	Interactive Call Distribution	. . .
	re: Telephone system message handling	
ICD	Interactive Cartridge Debugger	. . .
ICE	International Electro-Technical Commission	. . .
ICE	In-Circuit Emulator	. . .
ICES	Integrated Civil Engineering Software System	. . .
ICF	Inertial Confinement Fusion	. . .
	re: Fusion reactor technology	
ICF	Integrated Catalog Facility	IBM
ICFD	Image Capture, Formatting, and Display	. . .
ICLAS	International Coordination Group on Laser Atmospheric Studies	. . .
ICLID	Incoming Call Line Identifier	AT&T
ICMASD	Integrated Circuit Master Directory	Hearst
ICMP	Internet Control Message Protocol	DoD
ICMS	Instrument Calibration and Maintenance Schedule	Beckman
ICMS	Intelligent Chassis Management System	NEC America
ICN	International CUG Number	CCITT
	sa *CUG, Closed User Group*	

ICO	Integrated Communications Outlet	Fritz, J., WVU
ICOBOL	Interactive Common Business Oriented Language	Data General
ICP	In-Circuit Programming	. . .
ICP	Input/Output Control Processor Designated by *IOCP* in other systems	Ziatech
ICP	Integrated Channel Processor	NeXT
ICP	Intelligent Communications Processor	Equinox
ICS	Image Control System	. . .
ICS	Inbound Communications Server	. . .
ICS	Interactive Computer Systems	DEC
ICS	ISDN Communication Subsystem	Tandem Computers
	sa *ISDN, Integrated Services Digital Network*	
ICSTI	International Centre for Scientific and Technical Information	ICSTI
ICSU	Intelligent Channel Service Unit	. . .
ICT	In-Circuit Test(er)	Temco
ICTP	International Center for Theoretical Physics	ICTP
ICU	Instruction Cache Unit	IBM
ICX	Integrated Circuit Experiment	. . .
ID	Intelligent Device	. . .
IDA	Institute for Defense Analysis	. . .
IDA	Integrated Digital Access	British Telecom
IDASYS	Institute for Defense Analysis System Operating system for CDC 6600	IDA
IDB	Instruction Decode Buffer	IBM
IDB	Interrupt Dispatch Block	DEC
IDBN	Integrated Digital Backbone Network	. . .
IDC	Insulation Displacement Connector Method of terminating flat multiple-conductor cable	Samtec
IDCA	Integrated Dewar Cooler Assembly re: Chilled radiation detector	. . .
IDCMA	Independent Data Communications Manufacturers Association	. . .
IDD	Integrated Data Dictionary	. . .
IDD	International Direct Dial	. . .
IDDD	International Direct Distance Dialing	. . .
IDE	Independent Drive Electronics Self-contained control electronics for microcomputer hard disk	. . .
IDE	Integrated Device Electronics	. . .
IDEA	Iterative Design and Engineering Automation	. . .
IDEC	Integrated Dynamic Echo Cancellation	PictureTel
IDEPT	Image Document Entry Processing Terminal	HNC

IDF	Instrument Data Frame	NASA
IDF	Integrate and Dump Filter	JPL
IDF	Intermediate Distribution Frame	. . .
IDL	Interactive Distance Learning	. . .
IDLC	Integrated Digital Loop Carrier	Bellcore
IDLS	Image Display List System	VITec
IDMS	Interactive Database Management System	Cullinet Software
IDNX	Integrated Digital Network Exchange	NET
IDP	Initial Domain Part	DEC
IDP	Inosine Diphosphate	. . .
	A compound important in biochemistry	
IDP	Integrated Data Processing	ANDIP
IDP	Internet Datagram Protocol	. . .
IDPS	Integrated Design and Production System	. . .
	Methodology for design of application-specific integrated circuits (ASICs)	
IDRC	Improved Data Recording Capability	IBM
IDRP	Inter-Domain Routing Protocol	OSI
IDS	Intelligent Disk Server	. . .
IDS	Intensity-Dependent Spread	Odetics
	An image enhancement technology	
IDT	Integrated Device Technology	. . .
IDT	Interdigital Transducer	. . .
IDT	Interface Development Tool	DEC
IDT	Interrupt Descriptor Table	Intel
IDTV	Improved Definition Television	. . .
IDU	Indoor Unit	. . .
	re: Satellite communications amplifier	
IDU	Interface Data Unit	. . .
IE	Information Engineering	. . .
IEB 5	Information Engineering Bulletin 5	EIA
	EIA paper on signal quality sa *EIA, Electronics Industry Association*	
IEB 9	Information Engineering Bulletin 9	EIA
	EIA application notes on RS-232-C sa *EIA, Electronics Industry Association*	
IEB 12	Information Bulletin 12	EIA
	EIA application notes on RS-449/RS-232-C interface sa *EIA, Electronics Industry Association*	
IEC	Inter-Exchange Carrier	FCC
	FCC-registered interstate transmissions carrier sa *FCC, Federal Communications Commission*	
IEC	International Electrotechnical Commission	IEC

IEEE	Institute of Electrical and Electronics Engineers	IEEE
IEF	Information Engineering Facility	TI
IEMIS	Integrated Emergency Management Information System	. . .
IEN	Internet Experiment Note	NSF
IETF	Internet Engineering Task Force	Internet
IEU	Integer Execution Unit	. . .
IEW	Information Engineering Workbench	KI
IF	Intermediate Frequency	. . .
IF	Internal Focus re: Special photographic lenses such as long-focus lenses and mirror optics	. . .
IFC	Interface Clear IEEE Standard 488 bus command; sa *IEEE*	IEEE
IFI	Instrumentation Facility Interface	. . .
IFIP	International Federation for Information Processing	IFIP
IFL	Inter-Facility Link re: Cable connection between the outdoor unit (ODU) and IDU and the indoor unit (IDU) in satellite communications technology	. . .
IFM	Instantaneous Frequency Measurement	. . .
IFOG	Interferometeric Optical Gyro	. . .
IG	Interactive Graphics	. . .
IGA	Integrated Graphics Array	IIT
IGAS	Interactive Generalized Accounting System	NCR
IGBT	Insulated Gate Bipolar Transistor	. . .
IGCC	Integrated Gasification Combined Cycle re: Coal gasification technology	. . .
IGES	Initial Graphics Exchange Standard	ANSI
IGES	International Graphics Exchange Specification	. . .
IGFET	Insulated Gate Field Effect Transistor	. . .
IgG	Immunoglobulin G A compound important in biochemistry	. . .
IGOSS	Industry Government Open Systems Specification	NIST
IGP	Interior Gateway Protocol	IETF
IGRP	Interior Gateway Routing Protocol	Cisco Systems
IGRP	Internet Gateway Resolution Protocol	Internet
IGY	International Geophysical Year	. . .
IHD	Interharmonic Distortion	. . .
II	Integrated Circuit Interconnect	DEC
IICIT	International Institute of Connector and Interconnection Technology	IICIT

IIE	Institute of Industrial Engineers	IIE
IIOP	Intelligent Input/Output Processor	. . .
IIR	Infinite Impule-Response	. . .
	re: Digital filter design	
IIS	Interactive Instructional System	IBM
IKS	Imaging Kernel System	Univ. of Lowell
ILA	Integrated Laboratory Automation	. . .
ILAN	Integrated Local Area Network	. . .
ILAN	Israeli Academic Network	ILAN
ILD	Injection Laser Diode	Pirelli
Ile	Isoleucine	. . .
	A compound important in biochemistry	
ILF	Infra Low Frequency	. . .
	300 to 3000 Hz	
Illiac	Illinois Automatic Computer	Univ. of Illinois
	Clone of IAS computer	
	sa *IAS, Institute of Advanced Study*	
ILM	Intelligent Library Manager	Memorex Telex
ILO	Injection-Locked Oscillator	. . .
ILRC	International Laser Radar Conference	ILRC
ILS	Interdisciplinary Laser Science	Amer. Phys.
		Soc.
ILTA	International Laser Therapy Association	ILTA
ILU	Initiate Logical Unit	IBM
IM	Information Management	CDC
IM	Intensity Modulation	. . .
	re: Optical communication	
IM	Interconnection Medium	. . .
IM	Intermodulation [distortion]	. . .
IMC	Information Management Center	. . .
IMD	Intermodulation Distortion	. . .
IMKA	Initiative for Managing Knowledge Assets	DEC, et al.
IML	Interactive Matrix Language	SAS
IMOM	Improved Many On Many	US Air Force
	Networked defense software	
IMP	Image Management Processor	. . .
IMP	Interface Message Processor	BBN/ARPA
IMPACT	Ion-Implanted Advanced Composed Logic	TI
IMPATT	Impact Avalanche and Transmit Time [diode]	. . .
IMR	Integrated Multiport Repeater	ADM
IMR	Isolation Mode Rejection	. . .
IMS	ILAN Management Software	. . .
	sa *ILAN, Integrated Local Area Network*	
IMS	Information Management System	IBM
IMS	Integrated Measurement System	. . .

IMS	Inventory Management System	Honeywell, IBM
IMS/VS	Information Management System/Virtual System	IBM
IMSL	International Mathematics and Statistical Library	IMSL
IMSLIDF	International Mathematics and Statistical Library Interactive Documentation Facility	IMSL
IMT	Inter-Machine Trunk	. . .
IMTEC	Information Management and Technology	GSA
IMU	Inertial Measurement Unit	. . .
	Elementary unit of a gyro or accelerometer	
In	Indium	. . .
	Atomic element number 49	
IN	Information Network	IBM
IN	Intelligent Network	. . .
INC	Intelligent Network Controller	. . .
INCA	Interactive Controls Analysis	NASA
INEWS	Integrated Electronic Warfare System	Sanders Associates
INFOBANK	Information Bank	*NY Times*
	New York Times database	
Infoswitch	—Infoswitch	. . .
	Canadian packet/circuit-switched network	
INL	Integral Non-Linearity	. . .
INMACS	Integrated Network Management Administration and Control System	Amdahl
INMS	Integrated Network Management Service	MCI
INMS	Integrated Network Management System	DEC
INP	Independent Network Processor	. . .
INP	Internet Nodal Processor	. . .
INS	Instruction Set Simulator	. . .
INT	Interrupt	CCITT
	X.25 protocol packet assembly/disassembly (PAD) command sa *X.25*	
INTACK	Interrupt-Acknowledge(ment)	Intel
	re: Microprocessor control signal	
INTELSAT	International Telecommunications Satellite	INTELSAT
INTUG	International Telecommunications Users Group	INTUG
INV	Invalid [facility request]	CCITT
	X.25 protocol packet assembly/disassembly (PAD) service signal sa *X.25*	

INVERT	INVERT [circuit or logic gate] Electronic circuit which exhibits the Boolean INVERT logic function	. . .
IO	Input/Output Alternate; see *I/O*	. . .
IOB	Input/Output Block re: Integrated circuit (IC) layout design	. . .
IOC	Inter-Office Channel	. . .
IOCP	Input/Output Control Program sa *ICP, Input/Output Control Processor*	IBM
IOCS	Input/Output Control System	IBM
IOCTL	Input/Output Control	. . .
IOM	Information Output Management	. . .
IOM	ISDN Oriented Modular [interface architecture] Multiplexed channel in digital signal processing sa *ISDN, Integrated Services Digital Network*	Siemens
IOP	Input/Output Processor	. . .
IOS	Input/Output Subsystem	. . .
IOSB	Input/Output Status Block	DEC
IOWIT	International Organization of Women in Telecommunications	. . .
IP	Instrument Panel [connector]	AMP
IP	Information Processing re: Automotive industry	. . .
IP	Initialize Program TELNET command; sa *TELNET*	IBM
IP	Intelligent Peripheral	CCITT
IP	Interactive Processor	. . .
IP	Internet Protocol	. . .
IP	Interrupt Process	DoD
IPAC	Interface Protocol Asynchronous Cell	. . .
IPARS	International Passenger Airline Reservation System	IBM
IPB	Instruction Prefetch Buffer	IBM
IPC	Information Processing Center	. . .
IPC	Instructions Per Clock A measure of processor speed	. . .
IPC	Integrated Peripheral Controller	. . .
IPC	Integrated Product Catalog	Computer Associates
IPC	Inter-Processor Communications re: Multiple processor computers	nCUBE
IPD	Intelligent Power Device	. . .
IPDA	Intensified Photodiode Array	. . .

IPDS	Intelligent Printer Data Stream	IBM
IPF	Interactive Productivity Facility	IBM
	An IBM virtual machine (VM) facility	
IPG	Interactive Program Generator	Wayne Kerr
IPI	Intelligent Peripheral Interface	. . .
	High-level interface for optical storage devices	
IPIC	Intelligent Power Integrated Circuit	. . .
	re: Power integrated circuits with built-in logic	
IPICS	Initial Production Inventory Control System	IBM
IPK	Intrastromal Photorefractive Keratoplasty	. . .
	Medical use of lasers for ophthalmological rectification	
IPL	Initial Program Load	IBM
IPL	Interrupt Priority Level	DEC
IPM	Incremental Phase Modulation	. . .
IPM	Intelligent Power Module	. . .
IPN	Integrated Packet Network	. . .
IPNS	ISDN PBX Networking Specification	IPNS Forum
	sa *ISDN, Integrated Services Digital Network* and *PBX, Private Branch Exchange*	
IPO	Interactive Protocol Optimization	Xyplex
IPP	Internetwork Packet Protocol	Xerox
IPS	Information Protection System	IBM
IPS	Intelligent Power Supply	. . .
IPS	Intelligent Power System	Elgar
IPS	Invoice Processing Service	US Sprint
	Electronic billing system	
IPS	Item Processing System	Burroughs
	Data management system for the banking industry	
IPSE	Integrated Project Support Environment	IBM
IPTS	International Practical Temperature Scale	NIST
IPU	Instruction Processing Unit	. . .
IPV	Inverse Peak Voltage	. . .
	Alternate; see *PIV, Peak Inverse Voltage*	
IPX	Internet Packet Exchange [protocol]	Novell
IQ	Intelligent Query	Prog. Intell.
IQA	Information Quality Analysis	IBM
IQEC	International Quantum Electronics Conference	IQEC
IQL	Interactive Query Language	. . .
Ir	Iridium	. . .
	Atomic element number 77	
IR	Infrared	. . .
	Invisible radiation of wavelength greater than 700 nm	

IR	Instruction Register	. . .
IR	Insulation Resistance	. . .
IR	Internet Router	Interlan
IRAD	Industry Research and Development	DoD
IRAS	Infrared Astronomical Satellite	NASA
	Part of NASA's *Great Observatory Program, GOP,* which see	
IRC	Immediate Response Chain	IBM
IRC	Inductance-Resistance-Capacitance [circuit]	. . .
IRC	International Record Carrier	. . .
IRCCD	Infrared Charge-Coupled Device	. . .
IRDS	Information Resource Dictionary System	. . .
IRG	Inter-Record Gap	. . .
IRIG	Inter-Range Instrumentation Group	ASTIA
IRJE	Internet Remote Job Entry	NNSC
IRLD	Infrared Laser Diode	. . .
IRM	Information Resources Management	. . .
IRMS	Information Resources Management Service	GSA
IRP	I/O Request Packet	. . .
	sa *I/O, Input/Output*	
IRP	Inventory Requirements Planning	IBM
IRSS	Incident Resource Status System	USFS
IRX	ISDN Resource Exchange	Teleos
	sa *ISDN, Integrated Services Digital Network*	
IS	Immediate System	. . .
IS	Information Separator	CCITT
IS_n	Information Separator n ($n=1, 2, 3, 4$)	ISO
	Generic designation for ISO seven-bit code positions X1D through X1F; see IS_1 through IS_4	
IS_1	Information Separator 1	
	Underscore (US)	
IS_2	Information Separator 2	ISO
	Record separator (RS)	
IS_3	Information Separator 3	ISO
	Group separator (GS)	
IS_4	Information Separator 4	ISO
	File separator (FS)	
IS	Information System	. . .
IS	International Standard	. . .
IS	Interrupt Stack	DEC
IS-IS	Intermediate System-to-Intermediate System	NIST
IS-to-IS	Intermediate System-to-Intermediate System	DEC
ISA	Industry Standard Architecture	IBM
ISAAC	Information System for Advanced Academic Computing	IBM/Univ. of Wash.

ISAM	Indexed Sequential Access Method	IBM
ISC	Information Systems Command	US Army
ISC	International Service Carrier	AT&T
ISC	Intersystem Communication	IBM
ISD	Intelligent Snapshot Driver	Microsoft
ISDN	Integrated Services Digital Network	AT&T
ISE	Integrated Storage Element	DEC
ISFET	Ion-Sensitive Field Effect Transistor	. . .
ISHM	International Society for Hybrid Microelectronics	ISHM
ISI	Institute for Scientific Information	ISI
ISI	Intelligent Standard Interface	CDC
ISIS	Integrated Series IMPATT Structure sa *IMPATT*	. . .
ISIS	Integrated Scientific Information System	Molecular Design
ISLU	Integrated Services Logical Unit	. . .
ISM	Industrial-Scientific-Medical Designation given to radio frequency bands reserved for those purposes, specifically, 902–928, 2400–2483.5, and 5725–5858 MHz	. . .
ISMX	Integrated Subrate Multiplexer	BOC
ISN	Information System Network	AT&T
ISO	International Standards Organization	. . .
ISO *nnnn*	International Standards Organization *nnnn* Data communications standard, where *nnnn* is the standard number	ISO
ISODE	International Standards Organization Development Environment	ISO
ISP	In-Store Processor	. . .
ISP	Interrupt Stack Pointer	DEC
ISPF	Interactive System Productivity Facility	IBM
ispLSI	in-system programmable Large-Scale Integration re: Logic arrays	. . .
ISR	Interrupt Service Routine	DEC
ISS	Information System Services	IBM
ISS	Integrated Switching System	. . .
ISSCC	International Solid-State Circuits Conference	ISSCC
ISSR	Independant Secondary Surveillance Radar	. . .
ISSS	Initial Sector Suite System re: A segment of the FAA's Advanced Automation System (AAS)	FAA
ISTE	International Society of Technology in Education	ISTE

ISU	Integrated Service Unit	. . .
ISUP	ISDN User Part	. . .
	sa *ISDN, Integrated Services Digital Network*	
ISV	Independent Software Vendor	. . .
ISVS	International Switched-Voice Service	Decco
IT	Incomplete Transmission	. . .
	Equivalent to *NACK, No Acknowledgement*	
IT	Information Technology	. . .
ITAC	Information Technology Acquisition Center	US Navy
ITC	Intelligent Traffic Controller	Sequel Data Systems
ITCB	ISDN Terminal Co-Processor Board	. . .
	sa *ISDN, Integrated Services Digital Network*	
ITDE	Interchannel Time Displacement Error	. . .
	re: multi-channel tape recorder performance	
ITER	International Thermonuclear Experimental Reactor	USA, USSR, et al.
ITG	Interactive Test Generator	H-P
ITL	Independent Testing Laboratory	. . .
ITMS	Ingestible Thermal Monitoring System	Johns Hopkins Univ.
ITN	Image Transmission Network	FBI
ITN	Integrated Telecommunications Network	American Express
ITP	Industrial TEMPEST Program	. . .
	sa *TEMPEST*	
ITP	Inosine Triphosphate	. . .
	A compound important in biochemistry	
ITPS	International Practical Temperature Scale	ITPS
ITR	Internal Throughput Rate	IBM
	Computer performance measurement technology, roughly equivalent to industry-standard *MIPS*, which see	
ITRC	Information Technology Requirements Council	. . .
ITRR	Internal Throughput Rate Ratio	IBM
ITS	International Temperature Scale	NIST
	Also designated by *ITS-90* to indicate year of acceptance	
ITS-90	International Temperature Scale	NIST
	See *ITS*	
ITU	International Telecommunications Union	. . .
	An agency of the United Nations	
IU	Integer Unit	Burroughs
IUCRC	Industry/University Cooperative Research Center	NSF

IUPAC	International Union of Pure and Applied Chemistry	IUPAC
IUPAP	International Union of Pure and Applied Physics	IUPAP
IUS	Inertial Upper Stage	NASA
IUSS	Integrated Undersea Surveillance System	US Navy
IVA	Intra-Vehicular Activity re: Space flight	NASA
IVAN	International Value-Added Network	. . .
IVD	Inside Vapor Deposition	Corning
IVD	Integrated Voice and Data	. . .
IVDT	Integrated Voice-Data Terminal	. . .
IVHS	Intelligent Vehicle Highway System	ERIM
IVI	Interactive Video Instruction	. . .
IVPN	International Virtual Private Network	US Sprint, et al.
IVR	Instant Video Reception (or Receiver) re: Video signal reception in "compressed time"	. . .
IVR	Interactive (or Integrated) Voice Response	. . .
IWSDB	Integrated Weapons System Data Base	DoD
IXC	Interexchange Carrier	AT&T
IXR	Intelligent Transparent Restore	Computer Associates
I2ICE	Intel Integrated In-Circuit Emulator	Intel

J

J	Joule Unit of work, $= 10^7$ erg Named in honor of English physicist James Prescott Joule (1818–1889)	. . .
J-Band	J-Band Microwave frequency allocation of 10 to 20 GHz	. . .
JAD	Joint Application Development	. . .
JAERI	Japan Atomic Energy Research Institute	JAERI
JAN	Joint Army Navy	DoD
JARS	Job Accounting Record Statistics	Johnson
JARS	Job Accounting Report System	JSI
JASORS	Joint Advanced Special Operations Radio Systems	CECOM

JATO	Jet-Assisted Take-Off	US Air Force
	A modular add-on unit used to provide additional thrust to aircraft during take-off; sa *RATO, Rocket-Assisted Take-Off*	
JBIG	Joint Bi-Level Imaging Group	. . .
	An international electronic image networking compression standards group; also, the standard	
JCALS	Joint Computer-Aided Acquisition and Logistics Support	DoD
JCL	Job Control Language	IBM
JEDI	Joint Education Initiative	NASA, et al.
JES	Job Entry Subsystem	IBM
JET	Joint European Torus	Euorpean Community
	A large fusion research facility	
JFET	Junction Field-Effect Transistor	. . .
JFN	Job File Number	DEC
JI	Junction Isolation	. . .
JIB	Job Information Block	DEC
JICB	Junction-Isolated Complementary Bipolar Integrated circuit technology	. . .
JILA	Joint Institute for Laboratory Astrophysics	NIST
JIT	Just In Time	. . .
	Manufacturing method of maintaining a low stock level	
JNLT	Japan National Large Telescope	Nat'l. Astro. Observ.
	A 7.5-meter monolithic telescope	
Johniac	John [von Neumann] Integrator and Computer	Rand
	Clone of *IAS* computer (which see), and named in honor of American mathematician John von Neumann (1903–1957)	
JOVIAL	Jule's Own Version of International Algorithmic Language	. . .
JPEG	Joint Photographic Experts Group	. . .
	Standards committee for real-time video image compression and processing; also, the JPEG standard	
JRP	Joint Requirements Planning	. . .
JSTARS	Joint Surveillance Target Attack Radar System	US Navy
JTAG	Joint Test Action Group	JTAG
JTC³A	Joint Tactical Command, Control and Communications Agency	DoD

JTIDS	Joint Technical Information Distribution System	DoD
JUSTIS	Joint Uniform Services Technical Information System	DoD
JvNC	John von Neumann National [supercomputer] Center	JvNC

K

k	—Boltzmann constant 1.38054×10^{-16} erg deg^{-1} Named in honor of Austrian physicist Ludwig Boltzmann (1844–1906)	. . .
k	kilo Prefix for 10^3 In computer parlance, 2^{10}, or 1024, generally referred to as a "binary k," to distinguish from a "decimal k," which is equal to 1000	. . .
K	—Deflection parameter (symbol) Stated as a pure number; synchrotron undulator or "wiggler" property	. . .
K	—Stiffness [coefficient] (symbol)	. . .
K	Kalium Symbol for *potassium*, atomic element number 19	. . .
K	Kelvin Scale of temperature measurement Named in honor of Lord Kelvin (William Thompson) (1824–1907)	. . .
K-Band	K-Band Microwave frequency allocation of 18 to 27 GHz	. . .
K$_a$-Band	—K$_a$-Band Radar electromagnetic radiation in the 27 to 40 GHz range	. . .
KAPSE	Kernel Ada Programming Support Environment sa *Ada*	DARPA
KAR	Kodak Automated Registration [System]	Kodak
kb	kilobit 1024 bits ("Binary k")	. . .
kB	kiloByte 1024 bytes ("Binary k")	. . .
KBMS	Knowledge Base Management System	AI
kbps	kilobits per second Data rate—thousands of bits per second	. . .

KEE	Knowledge Engineering Environment	Intellicorp
KEEPS	Kodak Ektaprint Electronic Publishing System	Kodak
KEK	Key-Encrypting Key	. . .
KERMIT	Kermit	. . .
	File transfer protocol named after Kermit	
	the Frog, a Jim Henson creation	
KES	Knowledge Engineering System	Software A&E
keV	kiloelectron Volt	. . .
	10^3 electron volts	
KFLOPS	Kilo Floating Point Operations Per Second	. . .
kHz	kilohertz	. . .
	10^3 Hertz	
	sa *Hz, Hertz*	
KIP	Kinetics Internet Protocol	. . .
KIPP	Kofax Image Processing Platform	Kofax
KIPS	Kilo Instructions Per Second	IBM
	10^3 instructions per second	
KITES	Kids Interactive Telecommunications	. . .
	Experience by Satellite	
	A teleconferencing experimental project	
KLIPS	Kilo Logical Inferences Per Second	. . .
	10^3 logical inferences per second	
	sa *LIPS*	
KLM	Kerr Lens Modelocking	. . .
	re: Laser pulse generation	
KMC	Key Management Center	Racal-Milgo
	Encryption management hardware/software	
KOPS	Kilo Operations Per Second	. . .
KOS	Kent Operating System	Kent State
		University
Kr	Krypton	. . .
	Atomic element number 36	
KSDS	Key Sequenced Data Set	. . .
KSP	Kernel Stack Pointer	DEC
KSPS	Kilo Samples Per Second	. . .
	Usually used in reference to analog-to-digital	
	conversion (ADC) and digital-to-analog	
	conversion (DAC) technology	
KSR	Keyboard Send/Receive	. . .
	re: Teletype communications unit	
KSU	Keu Systems Unit	. . .
KTP	Kalium (Potassium) Titanyl Phosphate	. . .
	Non-linear crystal used in diode-pumped	
	lasers	
KTS	Key Telephone System	. . .

K$_u$-Band	K$_u$-Band Microwave frequencies in the approximate range 12–18 GHz	. . .
kV	kilovolt 10³ Volts	. . .
kVA	kilovolt-Amperes 10³ Volt-Amperes (VA) Preferred form; also appears as *KVA* in the literature	. . .
kW	kilowatt 10³ Watts	. . .
kWh	kilowatt-hour 10³ Watt-hours	. . .
KWIC	Keyword in Context	IBM
KWOC	Keyword Out of Context	IBM

L

l	length Usually expressed in *meters* (*m*) in scientific literature	. . .
l	liter Metric unit of capacity	. . .
L	—50 Roman numeral designation	. . .
L	—Inductance (symbol) Expressed in units of *Henries*; named in honor of American physicist Joseph Henry (1797–1878)	. . .
L	Lambert Unit of luminance, metric	. . .
L	Liter Alternate form; see *l*	. . .
L-Air	Liquid Air	. . .
L-Band	L-Band Radio high-frequency allocation of 1.0–2.0 GHz	. . .
L-He	Liquid Helium	. . .
La	Lanthanum Atomic element number 57	. . .
LAA	Locally Administered Address re: Token ring communication controller	IBM
LAB	Logic Array Block	. . .
LAB-C	Line Attachment Base-C IBM token ring attachment	IBM

LAD	Large Area Display	Greyhawk Systems
LAD	Listen Address Device IEEE Standard 488 bus command; sa *IEEE*	IEEE
LAD	Local Area Disk	. . .
LADD	Lens Antenna Deployment Demonstration	DoD
LADD	Local Area Data Distribution	. . .
LADDER	Language Access to Distributed Data with Error Recovery	SRI
Laddr	Layered Device Diver	Microsoft
LADT	Local Area Data Transport	IBM
LAG	Listen Address Group re: IEEE Standard 488; sa *IEEE*	IEEE
LAGEOS	Laser Geodynamic Satellite	NASA
LAM	LAN Access Module sa *LAN, Local Area Network*	AT&T
LAM	Lobe Access (or Attachment) Module re: Token ring network support	. . .
LAMN	Local Area Multiplexer Node	. . .
LAMPF	Los Alamos Meson Physics Facility	LANL
LAN	Local Area Network	. . .
LANA	Local Area Network Accelerator	. . .
LANGS	LAN Gateway Service sa *LAN, Local Area Network*	Fritz, J. WVU
LANL	Los Alamos National Laboratory	LANL
LANRES	Local Area Network Resource Extension	IBM
LANSP	Local Area Network Support Program	IBM
LAOS	Light Amplifying Optical Switch	. . .
LAP	Link Access Protocol sa *LAP-B* and *LAP-D*	. . .
LAP	Local Area Power	. . .
LAP-B	Link Access Protocol Balanced	. . .
LAP-D	Link Access Protocol D-channel re: ISDN D-channel protocol; sa *ISDN, Integrated Services Digital Network* and *D, D-channel*	CCITT
LAP-M	Link Access Procedure for Modems	CCITT
LAPB	Link Access Protocol Balanced Alternate; see *LAP-B*	. . .
LAPD	Link Access Protocol D-channel Alternate; see *LAP-D*	. . .
LAPM	Link Access Procedure for Modems Alternate; see *LAP-M*	. . .
LARC	Livermore Advanced Research Computer	LLNL
LARS	Labor Activity Reporting System	. . .
LARS	Laser Ranging System	. . .
LAS	Land Analysis System	NASA

LAS*	Logical Address Strobe [signal]	. . .
	Note: "*" indicates that a signal (called "active high") must be present at the circuit terminal in order for the described function to be activated.	
Laser	Light Amplification by Stimulation of Emitted Radiation	. . .
	Formerly capitalized, but now accepted as an English word	
LASER	Light Amplification by Stimulation of Emitted Radiation	. . .
	Now accepted as an English word: *laser*	
LASL	Los Alamos Scientific Laboratory	DoD
LAST	Local Area System Transport	. . .
LAT	Local Access Terminal	Sperry
LAT	Local Area Transport	DEC
LATA	Local Access and Transport Area	AT&T
LATCP	Local Area Transport Control Protocol	DEC
LAVC	Local Area VAX Cluster	DEC
	sa *VAX, Virtual Address Extension*	
LAVCS	Local Area VAX Cluster System	DEC
	sa *VAX, Virtual Address Extension*	
LAWN	Local Area Wireless Network	O'Neill Comm.
lb	libra	. . .
	Latin for *pound*	
LBC	Local Bus Controller	. . .
LBL	Lawrence Berkeley Laboratory	LBL
LBL	Line by Line	. . .
	A mathematical procedure for calculating radiation scattering	
LBN	Logical Block Number	DEC
LBO	Line Build Out [device]	Novell
LBO	Lithium Borate	. . .
	A non-linear laser crystal material	
LBR	Large Business Remote	. . .
	A large switching system ("super *PBX*") sa *PBX, Private Branch Exchange*	
LBRV	Low Bit Rate Voice	. . .
LC	Library of Congress	US Congress
LC	Liquid Crystal	. . .
LC	Inductance-Capacitance [circuit]	. . .
LC	Long Convolver	. . .
	An algorithm for processing electronic signals for introduction into a dispersive delay line (DDL)	
LCA	Logic Cell Array	. . .

LCC	Leadless Chip Carrier	. . .
LCC	Local Communications Controller	IBM
	Series 1 Chat ring	
LCCC	Leadless Ceramic Chip Carrier	. . .
	Chip mounting technology; as opposed to	
	socket mounting	
LCD	Liquid Crystal Display	. . .
LCLV	Liquid Crystal Light Valve	Greyhawk Systems
LCN	Logical Channel Number	CCITT
LCN	Loosely Coupled Network	CDC
LCP	Link Control Protocol	. . .
LCPL	Linear Complementary Problem Solving by	. . .
	Lemke [method]	
LCR	Inductance (symbol)-Capacitance-Resistance	. . .
LCR	Lead Calcium Rechargeable [battery]	
LCR	Least-Cost Routing	. . .
	Automatic selection of least cost (optimal)	
	routing in communications networks	
LCS	Liquid Crystal Shutter	. . .
	Device used in non-impact printers	
LCTV	Liquid Crystal Television	. . .
	re: Solid-state (SS) video display	
LCU	Lightweight Computer Unit	US Army
LD	Laser Diode	. . .
LD	Laser Disk	. . .
	Laser video recording on disk format; sa	
	CDV, Compact Disk Video	
LD	Long Distance	. . .
LD	Low Dispersion	. . .
	re: Optical glass, fiber-optic material	
LD_n	Lethal Dose n	. . .
	where n = value indicating median	
	percentage of death rate expected (after	
	exposure to radiation, etc.)	
LDA	Linear Discriminant Analysis	. . .
LDA	Live Data Analysis	TTC
LDA	Long Distance Adapter	Equinox
LDD	Lightly Doped Drain	. . .
	re: Integrated circuit production technology	
LDDC	Long Distance Direct Current [dialing system]	. . .
LDDS	Limited Distance Data Set	. . .
LDEF	Long Deposition Experimental Facility	NASA
LDF	Local Distribution Frame	AMP
	re: Telephone/data communications	

LDH	Lactate dehydrogenase A compound important in biochemistry	...
LDI	Local Data Interchange	...
LDM	Limited Distance Modem	...
LDM	Logical Data Modeling	...
LDO	Low Drop-Out re: Low input-to-output voltage drop in power supplies and voltage regulators	...
LDR	Local Distribution Radio	...
LDRPS	Living Disaster Recovery Planning System	Strohl Systems
LDT	Local Descriptor Table	Intel
LD2	Liquid Deuterium	...
LEA	Longitudinally Excited Atmosphere [laser]	...
LEC	Liquid Encapsulation Czochralski re: Single crystal growth for electronic circuit chip fabrication and optical applications	...
LEC	Local Exchange Carrier	...
LEC	Long External Cavity re: Laser construction	...
LED	Light-Emitting Diode	...
LEIS	Law Enforcement Information System	US Coast Guard
LEM	Lobe Expansion Module re: Token ring network support	AMP
LEN	Low-Entry Networking	IBM
LEO	Laser and Electro-Optics	...
LEO	Low Earth Orbit	...
LEOS	Lasers and Electro-Optics	LEOS
LEOS	Low Earth-Orbiting Satellite	...
LEP	Large Electron Positron [collider, physics] re: "Linear" (circular) accelerators, electron physics	CERN
LET	Linear Energy Transfer	...
Leu	Leucine A compound important in biochemistry	...
LEX	Leading Edge Extension	...
LF	Line Feed Format effector 2 (FE_2); a component of the binary code in CCITT Recommendation V.3; sa FE_n, *CCITT* and *V.3*	CCITT
LF	Low Frequency 30 to 300 kHz	...
LFSR	Linear Feedback Shift Register	...

LGA	Land Grid Array	. . .
	Microchip packaging and pin-out technology sa *PGA, Pin Grid Array* and *SMT, Surface Mount Technology*	
LGMSS	Large Gap Magnetic Suspension System	Langley Research Ctr.
LH	Light Helicopter	DoD
LH	Luteinizing Hormone	. . .
	A compound important in biochemistry	
LHC	Left-Hand Circular	
	re: Polarization of electromagnetic radiation	
LHCP	Left-Hand Circular Polarization	. . .
	re: Polarization of electromagnetic radiation	
LHOTS	Long-Haul Optical Transmission Set	. . .
LHX	Light Helicopter Experimental [aircraft]	Sikorsky Aircraft
LH2	Liquid Helium	. . .
Li	Lithium	. . .
	Atomic element number 3	
LIA	Laser Interferometric Alignment	Nikon
	re: Precision integrated circuit (IC) wafer overlay alignment	
LIB	Line Interface Base	IBM
	Pertains to software for the IBM 3705 Communications Controller	
LIC	Linear Interface Circuit	TI
LIC	Line Interface Coupler	IBM
LIC	Lowest Incoming Channel	CCITT
LICT	Low-Impurity-Channel Transistor	Hitachi
Lidar	Laser Intensity Detection and Ranging	. . .
	Alternate form; see *LIDAR*	
LIDAR	Laser Intensity Detection and Ranging	. . .
	Also designated by *Lidar*	
LIDB	Line Information Database	. . .
LIF	Laser Induced Fluorescence	. . .
LIF	Low Insertion Force	. . .
	Socket designed to accept integrated circuits (ICs) with minimum force	
LIFE	Laboratory for International Fuzzy Engineering	JMITI
LIFE	Long Instruction Format Engine	. . .
LIFO	Last In First Out	. . .
	Programming stacking technique; equivalent to *FILO, First In Last Out*	
LIGO	Laser Interferometry Gravitational [wave] Observatory	Caltech/MIT

LIM	Line Interface Module	Ericsson
	Time division switch for voice/data	
LIMS	Laboratory Information Management System	...
LIMS	Laser Ionization Mass Spectrometry	...
LINPACK	Linear [systems] Package	...
LINX	Logistics Information Exchange	Defense Logistics Agy.
LIOM	LAN I/O Module	...
	sa *LAN, Local Area Network* and *I/O, Input/Output*	
lips	logical inferences per second	...
	Alternate form; see *LIPS*	
LIPS	Logical Inferences Per Second	...
	Refers to rate of processing in knowledge-based systems sa *GLIPS, Giga Logical Inferences Per Second* Alternately designated by *lips*	
LIS	Library Information System	CMU
LISN	Line Impedance Stabilization Network	...
LISP	List Processor	...
LISREL	Linear Structural Relationship	SPSS
LITE	Laser Inter-satellite Transmission Experiment	MIT
LIU	Line Interface Unit	...
LKED	Linkage Editor	IBM
LLA	Library Look Aside	IBM
LLB	Local Loop Back	...
LLC	Logical Link Control [protocol]	IEEE
	sa *LLCn, Logical Link Control [sublayer] n*	
LLC*n*	Logical Link Control [sublayer] *n* (n=1 or 2)	IEEE
	re: Local area network (LAN) intercommunication	
LLD	Local Longitude Difference	...
	Difference between Local Mean Time (LMT) and Greenwich Mean Time (GMT)	
LLDPE	Linear Low-Density Polyethylene	...
	A soft plastic widely used in many technologies	
LLNL	Lawrence Livermore National Laboratory	LLNL
LLO	Local Lock Out	IEEE
	IEEE Standard 488 bus command; sa *IEEE*	
LLP	Lowest Level Processor	...
LLS	Lower Layers Service	Wollongong Group
	re: OSI protocol servicing; sa *OSI, Open Systems Interconnection*	

LLT	Large Lunar Telescope	NASA
	A multiple-aperture telescope; also called a multiple-mirror telescope, *MMT*, which see	
LM	LAN Manager	IBM
	sa *LAN, Local Area Network*	
LM	Linear Module	Nat'l. Semiconductor
LM	Long Multiplier	. . .
	An algorithm for processing electronic signals for intro- duction into a dispersive delay line *DDL*, which see	
LM/X	LAN Manager X	H-P
	sa *LAN, Local Area Network*	
LMB	Logical Memory Block	DEC
LMCC	Land Mobile Communications Council	. . .
LME	Layer Management Entity	. . .
LMF	License Management Facility	DEC
	re: Clustered processors	
LMI	Layer Management Interface	. . .
LMI	Link Management Interface	. . .
LMI	Local Management Interface	. . .
	Specification developed by Frame Relay Implementor's Forum	
LMN	Lossless Matching Network	. . .
	An impedance matching device with no insertion loss	
LMOS	Line Management Operating System	. . .
LMRS	Land Mobile Radio Service	FCC
LMS	Laser Magnetic Storage	. . .
LMS	Learning Management System	DEC
LMS	Least Mean Square	. . .
	A mathematical algorithm	
LMS	Library Management Software	. . .
LMT	Local Mean Time	. . .
LMU	Line Monitoring Unit	. . .
ln	logarithm, natural (or Naperian)	. . .
	Base $e = 2.71828\ldots$	
LNA	Low-Noise Amplifier	. . .
LNB	Low-Noise Block	. . .
	A measure of sensitivity limit in antennas, electronic circuits, etc.	
LNI	Line Network Interface	. . .
LNMS	Link Network Management System	Timeview
LNR	Low-Noise Receiver	. . .
LN_2	Liquid Nitrogen	. . .
LO	Local Oscillator	. . .

LOC	Loss Of Carrier	Bellcore
	re: Communications reliability technology	
LOC	Lowest Outgoing Channel	CCITT
LOCCB	Lead-On-Chip with Center Bond	. . .
	re: Integrated circuit fabrication technology	
log	logarithm	. . .
	Common; base = 10	
LON	Local Operating Network	Echelon
LONS	Local On-line Network System	US Air Force
LOP	Loss of Power	. . .
Loran-C	Long range navigation-C	. . .
	A system of low frequency (LF; 100 kHz) broadcast stations used for the dissemination of precise frequency, time, and navigational information (accuracies within 1 part in 10^{13})	
	sa *Shoran, Short Range Navigation*	
LORRA	Land, Ocean and Rain Radar Altimeter	. . .
LOS	Line Of Sight	. . .
	re: Radar ranging determination, microwave transmission and reception capability or restriction	
LOS	Loss of Signal	. . .
LOX	Liquid Oxygen	. . .
LP	Line Printer	. . .
LP	Linear Polarization (or Linearly Polarized)	. . .
	re: Fiber-optic communications	
LP	Linear Programming	. . .
LP	Liquid Petroleum	. . .
	viz., propane; also *LPG, Liquid (or Liquified Petroleum Gas)*	
LP	Long-Play(-ing)	. . .
	re: Audio or video recordings	
LPA	Line Powered Amplifier	. . .
LPA	Link Pack Area	IBM
LPAR	Logical Partition	IBM
LPBLAS	Linear Programming Basic Linear Algebra Subroutine	DEC
LPC	Laboratory Precision Connector	. . .
LPC	Linear Predictive Coding	. . .
LPCVD	Low-Pressure Chemical Vapor Deposition	. . .
LPDA	Link Problem Determination Aid	IBM
LPDA	Linear Photo-Diode Array	. . .
LPE	Liquid Phase Epitaxy	. . .
	re: Fiberoptic/laser crystal-growing technology	

LPF	Long-Period Focussing re: Design of traveling wave tubes	. . .
LPG	Liquid (or Liquified) Petroleum Gas Also designated by *LP, Liquid Petroleum*	. . .
lpm	lines per minute Speed rating of computer line printers	. . .
LPM	Laser Processing Machinery	. . .
LPM	Linear Power Module	. . .
LPM	Low-Power Microcomputer	. . .
LPP	Link Peripheral Processor	Northern Telecomm
LPSA	Licensed Program Support Agreement	IBM
LPT	Line Printer	. . .
LQ	Letter Quality re: Printer with high resolution typeface	. . .
LQG	Linear Quadratic Gaussian [smoothing] re: Statistical treatment of raw data	. . .
Lr	Lawrencium Atomic element number 103 Named in honor of American physicist Ernest O. Lawrence (1901–1958), inventor of the cyclotron	. . .
LR	Link Register	IBM
LR	[Inductance] Resistance	. . .
LR	Longitudinal Recording A magnetic recording technique, standard through the 1970s	. . .
LRC	Inductance (symbol)-Resistance-Capacitance (circuit)	. . .
LRC	Local Register Cache	. . .
LRC	Longitudinal Redundancy Check A method of checking received data for accuracy sa *CRC, Cyclic Redundancy Check* and *VRC, Vertical Redundancy Check*	. . .
LRECL	Logical Record Length	IBM
LRM	Line-Reflect-Match Vector network analyzer calibration methodology	. . .
LRP	Logical Request Package	. . .
LRPD	Low-Repetition-Rate Pulse Doppler	. . .
LRU	Least Recently Used Algorithm used in cache memories; opposite of *MRU, Most Recently Used*	. . .
LRU	Line-Replaceable Unit	. . .
LRV	Lunar Roving Vehicle	NASA

LS	Least Squares	...
	Statistical process, frequently used in curve-fitting	
LS	Linkage Stack	IBM
LS	Low-Power Schottky	...
	re: Low-power high-speed integrated circuit (IC) technology sa *S, Schottky*	
LSB	Large-Scale Bypass	AT&T
LSB	Least Significant Bit	...
LSB	Low Surface Brightness	...
	re: Relative intensity of galaxies	
LSB	Lower Sideband	...
LSC	Liquid Scintillation Counting	...
LSE	Language-Sensitive Editor	DEC
LSE	Linkage Stack Entry	IBM
LSE	Local System Environment	CCITT
LSI	Large-Scale Integration	...
	IC technology developed in 1970s; Contains 10^4 to 10^5 gates	
LSM	Laser Section Microscope	CyberOptics
LSM	Line Switch Module	...
LSO	Limited Service Offering	...
	Customized network service provided by a major communications vendor	
LSR	Local Shared Resources	IBM
LSSD	Level-Sensitive Scan Detector	IBM
	An on-chip test logic facility	
LST	Large Space Telescope	NASA
	Early consideration; replaced by the *Hubble Space Telescope, HST*	
LSTTL	Low-power Schottky Transistor-Transistor Logic	...
	re: Low power high-speed integrated circuit (IC) technology sa *S, Schottky*	
LSU	Laser Scanning Unit	...
	sa *Laser*	
LT	Line Termination	...
	re: *ISDN, Integrated Services Digital Network*	
LTB	Local Token-Ring Bridge	...
LTC	Lowest Two-Way Channel	CCITT
LTH	Leaded Through Holes	...
	Designation given to conductive holes in an electronic circuit board; also designated by *PTH, Plated Through Holes*	

LTM	Lighted Termination Module	. . .
	re: Bare circuit board testing	
LTM	LAN Traffic Manager	. . .
	sa *LAN, Local Area Network*	
LTP	Long-Term Prediction	. . .
	Statistical procedure	
LTSS	Lawrence Timesharing System	LLNL
LTTS	Launch Test Training System	Lockheed
Lu	Lutetium	. . .
	Atomic element number 71	
LU	Logical Unit	IBM
	An element of IBM's *Systems Network*	
	Architecture, SNA	
LUF	Lowest Usable Frequency	. . .
LUI	Logical Unit Interface	IBM
LURE	Laboratoire pour l'Utilisation du	LURE
	Rayonnement Electromagnetique	
	(Laboratory for the Utilization of	
	Electromagnetic Radiation)	
LUT	Logic Under Test	. . .
	sa *DUT, Device Under Test* and *UUT, Unit*	
	Under Test	
LUT	Look-Up Table	. . .
LUW	Logical Unit of Work	IBM
LU6.2	Logic Unit [type] 6.2	IBM
	re: IBM's *Systems Network Architecture,*	
	SNA	
LV	Laser Velocimeter(-try)	. . .
	re: Digital signal processing (DSP) of	
	photons sensed by a photo-multiplier or	
	other photoelectric device	
LV	Linear Video	. . .
LVDT	Linear Variable Differential Transformer (or	. . .
	Transducer)	
LVDT	Linear Velocity/Displacement Transducer (or	. . .
	Transmitter)	
LVS	Layout Vs. Schematic	. . .
	re: Computer-aided circuit design technology	
LWIR	Long-Wavelength Infrared	. . .
	Infrared radiation in the range	
	approximately 10^{12} to 10^{14} Hertz (Hz)	
LWR	Laser Write Read	
LWX	LAN/WAN Exchange	. . .
	sa *LAN, Local Area Network* and *WAN,*	
	Wide Area Network	

lx	lux	
	Unit of illumination	
ly	light-year	. . .
	Approximately 9.45×10^{17} cm, or 5.879×10^{12} miles	
Lys	Lysine	. . .
	A compound important in biochemistry	
LZA	Leading Zero/One Anticipator	IBM
	re: Reduced instruction set computer (RISC) hardware design	
LZA	Lempel-Ziv Algorithm	Lempel, Ziv
	Mathematical algorithm used in a data compression technique	
LZ*n*	Lempel-Ziv [algorthm] *n*	Lempel, Ziv
	where $n = 1$ or 2, representing two techniques for achieving data compression	
LZS	Lempel-Ziv Stack	. . .
	re: Data compression technology	
LZW	Lempel-Ziv-Welch	Lempel, Ziv, Welch
	A data compression algorithm, named after its co-developers	

M

m	mass	. . .
	Expressed in grams (g) in the *cgs* system of units, which see	
m	minute	. . .
m	meter	. . .
	Metric unit of length	
m	milli	. . .
	Prefix for 10^{-3}	
M	−1000	. . .
	Roman numeral designation	
M	Mega	. . .
	Prefix for 10^6	
M	Molar (Mole, Molarity)	. . .
	re: Solution concentration	
M	More	CCITT
	Data bit in *X.25* protocol, which see	
M-Band	M-Band	. . .
	Microwave frequency allocation of 10–15 GHz	
M/O	Magneto-Optic	. . .

M-ST	Monochrome Super Twist	Toshiba
	High-contrast liquid crystal display (LCD)	
mA	milliampere	. . .
	10^{-3} Ampere	
MA	Materials Analysis	. . .
MAC	Mandatory Access Control	. . .
	re: *UNIX* file access control per Department of Defense criteria	
MAC	Media Access Control	. . .
MAC	Memory Access Controller	. . .
MAC	Message Authentication Code	. . .
	re: Message encryption	
MAC	Multiplexed Analog Component	. . .
	Satellite data transmission protocol	
MAC	Multiplier Accumulator	. . .
MAC	Multiply-and-Accumulate	. . .
	re: Mathematical procedure used in digital signal processing	
Mach	Mach	UC-Berkeley
	A multi-processing operating system	
Mach	Mach [number]	. . .
	A number representing the ratio of the velocity of an object in a medium to the speed of sound in that medium at standard conditions; in air, at standard temperature and pressure, *STP*, Mach 1 is equal to approximately 742 miles per hour (mph). Named in honor of Austrian physicist Ernst Mach (1838–1916)	
MACSAT	Multiple Access Communications Satellite	NASA
MAF	Multiply-Add-Fused	IBM
	IBM RS/6000 RISC (Reduced Instruction Set Computer) processor hardware component	
MAGIC	Master Graphics Interactive Console	NASA
MAI	Multiple Applications Interface	The Systems Center
MAISRC	Major Automated Information Systems Review Council	US Army
MAN	Metropolitan Area Network	TPT
MAN	Multiple Area Network	Bridge
MANCOVA	Multiple Analysis of Co-Variance	. . .
	re: Statistical analysis	
MANIAC	Mechanical and Numerical Integrator and Computer	. . .
	Clone of John von Neumann's *IAS* computer	
	sa *IAS, Institute for Advanced Study*	

MANOVA	Multiple Analysis of Variance	. . .
MAP	Manifold Absolute Pressure	. . .
MAP	Manufacturing Automation Protocol	General Motors
MAP	Measurement Assurance Program	NIST
MAP	Message Administration Procedure	. . .
MAPC	Multi-Access Protocol Converter	JBM Electronics
MAPI	Mail Applications Interface	Microsoft
MAPI	Messaging Application Programming Interface	Microsoft
MAPPER	Maintaining, Preparing and Producing Executive Reports	Unisys
MAPSE	Minimal Ada Programming Support Environment sa *Ada*	DARPA
MAR	Memory Address Register	. . .
MARC	Machine-Readable Cataloging	. . .
MARS	[University of] Missouri Automated Radiology System	Univ. of MO
MASELA	Matrix Addressable Surface Emitting Laser Array	. . .
MASER	Microwave Amplification by Stimulated Emission of Radiation	. . .
MASM	Macro Assembler	. . .
MATE	Modular Automated Test Equipment	IEEE
MAU	Media Access Unit	Microtest
MAU	Medium Attachment Unit re: Ethernet communications device; sa *Ethernet*	. . .
MAU	Multistation Access Unit IBM token-ring local area network (LAN) residency unit sa *CAU, Control Access Unit*	IBM
MAX	Multiple Array Matrix	Altera
MAXI	Modular Architecture for the Exchange of Information	DoD
Mb	Megabit 1,048,576 bits; $= 2^{20}$ bits	. . .
MB	Megabyte 1,048,576 Bytes; $= 8,388,608$ bits; $= 8 \times 2^{20}$ bits	. . .
MBC	Message Broadcast Controller	. . .
MBE	Molecular Beam Epitaxy Crystal-growing technology	AT&T

MBLT	Multiplexed Block Transfer	. . .
	A technology used to increase data transfer rate by combining data and address information;	
	sa *SSBLT, Source Synchronous Block Transfer*	
MBM	Magnetic Bubble Memory	. . .
MBP	Mail Box Protocol	. . .
Mbps	Megabits per second	. . .
	sa *Mb, Megabit*	
MBR	Master Boot Record	. . .
MBS	Media Broadband Service	NYNEX
MBT	Multilayer Bonding Technique	. . .
	Solid-state (SS) chip assembling technology for stacking chips to increase circuit density; see also the following: *MCM-C, Multichip Module—Ceramic, MCM-D, Multichip Module—Deposited, MCM-L, Multichip Module—Laminate, SiCB, Silicon Circuit Board* and *VIL, Vertical In-Line*	
MBV	Model-Based Vision	. . .
	re: Machine vision	
MCA	Micro Channel Architecture	IBM
MCAE	Mechanical Computer-Aided Engineering	. . .
MCAV	Modified Constant Angular Velocity	. . .
	re: Optical disk drive mechanism	
MCC	Main Cross-Connect	. . .
MCC	Management Control Center	DEC
MCC	Multiple Chip Carrier	Amdahl
MCD	Multichannel Communications Device	. . .
MCDN	Marine Corps Data Network	US Marines
MCET	Massachusetts Corporation for Educational Telecommunications	MCET
MCGA	Multi-Color Graphics Adapter	IBM
MCM	Multichip Module	. . .
MCM-C	Multichip Module—Ceramic	. . .
	Integrated circuit technology in which substrates are co-fired ceramics; sa *MBT, Multilayer Bonding Technique, MCM-D, Multichip Module—Deposited, MCM-L, Multichip Module—Laminate, SiCB, Silicon Circuit Board* and *VIL, Vertical In-Line*	

MCM-D	Multichip Module—Deposited Integrated circuit technology in which substrates are deposited sa *MBT, Multilayer Bonding Technique,* *MCM-C, Multichip Module—Ceramic,* *MCM-L, Multichip Module—Laminate,* *SiCB, Silicon Circuit Board* and *VIL,* *Vertical In-Line*	...
MCM-L	Multichip Module—Laminate Integrated circuit technology in which substrates are bonded sa *MBT, Multilayer Bonding Technique,* *MCM-C, Multichip Module—Ceramic,* *MCM-D, Multichip Module—Deposited,* *SiCB, Silicon Circuit Board* and *VIL,* *Vertical In-Line*	...
MCN	Metropolitan Campus Network	CMU/Bell of PA
MCN	Monopulse Comparator Network Microwave antenna signal processing system	...
MCNIU	Multicompatible Network Interface System	Honeywell
MCP	Macintosh Co-processor Platform	Apple
MCP	Master Catalog Program	Burroughs
MCP	Master Control Program	Burroughs
MCP	Micro Channel Plate Cathode ray tube construction technology	Tektronix
MCP	Modular Communications Processor	...
MCP	Multichannel Plate re: Image intesifiers and processors	...
MCR	Magnetic Character Reader	...
MCR	Magnetic Character Recognition	...
MCR	Monitor Console Routine	DEC
MCRR	Machine Check Recording and Recovery	IBM
MCS	Maneuver Control System	US Army
MCS	Multichip System	Intel
MCS	Multifunction Communication Service	AT&T
MCS	Multipoint Communications Service	Bell of Canada
MCT	Mercury-Cadmium-Telluride Image detector photosensitive material	...
MCT	Metal-oxide [semiconductor]-Controlled Thyristor	...
MCT	Motion Compensating Transform A coding technique used in video compression technology	...
MCTS	Multiple Console Timesharing System	GM
MCU	Memory Control Unit	TI

MCU	Micro-Controller Unit	. . .
MCU	Multichip Unit	DEC
MCVD	Modified Chemical Vapor Deposition	. . .
	Technique for manufacturing optical fiber	
MCXO	Microcomputer Compensated Crystal	Frequency
	Oscillator	Electronics
Md	Mendelevium	. . .
	Atomic element number 101	
	Named in honor of Russian chemist Dmitri	
	Mendeleev (1834–1907)	
MDA	Manufacturing Defects Analyzer	. . .
MDA	Modulation-Domain Analysis	H-P
MDA	Monochrome Display Adapter	IBM
MDA	Monolithic Diode Array	. . .
MDA	Multi-Dimensional Analysis	. . .
MDAC	Multiplying Digital-to-Analog Converter	. . .
MDC	Modification Detection Code	. . .
	re: Message encryption technology	
MDC	Multistage Depressed Cathode	. . .
MDE	Magnetic Decision Element	. . .
MDE	Modular Design Environment	. . .
MDF	Main Distribution Frame	. . .
MDH	Malate Dehydrogenase	. . .
	A compound important in biochemistry	
MDNS	Managed Data Network Service	. . .
MDNS	Meridian Data Networking System	Northern
		Telecom
MDOS	Multi-User Disk Operating System	. . .
MDPSK	Multilevel Differential Phase Shift Keying	. . .
MDPSK	Multiple Doppler Phase Shift Keying	JPL
MDS	Multiple Data Set	Racal-Vadic
MDT	Michigan Data Translator	. . .
MDT	Mobile Data Terminal	. . .
MDX	Multi-Indexing	. . .
ME	Metal Evaporated	. . .
	re: Magnetic recording tape, disk, etc.	
	construction technology;	
	sa *MP, Metal Particle*	
MEDIPHOR	Monitoring and Evaluation of Drug	. . .
	Interactions by Pharmacy-Oriented	
	Reporting	
MEG	Magneto Encephalography	Bloom, F., &
		Young, W.
MEM	Maximum Entropy Method	. . .
	re: Spectral analysis	
MEMDB	Medieval and Early Modern Data Bank	Rutgers Univ.

MEPIV	Multiple Exposure Particle-Image Velocimetry	. . .
MERA	Modular Electronics for Radar Application	TI
MESA	Modular Equipment Standards Architecture	. . .
	A movement to standardize interfunctionality of modular electronics devices	
MESCH	Multi-Environment Scheme	. . .
MESFET	Metal Enhancement Semiconductor Field Effect Transistor	. . .
Met	Methionine	. . .
	A compound important in biochemistry	
META	Megachannel Extraterrestrial Assay	. . .
METRAN	Managed European Transmission Network	METRAN
	A fiber-based network for *CEPT*, which see	
Metro I	Metro I	WU
	Western Union long-distance communications service	
MeV	Million Electron Volts	. . .
MF	Medium Frequency	. . .
	300 to 3000 kHz	
MFD	Master File Directory	DEC
MFDC	Main Facility Device Controller	AT&T
MFEL	Medical Free-Electron Laser	DoD
MFENET	Magnetic Fusion Energy Network	. . .
MFLOPS	Millions of Floating Point Operations Per Second	. . .
MFM	Modified Frequency Modulation	. . .
	Microcomputer hard disk-encoding technology	
MFS	Macintosh File Structure	Apple
MFS	Message Format Services	IBM
	For use under *IMS/VS, Information Management System/ Virtual System*	
MFS	Metropolitan Fiber System	. . .
MFT	Metallic Facility Terminal	AT&T
MFT	Multiprogramming with Fixed Number of Tasks	IBM
Mg	Magnesium	
	Atomic element number 12	
MG	Motor Generator	. . .
MGA	Monochrome Graphics Adapter	. . .
MGTS	Message Generator Traffic Simulator	Tekelec
MHDL	Microwave Hardware Description Language	. . .
MHS	Message Handling Service	. . .
MHS	Message Handling System	. . .

mHz	millihertz 10^{-3} Hertz	. . .
MHz	Megahertz 10^6 Hertz	. . .
MI	Memory Interconnect	DEC
MIB	Management Information Base	. . .
MIC	Microwave Integrated Circuit	. . .
MIC	Media Interface Connector	. . .
MICA	Multimedia Interactive Conferencing Application	Bell-Northern
MICE	Micro In-Circuit Emulator	. . .
MICR	Magnetic Ink Character Recognition	. . .
MICS	Marketing Information and Communication System	IMC
MIDI	Music Information Digital Interface	. . .
MIDS	Management Information Decision Support	. . .
MIDS	Multi-Function Information and Distribution System	US Air Force
MIF	Minimum Internetworking Functionality	ISO
MIG	Metal-In-Gap re: tape recorder head construction	. . .
MIIS	Meditech Interpreter Information System	. . .
MIL	Military [specification]	DoD
MIL-STD	Military Standard	DoD
MILNET	Military Network	DoD
MIM	Media Interface Management	. . .
MIM	Metal-Insulator-Metal re: Chip capacitor construction	. . .
MIMD	Multiple Instruction Multiple Data [processor] re: Computer architecture	. . .
MIMS	Mincom Information Management System	Mincom
MIND	Modular Interactive Network Designer	Contel
MINET	Movements Information Network A component of the Department of Defense *DDN, Defense Data Network*	DoD
MINOS	Modular In-Core Nonlinear Optimization System	Stanford University
MINX	Multimedia Information Network Exchange	Datapoint
MIOP	Master Input/Output Processor	Cray Research
MIP	Mixed-Integer Programming A process of *MPSX, Mathematical Programming System Extended*	IBM
MIP	Multimission Interactive Picture [planner]	NASA
MIPAS	Michelson Interferometer Passive Atmospheric Sounding	IMCR/NRCK
MIPL	Multi-mission Image Processing Lab	NASA

MIPS	Millions of Instructions Per Second	. . .
	sa *ITR, Internal Throughput Rate*	
MIR	Management Information Repository	DEC
MIS	Management Information System	. . .
MIS	Metal Insulator Semiconductor	. . .
MIS	Modular Interconnect System	. . .
MISC	Minimum Instruction Set Computer	. . .
	re: Computer architecture with minimum number of instructions; complexity somewhere between *RISC, Reduced Instruction Set Computer* and *CISC, Complex Instruction Set Computer*	
MISC	Minuscule Instruction Set Computer	TeraPlex
	Nine instruction set computer, as compared to approximately 30 for a RISC machine sa *CISC, Complex Instruction Set Computer* and *RISC, Reduced Instruction Set Computer*	
MISD	Multiple Instruction Single Data [processor]	. . .
	re: Computer architecture	
MISR	Multiple-Input Signature Register	IBM
MISTS	Management Information Systems Technical Information System	US Air Force
MIVPO	Modified Inside Vapor Phase Oxidation	. . .
	Technique for manufacturing optical fiber	
MIX	Modular Interface Extension	Intel
MKS	Meters-Kilograms-Seconds [system of units]	. . .
	Metric units of length, mass, and time	
ml	milliliter	. . .
	Metric unit of capacity; 10^{-3} liter (l)	
MLA	My Listen Address	IEEE
	re: IEEE Standard 488; sa *IEEE*	
MLB	Multi-Layer Board	. . .
	re: Multi-layered printed circuit boards	
MLC	Multi-Layer Ceramic [capacitor, substrate, etc.]	. . .
	A surface mount technology (SMT) electronic component	
MLC	Multi-Line Controller	. . .
MLC	Multi-Link Control [field]	CCITT
	re: *X.75* protocol, which see	
MLCP	Multi-Location Calling Plan	AT&T
MLG	Macro Layout Generator	IBM
MLIS	Molecular Laser Isotope Separation	. . .

MLOCR	Multi-Line Optical Character Reader	. . .
	Advanced optical character device for reading US mail	
MLP	Multi Link Procedure	CCITT
MLS	Maximum Length Sequence	NIST
	re: National Institute of Standards and Technology (NIST) time and frequency broadcasts in binary-coded decimal (BCD) format	
MLS	Microwave Landing System	US Air Force
MLS	Multi-LAN Switch	Alantec
	sa *LAN, Local Area Network*	
MLS	Multi-Level Secure	DoD
	Name applied to a center capable of handling information of differing sensitivities (security classifications)	
MLSS	Mechanized Letter Sorting System	Hong Kong
mlt	mass, length, time	. . .
	Fundamental dimensions of physical measurement	
mm	millimeter	. . .
	Metric unit of linear measure; 10^{-3} meter (m)	
mm	millimeter [band]	. . .
	Designation given to radar frequencies of millimeter wavelength: 40 to 300 GHz	
MM	Machine Model	. . .
	A set of specifications used as test parameters	
MMA	Microcomputers Managers Association	MMA
	Also, standards produced by that organization	
MMAC	Multi-Media Access Center	Cabletron Systems
MMAS	Material Management and Accounting System	DoD
MMD	Mobile-to-Mobile Direct	. . .
MME	Memory Mapping Enable	. . .
MMF	Multi-Mode Fiber	. . .
MMFS	Manufacturing Message Format Standard	. . .
MMI	Mobile-to-Mobile Indirect	. . .
MMIC	Monolithic Microwave Integrated Circuit	. . .
MMR	Multi-Mode Radar	. . .
MMS	Manufacturing Message Service (or Specification, or System)	. . .
MMS	Message Management System	. . .
MMS	Module Managemnent System	DEC

MMSE	Minimum Mean Square Error	. . .
	re: Mathematical statistics	
MMSS	Maritime Mobile Satellite Service	FCC
MMT	Multiple-Mirror Telescope	. . .
	An optical telescope consisting of many smaller main mirrors; the opposite of *monolithic*—having *one* main mirror	
MMU	Memory Management Unit	. . .
MMW	Millimeter Microwave	. . .
Mn	Manganese	. . .
	Atomic element number 25	
MN(S)	Multilink Sequence Number	CCITT
MNN	Main Network Node	. . .
MNOS	Metal-Nitride Oxide Semiconductor	. . .
	Metal oxide semiconductor (MOS) utilizing silicon nitride semiconductor material	
MNP	Microcom Networking Protocol	Microcom
MNT	Mercury-Manganese-Telluride	. . .
	Photosensitive material used in image detectors	
Mo	Molybdenum	. . .
	Atomic element number 42	
MO	Magneto-Optic(or Optical, or Optics)	. . .
MOC	Minimum Oxygen for Combustion	. . .
MOCA	Mixed Object Document Content Architecture	IBM
	Protocol that includes mixture of text, graphics, bar code, and voice	
MOCVD	Metalorganic Chemical Vapor Deposition	. . .
MOCVD	Metal Oxide Chemical Vapor Deposition	. . .
MOD	Magneto-Optic Disk	NeXT
MOD	Message Output Descriptor	IBM
MOD	Metallo-Organic Deposition	. . .
	re: Vacuum deposition of thin films	
Modem	Modulator Demodulator	. . .
MOI	Moment of Inertia	. . .
mol	mole	. . .
	Chemistry: quantity of a chemical substance, equal to its atomic weight in grams (g)	
MOL	Machine-Oriented Language	. . .
MOM	Method of Moments	. . .
	Mathematical analysis tool	
MOMBE	Metal-Organic Molecular Beam Epitaxy	Varian/H-P
MOP	Maintenance Operation Protocol	DEC
MOPA	Master Oscillator Power Amplifier	. . .
	re: Solid-state (SS) laser technology	

MOPS	Millions of Operations Per Second	. . .
MORIE	Metal-Organic Reactive Ion Etching	Cambridge/ Oxford
MOS	Macintosh Operating System	Apple
MOS	Metal Oxide Semiconductor	. . .
MOSFET	Metal Oxide Semiconductor Field-Effect Transistor	. . .
MOSLM	Magneto-Optic Spatial Light Modulator	. . .
MOTIF	Maui Optical Tracking and Identification Facility	NASA
MOTIS	Message-Oriented Text Interchange System	. . .
MOTR	Multiple Object Tracking Radar	. . .
MOV	Metal Oxide Varistor	. . .
MOVPE	Metal Organic Vapor Phase Epitaxial re: Electronic circuit wafer fabrication	. . .
MP	Metal Particle re: Magnetic recording tape, disk, etc. construction technology; sa *ME, Metal Evaporated*	. . .
MP	Multi-Processing(-or) re: Computers with multiple central processing units (CPUs)	. . .
MP/OS	Microprocessor Operating System	Data General
MPa	Megapascals Unit of pressure; 10^6 Pascals (Pa)	. . .
MPAX	Multi-Processor Architecture Extension	Chips & Technologies
MPB	Memory Processor Bus	. . .
MPC	Message Passing Coprocessor	Intel/VLSI Technology
MPC	Multi-Personal Computer	Motorola
MPCSU	Multiport Channel Service Unit re: fractional T1 multiplexers; sa *T1* and *FT1, Fractional T1*	Taylor, S.A.
MPD	Maximum Permissible Dose re: Human ingestion of toxins	. . .
MPE	Maximum Permissible Exposure	Laser Technology
MPEG	Motion Picture Experts Group re: Standard for real-time video (RTV) storage and retrieval	MPEG
MPG	Microwave Pulse Generator	. . .
MPG	Multi-Protocol Gateway	Hudson Laboratories
mph	miles per hour	. . .
MPI	Multibus Peripheral Interface	Intel

MPLPC	Multipulse Linear Predictive Coding	JPL (NASA)
	Algorithm used in speech encoding technology	
MPN	Manufacturer's Productivity Network	H-P
MPP	Massively Parallel Processing(-or)	. . .
MPP	Multi-Pinned Phase	NASA
	A technique for operating charge-coupled devices (CCDs) to eliminate dark current	
MPP	Multi-Protocol PAD	. . .
	sa *PAD, Packet Assembler/Disassembler*	
MPR	Mat Och Provradet	Sweden
	A Swedish standard (under consideration for use in the USA) describing acceptable tolerances for electromagnetic (EM) fields, X-rays, and static electricity	
MPR	Multi-Port Repeater	Micro Linear
MPR	Multi-Protocol Router	. . .
	re: Communications networks	
MPSK	Multiple Phase Shift Keying	. . .
MPSX	Mathematical Programming System Extended	. . .
MPT	Ministry of Posts and Telecommunications	Japan
MPW	Metallized Polypropylene Wrap	Illinois Capacitor
	Material used in capacitor manufacturing	
MPX	Multiplexer	. . .
	Alternate form; see *MUX*	
MPX	Multiprogramming Executive	. . .
MQW	Multi- (or Multiple) Quantum Well	. . .
	re: Laser technology	
mR	milliroentgen	. . .
	Unit of electromagnetic (EM) radiation; 10^{-3} Roentgen	
	sa *R, Roentgen*	
MR	Magnetic Resonance	. . .
MR	Modem Ready	. . .
MRAM	Mapping Random Access Memory	. . .
MRD	Manual Ringdown	. . .
MRDS	Mineral Resources Data System	US Dept. of Interior
MRI	Magnetic Resonance Imaging	. . .
mRNA	messenger Ribonucleic Acid	. . .
	sa *RNA, Ribonucleic Acid*	
MRNet	Minnesota Regional Network	MRNet
MRO	Multiple Region Operation	IBM
MRP	Manufacturing Resource Planning	General Motors

MRP	Materials Requirements Planning An automation procedure	. . .
MRPD	Medium Repetition-Rate Pulse Doppler	. . .
MRS	Magnetic Resonance Spectrometry	. . .
MRT	Minimum Resolveable Temperature re: Bolometry	. . .
MRU	Most Recently Used Algorithm used in cache memories; opposite of *LRU, Least Recently Used*	. . .
ms	millisecond 10^{-3} second; alternate form: *msec*	. . .
MS	Mass Spectroscope(-scopy)	. . .
MS	Message Store	CCITT
MS	Multi-Spectral re: Satellite image data	. . .
MS-DOS	MicroSoft Disk Operating System	Microsoft
MS/s	Mega Samples per Second 10^6 samples per second re: Digital oscilloscope input, analog-to- digital conversion (ADC), and other data acquisition technology	. . .
MSAG	Multifunction Self-Aligned Gate re: Gallium arsenide chip fabrication technology	. . .
MSAR	Mass Storage Analysis and Relocation	Unisys
MSAT-X	Mobile Satellite Experiment	NASA
MSAU	Multi-Station Access Unit	. . .
MSB	Most Significant Bit	. . .
MSBLS	Microwave Scanning Beam Landing System	. . .
MSBS	Magnetic Balance and Suspension System	Langley Research Ctr.
MSC	Multiple System Coupling	IBM
MSCC	Multiple System Communication Control	Amdahl
MSCP	Mass Storage Control Protocol	DEC
MSD	Mass Storage Device	. . .
MSD	Most Significant Digit	. . .
MSDC	Multi-Stage Depressed Collector High efficiency klystron for television transmission	NASA
MSDS	Material Safety Data Sheet re: Toxic chemical or other hazard	. . .
MSDS	Mixed-Signal Design Solution	Gould Electronics
MSE	Mobile Subscriber Equipment	US Army
msec	millisecond 10^{-3} second; alternate form; sa *ms*	. . .

MSH	Melanocyte-Stimulating Hormone A compound important in biochemistry	. . .
MSI	Medium Scale Integration IC technology developed in 1960s; Contain 10^3 to 10^4 gates	. . .
MSIC	Mixed-Signal Integrated Circuit re: Mixed analog and digital signals on a single integrated circuit (IC) chip	Silicon Systems
MSIS	Marine Safety Information System	US Coast Guard
MSITTL	Medium Scale Integration Transistor- Transistor Logic	. . .
MSK	Multi-Shift Keying	. . .
MSNF	Multiple Systems Networking Facility	IBM
MSO	Main Storage Occupancy A measure of memory usage in virtual memory systems	IBM
MSO	Multivendor Support Operation	H-P
MSPS	Megasamples per Second 10^6 samples per second Alternate form; see *MS/s*	
MSRE	Molten Salt [converter] Reactor Equipment	. . .
MSS	Mass Storage System (or Subsystem)	IBM
MSS	Mobile Satellite Service	FCC
MSS	Multi-Spectral Scanner re: Scanning of multispectral satellite image data	. . .
MSSR	Monopulse Secondary Surveillance Radar	Westinghouse
MST	Mountain Standard Time	. . .
MST	Multi-Sensor Track re: Oceanography	. . .
MSTS	Maui Satellite Tracking Site	NASA
MT	Message Transfer	CCITT
MTA	Message Transfer Agent	. . .
MTA	Multi-Terminal Access	Comm-Pro
MTACP	Magnetic Tape Ancillary Control Process	DEC
MTAE	Message Transfer Agent Entity	. . .
MTBCF	Mean Time Between Critical Failures	. . .
MTBF	Mean Time Between Failures	. . .
MTBSF	Mean Time Between System Failure	. . .
MTC	Manufacturing Technology Center	NIST
MTC	Midwestern Telecommunications Association	MTC
MTCXO	Mathematically Temperature-Compensated Crystal Oscillator	Fluke
MTDA	Mean Time for Data Availability	. . .

MTF	Modulation Transfer Function	. . .
	re: Optical design	
MTF	Multitasking Facility	IBM
MTI	Moving Target Indicator	. . .
	re: Radar	
MTIE	Maximum Time Interval Error	ANSI
MTO	Master Terminal Operator	. . .
MTS	Message Telephone Service	. . .
MTS	Message Transfer System	. . .
MTS	Multichannel Television Stereo	Zenith
MTSO	Mobile Telephone Switching Office	. . .
	re: cellular radio	
MTT	Magnetic Tape Transport	. . .
MTTA	Multi Tenant Telecommunications Association	MTTA
MTTD	Mean Time to Diagnose	. . .
MTTF	Mean Time to Failure	. . .
	sa *MTBCF, Mean Time Between Critical Failures*; *MTBF, Mean Time Between Failures*; and *MTBSF, Mean Time Between System Failures*	
MTTR	Mean Time To Repair	. . .
	To be distinguished from *MTBF, Mean Time Between Failures*, which see	
MTVS	Multilayer Transient Voltage Suppressor	Harris Semi-conductor
MUF	Maximum Usable Frequency	. . .
MUMPS	Massacheussetts [General Hospital] Utility Multi-Programming System	Mass. Gen. Hosp.
MUPID	Multipurpose Universally Programmable Intelligent Decoder European Videotex protocol	. . .
mux	multiplexer Alternate form; see *MUX*	. . .
MUX	Multiplexer Also used as a word, in lower-case: *mux*	. . .
MV	Multivibrator An electronic switching circuit, also called a *flip-flop, FF*	. . .
MV(R)	Multilink Variable—Received Received multilink state variable in X.75 protocol	CCITT
MV(S)	Multilink Variable—Send-state	CCITT
MV(T)	Multilink Variable—Transmitted Transmitted multilink frame acknowledged variable in X.75 protocol	CCITT

MVL	Metal Vapor Laser	. . .
MVM	Multiple Virtual Modem	Paradyne
MVS	Multiple Virtual Storage	IBM
MVS	Multiple Virtual Systems	IBM
MVS/SP	Multiple Virtual Storage/System Product	IBM
MVS/XA	Multiple Virtual Systems/Extended Architecture	IBM
MVT	Multiprogramming with Variable Number of Tasks	IBM
MVTL	Modified Variable Threshold Logic	. . .
mW	Milliwatt 10^{-3} watt	. . .
MW	Megawatt 10^6 watts	. . .
MW	Microwave Electromagnetic wave of wavelength 0.003 to 3 meters (m)	. . .
MW	Molecular Weight	. . .
MW	Multilink Window Multilink window size in X.75 protocol	CCITT
MX	Mail Exchange	. . .
MXIbus	Multisystem Extension Bus	National Instruments
	Open architecture for interconnection of VXIbus and personal computers (PCs); sa *VXI*	
MZF	Multi-Zone Furnace	Soterem
MZIM	Mach-Zehnder Interferometeric Modulator A laser beam modulator	. . .
MZR	Multi-Zone Recording re: Disk data recording technology	. . .
MZT	Mercury-Zinc-Telluride Photosensitive material used in image detectors	. . .
M24	Multiplexer-24 Frame encoding for T1 data circuits; sa *T1*	AT&T
M44	Multiplexer-44 44 voice channels on a T1 transmission facility; sa *T1*	. . .

N

n	nano Prefix for 10^{-9}	. . .

n	negative (or *n*-channel) [doping]	. . .
	Solid-state (SS) semiconductor using electron flow as the primary conduction medium	
N	Newton	. . .
	Unit of force	
	Named in honor of English mathematician and physicist Sir Isaac Newton (1642–1727)	
N	Nitrogen	. . .
	Atomic element number 7	
N-Chip	N-Chip	Fairchild Space
	Three-dimensional very large scale integration (VLSI) mass memory technology	
n-MOS	negative (or n-channel) Metal Oxide Semiconductor	. . .
	Semiconductor material utilizing electron conduction	
	sa *n, negative* and *NMOS, Negative (or n-channel) Metal Oxide Semiconductor*	
n-p-n	negative-positive-negative	. . .
	Alternate form for *npn*, which see	
N(R)	Number (Receive)	CCITT
	Sequence number in X.25 protocol control field	
	sa *X.25*	
N(S)	Number (Send)	CCITT
	Sequence number in X.25 protocol control field	
	sa *X.25*	
Na	Natrium	. . .
	Symbol for *sodium*, atomic element number 11	
NA	Not Accessible	CCITT
	X.25 protocol packet assembly/disassembly (PAD) service signal;	
	sa *X.25*	
NA	Numerical Aperture	. . .
	Optical term relating to light cone angle; stated as a functionality in lenses, fibers, and other optical devices	
NAB	National Association of Broadcasters	NAB
	Standards organization for setting general broadcasting standards, tape recording standards, etc.	
NABTS	North American Broadcast Teletext Specification	. . .
	Proposed Teletext standard	

NAD⁺	Nicotinamide Adenine Dinucleotide A compound important in biochemistry	. . .
NADH	Nicotinamide Adenine Dinucleotide [reduced] A compound important in biochemistry	. . .
NADP⁺	Nicotinamide Adenine Dinucleotide Phosphate A compound important in biochemistry	. . .
NADPH	Nicotinamide Adenine Dinucleotide Phosphate [reduced] A compound important in biochemistry	. . .
NAEB	North American EDIFACT Board sa *EDIFACT, Electronic Data Interchange for Administration, Commerce and Transport*	NAEB
NAG	Numerical Algorithms Group (programs)	NAG
NAIS	National Association for Information Systems	NAIS
NAK	Negative Acknowledgement Transmission control 8 (TC_8) under CCITT Recommendation V.3; sa *CCITT, V.3* and *TC_n*	CCITT
NAL	National Agricultural Library	US
NAM	Numeric Assignment Module re: cellular radio	. . .
NAMPS	Narrowband Advanced Mobile Phone Service A digitally enhanced system combining analog voice with digital signalling	Motorola
NAN	N-Acetylneuraminic [acid] A compound important in biochemistry; also designated by *NANA*	. . .
NANA	N-Acetylneuraminic Acid A compound important in biochemistry; also designated by *NAN*	. . .
NAND	Negative (or NOT) AND [circuit or logic gate] Electronic circuit which exhibits the Boolean NAND logic function (inverse of the AND logic function); sa *AND*	. . .
NANP	North American Numbering Plan ISDN subscriber line numbering scheme sa *ISDN, Integrated Services Digital Network*	AT&T/CCITT
NANPA	North America Numbering Plan Administration The entity which assigns and manages telephone area codes, SS7 point codes, and other telephone standards; sa *SS7*	NANPA

NAP	Network [management] Access Program	IBM
NAP	Network Applications Platform	Unisys
NAPLPS	North American Presentation Level Protocol Syntax	US/Canada
NARA	National Archives and Records Administration	NARA
NARDAC	Navy Regional Data Automation Center	US Navy
NARTE	National Association of Radio and Telecommunications Engineers	NARTE
NARUC	National Association of Regulatory Utilities Commissioners	NARUC
NAS	National Airspace System	FAA
NAS	Network Application Support	DEC
NASA	National Aeronautics and Space Administration	NASA
Nascom	NASA Communications Network sa *NASA*	NASA
NASP	National Aero-Space Plane	NASA
NASTD	National Association of State Telecommunications Directors	NASTD
NASTRAN	NASA Structural Analysis System sa *NASA*	NASA
NATA	North American Telecommunications Association	NATA
NATC	[US] Naval Air Test Center	US Navy
NAU	Network Addressable Unit re: IBM's *Systems Network Architecture*, *SNA*	IBM
NAVMAT	Navy Materials	US Navy
Nb	Niobium Atomic element number 41 Also known as *Columbium*	. . .
NBP	Netbios Protocol A high-speed data communications transport system	3Com
NBS	National Bureau of Standards Now NIST—National Institute of Standards and Technology	NBS
NBVC	Narrow Band Video Conferenncing	. . .
NC	National Coarse [thread] Machine screw thread; sa *NF, National Fine [thread]*	. . .
NC	Network Congestion X.25 protocol packet assembly/disassembly (PAD) service signal; sa *X.25*	CCITT

NC	Noise Cancelling	. . .
NC	Normally Closed re: Switch contacts, relays, and solid-state (SS) circuit equivalents	. . .
NCAR	National Center for Atmospheric Research	NCAR
NCB	Network Connect Block	. . .
NCBN	National Carriers Buyers Network	NCBN
NCC	National Computer Conference	NCC
NCC	Network Communications Controller	Coastcom
NCC	Network Control Center	. . .
NCC	Network Control Console	. . .
NCCCD	National Center for Computer Crime Data	NIST
NCCF	Network Communications Control Facility	IBM
NCCS	Navy Command and Control System	US Navy
NCF	Network Configuration Facility	IBM
NCF	Neutral Code Format	. . .
NCGA	National Computer Graphics Association	NCGA
NCHSR	National Center for Health Services Research	. . .
NCIC	National Crime Information Center	FBI
NCL	Network Control Language	Systems Center
NCM	Network Configuration Management	DEC
NCMD	Noncritical-Matching Doubler re: Laser frequency doubling	. . .
NCMS	Network Control and Management System	NEC
NCO	Numerically Controlled Oscillator	. . .
NCP	NetWare Core Protocol	Novell
NCP	Network Control Point	AT&T
NCP	Network Control Program Pertains to software for the IBM 3705 Communications Controller	IBM
NCPM	Non-Critical Phase Matching re: Laser beam frequency-doubling crystals	. . .
NCS	National Communications System	NCS
NCS	Network Communication (or Control) Server	. . .
NCS	Network Computing Services	. . .
NCS	Network Computing System	OSF
NCS	Network Coordination Station	US Navy
NCSA	National Center for Supercomputing Applications	NCSA
NCSA	National Computer Security Association	NCSA
NCSAnet	National Center for Supercomputing Applications Network	NCSA
NCSC	National Computer Security Center	DoD
NCSL	National Computer Systems Laboratory	NCSL
NCSL	National Council of Standards Laboratories	NCSL

NCTC	Naval Computer and Telecommunications Command	US Navy
NCTE	Network Channel Terminating Equipment	AT&T
NCU	Node Coupling Unit	. . .
NCUG	National Centrex Users Group	NCUG
Nd	Neodymium Atomic element number 60	. . .
Nd:YAG	Neodymium Yttrium-Aluminum-Garnet A crystalline material used in lasers	. . .
NDAC	No Data Accepted re: IEEE Standard 488; sa *IEEE*	IEEE
NDE	Non-Destructive Evaluation	. . .
NDF	NCP/EP Definition Facility sa *NCP, Network Control Program* and *EP, Emulation Program*	IBM
NDIS	Network Device Interface Specification	IBM
NDIS	Network Driver Interface Standard	Microsoft
NDM	Network Data Mover	Systems Center
NDOS	Nested Distributed Operating System	Lambda
NDPD	National Data Processing Division	EPA
NDRO	Non-Destructive Read-Out	. . .
NDT	Non-Destructive Test(-ing)	. . .
NDT	Non-Linear Decoupling Theory Mathematical theory	. . .
Ne	Neon Atomic element number 10	. . .
NE	Network Equipment	CCITT
NEARnet	New England Academic and Research Network	NEARnet
NEAT	New Enhanced Advanced Technology	Chips & Technologies
NEC	National Electrical Code	. . .
NECA	National Exchange Carriers Association	FCC
NEFA	Nonesterified Fatty Acid A compound important in biochemistry	. . .
NEI	Noise Equivalent Irradiance	. . .
NELC	Naval Electronics Laboratory Center	NELC
NELINET	New England Library Information Network	. . .
NEMA	National Electrical Manufacturers Association A standards-defining organization	NEMA
NEMOS	Network Management Operational Support [system]	AT&T
NEMP	Nuclear Electromagnetic Pulse	. . .
NEP	Noise Equivalent Power re: Fiber-optic communications	. . .

NERSC	National Energy Research Supercomputer Center	LLNL
NESC	National Energy Software Center Defunct; responsibilities assumed by *ESTSC*, which see	DoE
NEST	Network Simulation Testbed	Columbia Univ.
NETA	New England Telecommunications Association	NETA
NETBIOS	Network Basic Input/Output System IBM's token ring local area network (LAN) input/output system (I/O or IOS)	IBM
NETID	Network Identification	. . .
NETNORTH	Network of the North Canadian network	. . .
NETS	Nationwide Emergency Telecommunications System	NCS
NEU	Network Extension Unit	. . .
neuMOS	neuron Metal Oxide Semiconductor A device which mimics a biological neuron	Ohmi/Shibata
NEWS	Network Extensible Window System	Sun Microsystems
NEXRAD	Next [generation] Radar	US Air Force
NEXT	Near-End Cross-Talk	. . .
NF	National Fine [thread] Machine screw thread; sa *NC, National Coarse [thread]*	. . .
NF	Noise Figure re: performance of electronic components or circuits	. . .
NFB	Negative Feedback	. . .
NFOV	Narrow Field of View re: Optical system coverage	. . .
*n*fs	*n*(times oversampled digital) filter sampling re: Digital audio recording (DAR) technology	. . .
NFS	Network File System (or Server)	Sun Microsystems
NFT	Network File Transfer	. . .
NGA	Next Generation Architecture	VME Int'l. Trade Assoc.
NGMF	NetView Graphic Monitor Facility	IBM
NGST	Next Generation Space Telescope	NASA
Ni	Nickel Atomic element number 28	. . .
NI	Network Interconnect	DEC

NIC	Near-Instantaneous Companding (Nearly) real-time digitization of analog signal	. . .
NIC	Network Information Center	. . .
NIC	Network Interface Card	Datability Software
NIC	Numerically Intensive Computing	. . .
NICE	Network Information and Control Exchange	DEC
NICENET	Naval [Research Laboratory] Integrated Communications Environment Network	US Navy
NICS	Network Image Computing System	VITec
NIEHS	National Institutes of Environmental Health Studies	. . .
NIF	Network Interface	. . .
NIM	Nuclear Instrument Module	. . .
NIOSH	National Institute of Occupational Safety and Health	CDC
NIP	Negative Intrinsic Positive [diode]	. . .
NIP	Nucleus Initialization Program	IBM
NIR	Near Infrared	. . .
NIS	Network Information Service	. . .
NISO	National Information Standards Organization	NISO
NIST	National Institute of Standards and Technology Formerly, *National Bureau of Standards, NBS*	US Dept. of Commerce
NIU	Network Interface Unit	. . .
NJE	Network Job Entry	IBM
NJEF	Network Job Entry Facility	CDC
NLC	Next Linear Collider	Stanford Univ.
NLDM	Network Logical Data Manager Program product in IBM's *Network Communications Control Facility, NCCF*	IBM
NLH/E	Natural Language Help/EDGE	Univ. of Karlsruhe
NLM	National Library of Medicine	. . .
NLM	NetWare Loadable Module	Novell
NLM	Network Level Module	US Air Force (SAC)
NLOP	Non-Linear Optical Polymer	NWC
NLQ	Non-Letter Quality re: printer typeface with low resolution	. . .
NLS	National Language Support	IBM
NLS	Network Library System	Univ. of Wisconsin
NLS	Network License System	DEC

nm	nanometer Metric unit of linear measure; 10^{-9} meter (m)	. . .
NM	Network Management	. . .
NMC	Network Monitoring (or Management) Center	. . .
NMCC	Network Management Control Center	GTE
NMCC	Non-digital Management Control Center	DEC
NMEF	Network Management Extended Facility	Mitek
NMI	Non-Maskable Interrupt re: Microprocessor control signal	. . .
NMM	Network Management Module	SynOptics
NMML	National Marine Mammal Laboratory	NOAA
NMN$^+$	Nicotinimide Mononucleotide A compound important in biochemistry	. . .
NMNH	Nicotinimide Mononucleotide [reduced] A compound important in biochemistry	. . .
NMOS	Negative (or n-Channel) Metal Oxide Semiconductor Alternate form; see *n-MOS*	. . .
NMP	N-Methylpyrrolidone A solvent used in the production of microchips, printed circuit boards, and other electronic devices	. . .
NMR	Nuclear Magnetic Resonance	. . .
NMS	NetWare Management System	Novell
NMS	Network Management Server	H-P
NMS	Network Management Software	DEC
NMS	Network Management System	Northern Telecom
NMVT	Network Management Vector Transport	IBM
NN	Network Node	. . .
*n*NF	*n*th Normal Form re: Relational databases (RDBs); where $n=1$ implies "First Normal Form," etc.	. . .
NNF	National Nanofabrication Facility	Cornell Univ.
NNI	Network Node Interface	. . .
NNN	Nearest Neighbor Notification re: Fiber-distributed data interface (FDDI) standard	. . .
NNSC	NSF Network Service Center sa *NSF, National Science Foundation*	NNSC
NNT	National Networking Testbed	DoD
No	Nobelium Atomic element number 102 Named in honor of Alfred Bernhard Nobel (1833–1896), discoverer of dynamite, and benefactor of the highly coveted Nobel Prize	. . .

NO	Normally Open	. . .
	re: Switch contacts, relays, and solid-state (SS) circuit equivalents	
NO	Not Obtainable	CCITT
	X.25 protocol packet assembly/disassembly (PAD) service signal	
	sa *X.25*	
NOAA	National Oceanic and Atmospheric Administration	NOAA
NOAO	National Optical Astronomy Observatory(-ies)	NOAO
NOC	Navy Oceanographic Command	US Navy
NOP	No Operation	. . .
NOR	Negative (or NOT) OR [circuit or logic gate)	. . .
	Electronic circuit which exhibits the Boolean NOR logic function (inverse of the OR function)	
NORC	Naval Ordinance Research Computer	IBM
	An early (1956) "large scale" computer	
NOS	Network Operating System	CDC
NOS/BE	Network Operating System/Basic Environment	CDC
NOS/VE	Network Operating System/Virtual Environment	CDC
NOSC	Naval Ocean Systems Center	NOSC
NOT	NOT [circuit or logic gate)	. . .
	Electronic circuit which exhibits the Boolean NOT logic function; equivalent to *INVERT*, which see	
NOx	Nitrogen Oxide	NASA
Np	Neptunium	. . .
	Atomic element number 93	
NP	Number Plan	CCITT
NPC	North Pacific Cable	. . .
	US-to-Japan fiber-optic cable (FOC)	
NPDA	Network Problem Determination Application	IBM
NPDU	Network Protocol Data Unit	. . .
NPL	National Physical Laboratory	NPT, UK
NPM	Network Performance Monitor	IBM
npn	negative-positive-negative	. . .
	re: Transistor fabrication where the emitter, base, and collector are intrinsic negative, positive, and negative semiconductor material, respectively Alternate: *n-p-n*	
nPnT	*n*-Pole *n*-Throw [switch]	. . .
	Generic form for *n* circuits with *n* positions where the number of circuits is not necessarily equal to the number of positions	
NPR	National Public Radio	NPR

NPSI	NCP Packet Switching Interface	IBM
	sa *NCP, Network Control Program*	
NPT	National Pipe Taper	. . .
	Standard pipe thread (US)	
NQS	Network Queueing System	. . .
NRAO	National Radio Astronomy Observatory	. . .
NRC	National Replacement Character	ASCII
	Seven-bit ASCII code allowing interchange	
	of national characters;	
	sa *ASCII*	
NRC	Noise Reduction Coefficient	. . .
NRC	Nuclear Regulatory Commision	NRC
NRE	Non-Recoverable Engineering	. . .
NREN	National Research and Education Network	US Congress
NRFD	Not Ready For Data	IEEE
	re: IEEE Standard 488;	
	sa *IEEE*	
NRI	National Research Institute	NRI
NRL	Naval Research Laboratory	US Navy
NRM	Normal Response Mode	OSI
NRMS	Network Reconfiguration and Monitoring	Metro. Fiber
	Service	Sys.
NRN	National Research Network	NRN
	Predecessor to *NREN*, which see	
nRNA	nuclear Ribonucleic Acid	. . .
NRP	Network Resource Planning	DCA
NRRFSS	National Research Facility for Submicron	. . .
	Structures	
NRS	Network Registration Service	OSI
	A database (DB) containing information on	
	interoperability tests	
NRTL	Nationally Recognized Testing Laboratory	OSHA
NRZ	Non-Return to Zero	. . .
	A method of encoding magnetic tape	
	whereby the flux changes in one direction	
	only for a corresponding binary "one"	
	sa *NRZI, Non-Return to Zero Inverted*	
NRZI	Non-Return to Zero Inverted	. . .
	A method of encoding magnetic pulses on	
	tape	
	sa *NRZ, Non-Return to Zero*	
ns	nanosecond	. . .
	10^{-9} second; alternate form: *nsec*	
NS	Network Support	IBM
NSA	National Security Agency	DARPA
NSAP	Network Service Access Point	. . .

NSC	National Supercomputer Center	NSC
NSC	Network Steering Committee	NASA
NSCAT	NASA Scatterometer	NASA
	sa *NASA*	
NSD	National Service Division	IBM
nsec	nanosecond	. . .
	10^{-9} second; alternate form: *ns*	
NSF	National Science Foundation	NSF
NSFNET	National Science Foundation Network	NSF
NSI	NASA Science Internet	NASA
	sa *NASA*	
NSLS	National Synchrotron Light Source	BNL
	A "third generation" synchrotron	
NSM	Network Security Monitor	Network-1
NSN	NASA Science Network	NASA
	sa *NASA*	
NSP	Network Services Protocol	. . .
NSSDC	National Space Science Data Center	NASA
NSTL	National Software Testing Laboratories	NSTL
NSW	National Software Works	. . .
NT	Network Termination	. . .
	re: AT&T's *Integrated Services Digital Network, ISDN*	
NT-1	Network Terminator [type] One	. . .
NTC	Negative Temperature Coefficient	. . .
NTDS	Naval Tactical Data Systems	US Navy
NTE	Network Terminating Equipment	. . .
NTF	National Transonic Facility	Langley Research Ctr.
	Transonic (greater than speed of sound) wind tunnel	
NTIA	National Telecommunications and Information Administration	NTIA
NTIS	National Technical Information Service	US Dept. of Commerce
NTM	Networking T1 Multiplexer	. . .
	sa *T1*	
NTN	National Telecommunications Network	NTN
NTN	Neutralized Twisted Nematic [LCD]	. . .
	A solid-state (SS) liquid crystal display (LCD) technology exhibiting crisp contrast and 16 shades of grey scale	
NTO	Network Terminal Option	IBM
NTP	National Toxicology Program	NTP
	An organization concerned with toxic materials safety standards	

NTS	Network Tracking System	The Systems Center
NTS	Non Traffic Sensitive re: Communications services, etc., where cost is independent of traffic	. . .
NTSC	National Television Standards Committee Also, the video transmission standard	. . .
NTSYS	Numerical Taxonomy System	Rohlf, Kishpaugh & Kirk
NTT	New Technology Telescope	. . .
NTT	Nippon Telegraph and Telephone	NTT
NTWA	Near Traveling Wave Amplifier Optical amplifier	. . .
NUA	Network Users Association	. . .
NuBus	New Bus New bus architecture of the NeXT computer	NeXT
NUI	Network User Identification re: *X.25* protocol, which see	CCITT
NUL	Null A component of the binary code in CCITT Recommendation V.3 sa *CCITT* and *V.3*	CCITT
NUTN	National University Teleconference Network	. . .
NUV	Near Ultraviolet	. . .
NVIS	Night Vision Imaging System	. . .
NVM	Non-Volatile Memory Memory chip that will retain data after power-down	. . .
NVRAM	Non-Volatile Random Access Memory	. . .
NVT	Network Validation Testing	AT&T
NVT	Network Virtual Terminal	. . .
NWC	New Wave Computing	H-P
NWG	Network Working Group	. . .
NWNet	NorthWest Network	NSF
NWS	National Weather Service	NOAA
N_0	—Avogadro's Number (symbol) 6.02252×10^{23} The number of molecules in one mole (or gram-molecular weight) of a substance Named in honor of Italian physicist Count Amedeo Avogadro (1776–1856)	. . .

O

O	Oxygen	. . .
	Atomic element number 8	
O&M	Operation and Maintenance	DARPA
OA	Office Automation	. . .
OA	Operational Amplifier	. . .
OA	Outgoing Access	CCITT
	Refers to public data network call routing	
OAA	Oxaloacetic Acid	. . .
	A compound important in biochemistry	
OACS	Office Automation Communications Services	. . .
OACS	Open Architechture CAD System	Motorola
	sa *CAD, Computer-Aided Design*	
OAI	Open Application Interface	NEC
OAM	Operations, Administration and Maintenance	. . .
	re: CCITT Recom. 1.610 on braodband	
	applications of *ISDN*, which see	
OASIS	Office Automation Systems Informational	WVNET
	Symposium	
OATS	Office Automation Technology Services	AT&T
OBB	On-Board Buffer	. . .
	re: Integrated circuit (IC) technology	
OBD	On-Board Diagnostics	. . .
	re: Diagnostic circuit included on a chip	
OBIOS	Open Basic Input/Output System	. . .
OBS	Object-Based Systems	Apple/IBM
OC	Open Connect	. . .
OC	Optical Carrier	. . .
	sa *OC-n*)	
OC-*n*	Optical Carrier [level] *n*	. . .
	where $n=1$ implies 51.84 Mbps; $n=3$	
	implies 3 times OC-1, or 155.5 Mbps, etc.,	
	for $n=9, 12, 18, 24, 36$; $n=48$ implies 48	
	times OC-1, or 2.4 Gbps.	
OCA	Open Communication Architecture	. . .
OCA	Operational Conveyor Amplifier	Derek Bowers
OCA	Optical Connector Adapter	Philips Telecom
OCC	Other Common Carrier	. . .
OCCA	Open Cooperative Computing Architechture	NCR
OCCF	Operator Communications Control Facility	IBM
OCDD	On-line Call Detail Delivery	AT&T
OCE	Open Collaborative Environment	Apple
OCE	Open Communications Environment	CCITT

OCEANIC	Ocean Network Information Center	Univ. of Delaware
OCL	Operation Control Language	. . .
OCLC	On-line Computer Library Center Formerly Ohio College Library Center	OCLC
OCP	Over-Current Protection	. . .
OCR	Optical Character Recognition (or Reader) sa *MLOCR, Multi-Line Optical Character Recognition*	. . .
OCS	On-Card Sequencer	. . .
OCS	Operator Control Station	Burroughs
OCS	Open Connect Server	Mitek
OCTS	Open Cooperative Test System	NCR
OCU	Office Channel Unit	. . .
OCU	Optical Conversion Unit	Ten X Technology
OCXO	Optically Controlled Crystal Oscillator	. . .
OC12	Optical Carrier 12	. . .
OD	Optical Density	. . .
ODA	Office Document Architecture	. . .
ODAPS	Oceanic Display and Planning System	FAA
ODBC	Open Database Connectivity	Microsoft
ODBMS	Object-Oriented Database Management System	. . .
ODFS	Optical Disk Filing System	Hitachi
ODI	Open Datalink Interface	Novell/Apple
ODI	Open Driver Interface re: Local area network (LAN) interfacing	Novell
ODIF	Office Document Interchange Format	. . .
ODIS	Optical Digital Image System	US Army
ODISS	Optical Digital Image Storage System	Unisys
ODLI	Open Data Link Interface	Novell
ODP	Open Distributed Processing Simultaneous multiprocessor, multidatabase communications	ISO
ODP	Ozone Depletion Potential	. . .
ODT	Open Desktop A UNIX implementation; sa *UNIX*	SCO
ODU	Outdoor Unit re: Satellite communications antenna-mounted amplifier	. . .
OE	Opto-Electronic	. . .
OEF	Original Element Field re: IBM's *Systems Network Architecture, SNA*	IBM

OEIC	Optoelectronic Integrated Circuit	. . .
OEM	Original Equipment Manufacturer	. . .
OFA	Optical Fiber Adapter	Philips Telecom
OFA	Optical Fiber Amplifier	. . .
OFC	Optical Fiber Communication	. . .
OFC	Oscillation Frequency Control	H-P
OFG	Overlay Frame Grabber	Imaging Technology
OFNR	Optical Fiber Non-conductive Riser	. . .
OFS	Optical File System	QStar
OFU	Object File Utility	. . .
OGL	Overlay Generation Language	IBM
OH	Off Hook	. . .
OHE	One Hot Encoding re: Architecture of state machines, commonly used in programmable logic devices (PLDs)	. . .
OHT	On-Hook Transmission re: Data transmission through open telephone circuits	. . .
OI	Opto- (or Optical) Isolator	. . .
OIF	Office Interconnect Facility	IBM
OISC	Optimum Instruction Set Computer see *MISC, Minimum Instruction Set Computer*	. . .
OIT	Operations Integration Testing	AT&T
OITDA	Optoelectronic Industry Technology Development Association	OITDA
OLC	On-Line Consultant	Computer Associates
OLCF	On-Line Customization Facility	Computer Associates
OLCSS	On-Line Customer Support System	Software AG
OLE	Object Linking and Embedding	. . .
OLQ	Outstanding Load Queue	IBM
OLTP	On-Line Transaction Processing	. . .
OMA	Object Management Architecture	OMG
OMA	Open Management Architecture	3Com
OMA	Optical Multichannel Analyzer	. . .
OMC	Optical Memory Card	. . .
OMG	Object Management Group	OMG Consortium
OMI	Open Messaging Interface	Lotus/IBM/ Apple
OMI	Open MUMPS Interconnect sa *MUMPS, Massachusetts [General Hospital] Utility Multi-Programming System*	Mass Gen Hosp

OMS	Operating Management System	. . .
OMVPE	Organo-Metallic Vapor-Phase Epitaxy	. . .
	re: laser and solid-state (SS) electronic	
	device technology	
ONA	Open Network Architecture	. . .
ONC	Open Network Computing	Sun
		Microsystems
ONC	Open Network Concentrator	. . .
OnCE	On-Chip Emulator [block]	. . .
ONEA	Office Network Exchange Architecture	Honeywell
ONI	Optical Network Interface	. . .
ONM	Open Network Management	. . .
ONN	Off-Network Node	. . .
ONP	Open Network Provision	. . .
ONR	Office of Naval Research	US Navy
ONS	Open Networking System	NCR
ONX	Open Network Exchange	. . .
OO	Object Orientation	. . .
	re: State-of-the-art computer operating	
	system (OS) design	
OOA	Object-Oriented Analysis	. . .
OOD	Object-Oriented Design	. . .
OODB	Object-Oriented Data Base	. . .
OODLE	Object-Oriented Design Language	. . .
OOF	Out Of Frame	. . .
	Communications transmission fault	
OOP	Object-Oriented Programming	. . .
OOPL	Object-Oriented Programming Language	. . .
OOPS	Object-Oriented Programming Style	IBM
OOPS	Object-Oriented Programming System	DEC
OOSD	Object-Oriented Structured Design	. . .
OOT	Out Of Tolerance	. . .
Op Amp	Operational Amplifier	. . .
	Alternate form; see *OA*	
OPA	Optical Parametric Amplifier	. . .
OPM	Optical Power Meter	. . .
OPO	Optical Parametric Oscillator	. . .
OPR	Optical Pattern Recognition	. . .
	sa *OCR, Optical Character Recognition*	
OPSSL	Optically Pumped Solid-State Laser	. . .
OQPSK	Offset Quaternary Phase Shift Keying	. . .
OR	OR [circuit or logic gate]	. . .
	Electronic circuit which exhibits the Boolean	
	OR logic function	
ORB	Object Request Broker	OMG
	See *CORBA, Common Object Request*	
	Broker Architecture	

ORD	Optical Rotatory Dispersion	. . .
ORIA	Office of Regulatory and Information Affairs	US Government
ORKID	Open Real-time Kernel Interface Definition	. . .
ORNL	Oak Ridge National Laboratory	ORNL
OROM	Optical Read Only Memory	. . .
ORT	Ongoing Reliability Test	DEC
ORT	Operational Readiness Testing	AT&T
ORU	Orbital Replacement Unit	. . .
	re: Orbiting platform maintenance	
ORVILLE	Orville	Stanford Univ.
	Text editor; converse of *WYLBUR*, which see	
Os	Osmium	. . .
	Atomic element number 76	
OS	Operating System	IBM
OS/2	Operating System 2	IBM
OSA	Open Systems Architecture	OSI
OSA	Optical Spectrum Analyzer	. . .
OSA	Optical Systems Architecture	. . .
OSAC	Optical Surface Analysis Code	. . .
	A measure of performance of an optical system	
OSAF	Origin Subarea Field	IBM
	re: IBM's *Systems Network Architecture, SNA*	
OSAM	Online System Activity Monitor	Unisys
OSC	Office of Science and Technology	. . .
OSC	Ohio Supercomputer Center	OSC
OSC	Operational Space Control	. . .
	Mathematical theory	
OSCA	Open Systems Cabling Architecture	BT
OSCAR	On-Line Student Communication and Registration	CFCC
OSCAR	On-Line Supreme Court Automated Resource	. . .
OSDIT	Office of Software Development and Information Technology	GSA
OSDP	Optical System Design Program	Gibson Optics
OSE	Open Systems Environment	OSI
OSEE	Optically Stimulated Electron Emission	. . .
OSF	Open Software Foundation	H-P et al.
OSHA	Occupational Safety and Health Administration	USDA
OSI	On-Screen Instrument(-ation)	. . .
OSI	Open Systems Interconnection	. . .
	Subcommittee of *ISO*, which see	

OSI/CS	OSI Communications Subsystem	IBM
	sa *OSI, Open Systems Interconnection*	
OSINet	Open Systems Interconnection Network	OSI
	Experimental computer network managed by the National Institute of Standards and Technology (NIST), and used for testing OSI-based communications products	
	sa *OSI, Open Systems Interconnection*	
OSIS	Ocean Surveillance Information System	US Navy
OSME	Open Systems Message Exchange	OSI
OSO	Orbiting Solar Observatory	. . .
OSP	Operator Service Provider	. . .
	re: Voice mail	
OSP	Optical Storage Processor	NeXT
OSPA	Open Signal-Processing Architecture	Spectron
OSPF	Open Shortest Path First	Proteon
	Protocol for efficient routing through multiple local area networks (LANs)	
OSS	Operational Support System	. . .
OSS	Optical Storage System	Data/Ware Development
OSSL	Optically Stabilized Semiconductor Laser	B. Dahmani et al.
OSTC	Open System Testing Consortium	OSI
OSTP	Office of Science and Technology Policy	US White House
OTA	Office of Technology Assessment	US Congress
OTA	Operational Transconductance Amplifier	. . .
OTDR	Optical Time Domain Reflectometry	. . .
OTEC	Ocean Thermal Energy Conversion	. . .
OTF	Optical Transfer Function	. . .
OTH	Over-The-Horizon [radar]	. . .
	Short form of *OTHR*	
OTH-B	Over-The-Horizon Backscatter	US Air Force
	A defensive radar system	
OTHR	Over-The-Horizon Radar	. . .
OTL	OSI Testing Liaison	OSI
	sa *OSI, Open Systems Interconnection*	
OTP	One-Time Programmable	. . .
	re: Electronic logic (or other) circuits field-programmable to a customized configuration	
OTP	One-Time Programmable	TI
	Memory integrated circuit (IC)	
OTPROM	One-Time Programmable Read Only Memory	. . .
	Memory integrated circuit (IC)	
OTV	Orbital Transfer Vehicle	NASA

OV	Overvoltage	. . .
OVCE	Operational Voltage-Controlled Element	. . .
OVD	Optically Variable Device	. . .
OVD	Outside Vapor Deposition	Corning
OVD	Over-Voltage Detector	. . .
OVLO	Over-Voltage Lock-Out	. . .
OVP	Over-Voltage Protection	. . .
OVPO	Outside Vapor-Phase Oxidation	. . .
	Manufacturing technique for optical fiber production	
oz	onza	. . .
	Italian for *ounce*	

P

p	pico	. . .
	Prefix for 10^{-12}	
p	positive (or p-channel) [doping]	. . .
	Solid-state (SS) semiconductor using hole flow as the primary conduction media	
p	pressure	. . .
	Expressed in units of *Pascals*, *Pa*, which see	
P	Peta	. . .
	Prefix for 10^{15}	
P	Phosphorus	. . .
	Atomic element number 15	
P	Power	. . .
	Expressed in *watts*, *W*	
P/AR	Peak to Average Ratio	. . .
P-Band	P-Band	. . .
	Radio high frequency allocation of 420–450 MHz	
P/F	Poll/Final	CCITT
	re: X.25 protocol control field; sa *X.25*	
P/FM	PBX Facilities Management	DEC
	sa *PBX, Private Branch Exchange*	
p-MOS	positive (or p-channel) Metal Oxide Semiconductor	. . .
	Semiconductor material utilizing holes as the primary conduction medium; alternately designated by *PMOS* sa *p, positive*	
p-n-p	positive-negative-positive	. . .
	Alternate form for *pnp*, which see	

P(R)	Packet Receive re: X.25 protocol, which see	CCITT
P(S)	Packet Sequence re: X.25 protocol, which see	CCITT
Pa	Pascal Unit of pressure Named in honor of French mathematician Blaise Pascal (1623–1662)	. . .
Pa	Protactinium Atomic element number 91	. . .
PA	Preamble	FDDI
PA	Program Access [key] Program function keys (PFKs) on IBM 3278 terminals, etc.	IBM
PA	Public Address [system] An amplification and loudspeaker system	. . .
PAB	p-Aminobenzoic Acid A compound important in biochemistry	. . .
PABB	Parameterized Analog Building Block	. . .
PABX	Private Automatic Branch Exchange	. . .
PAC	Programmable Array Controller	. . .
PAC	Public Access Computer	. . .
PACH	Plane Abberation-Correcting Holographic re: Optical interference grating technology	. . .
PACS	Picture Archiving and Communication System	Siemens Med. Sys.
PaCT	PBX and Computer Teaming Wide area network (WAN) services using integrated services digital network (ISDN) technology sa PBX, Private Branch Exchange	Siemens/ Gandalf
PACT	Private Access Communication Terminal	. . .
PAD	Packet Assembly/Disassembly re: Preparation of data prior to transmission over a packetized network and restoration of the data after receipt from the network; also, the X.25 protocol PAD service signal to "clear local PAD"	. . .
PAG	Polyazido-glycidyl An advanced rocket fuel	. . .
PAL	Paradox Applications Language	Borland
PAL	Phase Alteration by Line A video transmission standard	. . .
PAL	Postal Answer Line Automated voice response information system	USPS

PAL	Priviledged Architecture Library	DEC
PAL	Programmable Array Logic	Monolithic
	An integrated circuit (IC) which is user-programmable into a wide variety of logical configurations For other programmable logic devices (PLDs) see *EEPLD, EPLD, FPGA, FPLA, PEEL, PGA, PIC* and *PLA*	Mem.
PAL	Public Access Line	FCC
	Bulletin board service	
PAM	Patent Applicaion Management	PTO
PAM	Pulse Amplitude Modulation	. . .
PAPI	Pipes Application Program Interface	Lambda
PAPVD	Plasma-Assisted Physical Vapor Deposition	. . .
	C (diamond) insulation/thermal conductor deposition used for active electronic device manufacturing	
PAR	Parameter Request	CCITT
	X.25 protocol packet assembly/disassembly (PAD) command	
	sa *X.25*	
PARIS	Parallel Instruction Set	Syracuse Univ.
	A methodology used for testing faults in massively parallel processors	
PARS	Passenger Airline Reservation System	IBM
PAS*	Physical Address Strobe [signal]	. . .
	Note: "*" indicates that a signal (called "active high") must be present at the circuit terminal in order for the described function to be activated.	
PASCO	Panel Analysis and Sizing Code	NASA
	A finite element analysis method	
PASN-AL	Primary Address Space Name Access List	IBM
PASS	Personal Access Satellite System	NASA
PAT	Performance Analysis Tool	Intel
PAX	Parallel Architecture Extended	Intel
	A set of rules governing Intel 860 microprossor systems development	
Pb	Plumbum	. . .
	Symbol for *lead*, atomic element number 82	
PBC	Parallel Board Connector	. . .
PBE	Prompt By Example	Microrim
PBGACK*	Physical Bus Grant Acknowledge [signal]	. . .
	Note: "*" indicates that a signal (called "active high") must be present at the circuit terminal in order for the described function to be activated.	
PBMR	Pushbroom Microwave Radiometer	NASA

PBN	Pyrolitic Boron Nitride	. . .
	Compound commonly used for high temperature crucibles, etc.	
PBS	Public Broadcasting System	PBS
PBT	Permeable Base Transistor	. . .
PBW	Power By Wire	NASA
PBX	Private Branch Exchange	. . .
pc	parsec	. . .
	Astronomy: Distance at which an object portends one second of parallax; approx. 1.9174×10^{13} miles (mi) or 0.3066 light-year (ly)	
PC	Personal Computer	. . .
PC	Perspective Control	. . .
	Name applied to a lens with shiftable elements used for controlling perspective, especially in architectural and industrial photography	
PC	Phase Contrast	. . .
	re: Microscopy object illumination technology	
PC	Photoconductive(-tion)	. . .
PC	Plug Compatible	. . .
	re: Alternate vendor equipment compatibility	
PC	Printed Circuit	. . .
PC	Program Call	IBM
PC	Program Counter	. . .
	re: Computer hardware instruction address control	
PC	Protocol Controller	. . .
PC-DOS	Personal Computer Disk Operating System	IBM
PCA	Performance Coverage Analyzer	DEC
PCA	Personal Computer Architecture	. . .
PCA	Printed Circuit Assembly	Unisys
PCB	Polychlorinated Biphenyl	. . .
	High-dielectric-strength oil used in transformers and other high-density electrical applications	
PCB	Printed Circuit Board	. . .
	sa *PWB, Printed Wiring Board*	
PCB	Process Control Block	. . .
PCB	Program Communication Block	IBM
PCC	Parametric Cubic Convolution	. . .
PCC	Personal Computer Connection	. . .
PCEO	Personal Computer Enhancement Operation	Intel

PCET	Personal Computer Extended Technology	. . .
PCF	Packet Control Facility	NSC
PCG	Preconditioned-Cojugate-Gradient re: Mathematical iterative process used in finite element analysis	. . .
PCI	Personal Computer Instrumentation	. . .
PCI	Personal Computer Interface	American Mgt. Systems
PCI	Protocol Control Information	OSI
PCI	Pulsed Current Injection	. . .
PCIP	Personal Computer Instrument Product	Keithly
PCIP	Personal Computer Internet Protocol Personal computer (PC) version of *TCP/IP*, which see	. . .
PCL	Portable Common Loops	DEC
PCL	Printer Command Language	H-P
PCM	Photo Chemical Machining	. . .
PCM	Physical Connection Management	. . .
PCM	Plug-Compatible Mainframe	. . .
PCM	Protocol Converting Multiplexer	. . .
PCM	Pulse Code Modulation	. . .
PCMM	Plug-Compatible Mainframe Manufacturer	. . .
PCN	Personal Communications Network	. . .
PCN	Personal Computer Network	. . .
PCP	Plug-Compatible Peripheral	. . .
PCP	Primary Communications Processor	Merit Network
PCP	Primary Control Program	IBM
PCP	Programmable Communications Processor	. . .
PCR	Polymerase Chain Reaction re: Duplication of DNA segments used in genetic research sa *DNA, Deoxyribonucleic Acid*	. . .
PCS	Password Connection Security	. . .
PCS	Patient Care System	IBM
PCS	Personal Communications Services	FCC
PCS	Personal Communications System	Bell Canada
PCS	Personal Computer Support	IBM
PCS	Photon-Correlation Spectroscopy	. . .
PCS	Plastic-Clad Silica [fiber] re: Optical fiber construction	. . .
PCSA	Personal Computing Systems Architecture	DEC
PCSR	Parallel Channel Signalling Rate	. . .
PCSS	Photoconductive Semiconductor Switch	. . .
PCT	Personal Communications Terminal re: Terminals to aid hearing-impaired	Trident Technologies
PCT	Personal Computer Terminal	. . .
PCT	Process Control Table	DEC

PCT	Program Control Table	IBM
PCU	Peripheral Control Unit	NCR
PCU	Power Control Unit	. . .
PCVD	Polymer Chemical Vapor Deposition re: Fiber-optic production technology	. . .
PCXI	Personal Computer [bus] with Extensions for Instrumentation	. . .
PC²	Personal Computer Connection	. . .
Pd	Palladium Atomic element number 46	. . .
PD	Proportional/Derivative Variables involved in closed-loop controllers (as used in robotic control, etc.)	. . .
PD	Pulse Dialing	. . .
PDA	Parallel Drive Array re: Microcomputer storage technology	. . .
PDAU	Physical Delivery Access Unit	CCITT
PDB	Physical Data Base	. . .
PDB	Planar Doped Barrier re: doping technique used in producing solid-state (SS) electronic devices	. . .
PDC	Program Designator Code	DARPA
PDD	Performance Design and Debug	CAE Plus
PDES	Product Data Exchange Specification (or Standard)	IEEE
PDF	Packet-Data FIFO [buffer] sa FIFO, First In/First Out	. . .
PDF	Power Division Factor re: Power division in electronic bandpass filter circuits	. . .
PDF	Program Development Facility	IBM
PDGS	Product Design Graphics System	ITT
PDI	Picture Description Instruction	. . .
PDIP	Plastic Dual In-Line Package re: Integrated circuit packaging technology sa CDIP, Ceramic Dual In-Line Package	. . .
PDL	Page Description Language A code used for translating data for subsequent use by a printer or other "hard copy" device	. . .
PDL	Program Design Language	. . .
PDLC	Polymer Dispersed Liquid Crystal [display]	. . .
PDM	Physical Data Modeling	. . .
PDM	Pulse Duration Modulation re: Data recording technology	. . .
PDMA	Pipelined Direct Memory Access	Alantec

PDN	Public Data Network	...
PDP	Plasma Display Panel	...
PDP	Programmed Data Processor	DEC
PDS	Partitioned Data Set	IBM
	A data structuring format used in computer storage devices	
PDS	Power Distribution System	...
PDS	Premises Distribution System	AT&T
PDSS	Payload Data Services System	NASA
	re: NASA's space station support; sa *NASA*	
PDT	Peripheral Device Type	...
	re: SCSI standard inquiry; sa *SCSI, Small Computer Systems Interface*	
PDT	Photodynamic Therapy	...
	re: Use of light (usually from a laser) in conjunction with photosensitive drugs for cancer therapy	
PDT	Post Tuning Drift	...
PDU	Protocol Data Unit	ISO
PDV	Pulse Density Violation	...
	A digital communications fault	
PE	Performance Enhancement	IBM
PE	Phase Encoding(-ed)	...
PE	Photoelectric [effect]	...
PE	Photoelectron Equivalent	...
PE	Plasma Enhanced(-ment)	...
PE	Processing Element	...
PE	Professional Engineer	...
PE	Protocol Emulator	DEC
PEA	Phasic Excitation/Activation	...
PEC	Photoelectrochemical [cell]	...
PECL	Pseudo Emitter-Coupled Logic	Motorola
PECVD	Plasma-Enhanced Chemical Vapor Deposition	...
PEEL	Programmable Electrically Erasable Logic	...
	An integrated circuit (IC) which is user-programmable into a wide variety of logical configurations For other programmable logic devices (PLDs) see *EEPLD, EPLD, FPGA, FPLA, PAL, PGA, PIC* and *PLA*	
pel	picture element	...
	Variant of *pixel*, which see	
PEL	Permissible Exposure Level	OSHA
	re: Toxic chemical or other hazard exposure	
PELTS	Personal Emergency Locator Transmitter Service	FCC

PEM	Privacy Enhanced Mail	. . .
	Electronic mail with data security	
PEO	Program Executive Officer	. . .
PEP	Packetized Ensemble Protocol	Telebit
PEP	Partitioned Emulation Program	IBM
PEP	Peak Envelope Power	. . .
	re: Power supplied to an antenna during radio transmission	
PEP	Phosphpenolpyruvate	. . .
	A compound important in biochemistry	
PEP	Proposal Entry Processor	NASA
PERMS	Personnel Electronic Records Management System	US Army
PERT	Program Evaluation Review Technique	US Navy
PES	Positional Error Signal	. . .
	re: Computer disk drive actuator positioning accuracy	
PET	Polyethylene terephthalate	. . .
	A widely used plastic	
PET	Positron Emission Tomography	. . .
PEX	PHIGS Extension to X-Windows	. . .
	sa *PHIGS, "Programmer's Hierarchical Graphics Standard"*	
pF	picofarad	. . .
	Unit of capacitance; $= 10^{-12}$ farad	
PF	Program Function [key]	. . .
	Key on a personal computer (PC) or terminal that is software-interpreted	
PF	Programmable Function [key]	. . .
	Key on a personal computer (PC) or terminal or on an independent keyboard that is programmable to perform specific functions	
PFB	Parallel Filter Bank	. . .
	Mathematical analysis procedure	
PFC	Power Factor Correction	. . .
pFd	picofarad	. . .
	Alternate form; see *pF, picofarad*	
PFD	Phase and Frequency Detector	. . .
PFG	Pulsed-Field Gel	. . .
	A technique used in electrophoresis	
PFK	Program (or Programmable) Function Key	. . .
	Generic form for both definitions of *PF*, which see	
PFLL	Phase- and Frequency-Locked Loop	. . .
	sa *PLL, Phase-Locked Loop* and *FLL, Frequency-Locked Loop*	

PFMA	Protoflight Manipulator	NASA
PFPE	Perfluoropolyether	...
	Wide-temperature-range grease lubricant	
PGA	Pin Grid Array	...
	IC package system for dense pin connections	
	sa *LGA, Land Grid Array*	
PGA	Programmable Gain Amplifier	...
PGA	Programmable Gate Array	...
	An integrated circuit (IC) which is user-programmable into a wide variety of logical configurations For other programmable logic devices (PLDs) see *EEPLD, EPLD, FPGA, FPLA, PAL, PEEL, PIC* and *PLA*	
PGA	Pteroylglutamic Acid	...
	A compound important in biochemistry	
PGIA	Programmable Gain Instrumentation Amplifier	...
pH	—Hydrogen Ion Concentration	...
	where: pH 0 = acid < pH 7 = neutral < pH 14 = alkaline	
PH	Packet Handler	CCITT
PHA	Pulse Height Analyzer	...
Phe	Phenylalanine	...
	A compound important in biochemistry	
PHIGS	Programmer's Hierarchial Interactive Graphics Standard	ANSI
PHY	Physical [layer]	...
	re: Physical layer of ISO OSI seven-layer standard	
	sa *OSI*, and *ISO*	
pi	pi	...
	16th letter of the Greek alphabet (π) The mathematical constant 3.14159265359...	
PI	Polarization Intensity	...
PI	Proportional Integral	...
PIA	Peripheral Interface Adapter	Ciarcia
PIA	Programmable Interconnect Array	...
PIC	Particle In Cell	...
	Mathematical algorithm	
PIC	Picture [graphics standard]	...
PIC	Portable Industrial Computer	...
PIC	Power Integrated Circuit	...

PIC	Programmable Integrated Circuit	...
	An integrated circuit (IC) which is user-programmable into a wide variety of logical configurations For other programmable logic devices (PLDs) see *EEPLD, EPLD, EPLD, FPGA, FPLA, PAL, PEEL, PGA*, and *PLA*	
PICHTR	Pacific International Center for High Technology Development	Hawaii
PID	Personal Identification [number]	...
PID	Photo-Ionization Detector	...
PID	Process Identification [number]	DEC
PID	Proportional/Integral/Derivative	...
	Multivariate closed loop parameters (as used in robotic and industrial controls)	
PIF	Programmatic Interface Facility	...
PIK	Programmer's Imaging Kernel	ANSI
PIL	Picosecond Injection Laser	Technoexan
PIL	Pittsburgh Interpretive Language	...
PIM	Personal Information Manager	...
PIM	Process Inactivity Monitor	DEC
PIMP	Pluribus Interface Message Processor	DARPA
PIN	Personal (or Personnel) Identification Number	...
PIN	Positive-Intrinsic-Negative	...
	Solid-state (SS) diode photodetector	
PIND	Particle Impact Noise Detection	...
PING	Packet Internet Name Groper	...
PIO	Peripheral Input/Output [controller]	Ciarcia
PIO	Programmed Input/Output	...
PIP	Parallel Image Processor	...
PIP	Peripheral Interchange Program	DEC
PIRL	Polyimide Release Layer	...
	re: Integrated circuit production separation of photoresist material	
PIRLS	Probe Infrared Laser Spectrometer	...
PIU	Path Information Unit	IBM
PIV	Peak Inverse Voltage	...
	re: Voltage stress rating of diodes, vacuum tubes, etc.	
pix	picture	...
pixel	picture element	...
	In television, computer displays; the smallest element producing picture information. Thus, the simplest color element consists of three pixels: magenta (red), green, and cyan (blue), in appropriate intensities to produce the desired tint.	

	Sometimes designated by *pel*, but *pixel* is becoming widely accepted as an English word	
pK	—Potassium ion concentration	. . .
PKC	Public Key Cryptographic [system]	. . .
PKE	Public Key Encryption	DoD
PL/I	Programming Language I	IBM
PL/360	Programming Language 360	IBM
	Systems programming language for the IBM 360-series computers	
PLA	Programmed Logic Array	H-P
	An integrated circuit (IC) which is user-programmable into a wide variety of logical configurations For other programmable logic devices (PLDs) see *EEPLD, EPLD, FPGA, FPLA, PAL, PEEL, PGA* and *PIC*	
PLAR	Private Line Automatic Ringdown	. . .
PLB	Picture Level Benchmark	. . .
PLC	Power Line Conditioner	AT&T
PLC	Programmed Logic Controller	. . .
PLC	Project Life Cycle	. . .
PLCC	Plastic Leaded Chip Carrier	. . .
PLCP	Physical Layer Convergence Procedure	IEEE
	re: IEEE Standard 802.6 on metropolitan area networks (MANs) sa *IEEE, Institute of Electrical and Electronic Engineers*	
PLD	Programmable Logic Device	. . .
	An integrated circuit (IC) which is user-programmable into a wide variety of logical configurations For specific programmable logic devices see *EEPLD, EPLD, FPGA, FPLA, PAL, PEEL, PGA, PIC* and *PLA*	
PLD	Pulsed Laser Deposition	. . .
PLI	Paper-Like Interface	IBM
	Flat-panel display with digitizing tablet providing interactive computer access	
PLI	Private Line Interface	DARPA
PLL	Phase-Locked Loop	. . .
PLM	Pulse-Length Modulation	. . .
	re: Disk access technology	
PLO	Phase-Locked Oscillator	. . .
PLP	Presentation Level Protocol	AT&T
PLS	Partial Least Squares	. . .
	Statistical analysis procedure	
PLS	Programmable Logic Sequencer	TI

PLSA	Pulsed Laser Spectrum Analyzer	. . .
PLU	Primary Logical Unit	IBM
Pm	Promethium	. . .
	Atomic element number 61	
PM	Phase Modulation	. . .
PM	Presentation Manager	IBM
PM	Preventive Maintenance	. . .
PM	Programming Module	. . .
PMA	Performance Measurement and Accounting [system]	Computer Associates
PMC	Plug-In Memory Card	. . .
PMD	Physical [layer] Media Dependent	. . .
	A specification in the fiber distributed data interface standard *FDDI*	
PMDF	Pascal Memo Distribution Facility	DEC
PME	Photo-Magnetoelectric Effect	. . .
PMF	Panel Modification Facility	IBM
PMF	Parameter Management Frame	. . .
	An access method used in the fiber-distributed data interface (FDDI) standard	
PMF	Polarization-Maintaining Fiber	. . .
PML	Programmable Macro Logic	Signetics
PMMA	Polymethylmethacrylate	. . .
	re: Optical plastic	
PMMU	Paged Memory Management Unit	. . .
PMO	Program Management Optimizer	Duquesne Systems
PMOS	Positive (or p-channel) Metal Oxide Semiconductor	. . .
	Alternate form; see *p-MOS*	
PMS	Phenazine Methosulfate	. . .
	A compound important in biochemistry	
PMS	Project Management System	IBM
PMT	Photomultiplier Tube	. . .
PMT	Process Maturity Test	DEC
PMTS	Precision Multitarget Tracking System	. . .
PMU	Parametric Measuring Unit	Cadic
PMU	Power Management Unit	VIA Technologies
PMZF	Programmable Multi-Zone Furnace	MMSL
PN	Peripheral Node	. . .
PN	Pseudonoise	. . .
	re: Covert message detection sa *FH, Frequency-Hopped* and *TH, Time-Hopped* for related acronyms	

pnp	positive-negative-positive	. . .
	re: Transistor fabrication in which the emitter, base, and collector are intrinsic positive, negative, and positive semiconductor material, respectively	
	Alternate: *p-n-p*	
PNX	Private Network Exchange	Ztel
Po	Polonium	. . .
	Atomic element number 84	
POE	Point Of Entry	. . .
POF	Plastic Optical Fiber	Codenoll Tech./ GM
POFS	Private Operational-Fixed Service	. . .
POI	Probability of Intercept	. . .
	re: signal resolution capability of a compressive receiver *CR*, which see	
POMS	Plain Old Mail Service	. . .
POMS	Process Operations Management System	IBM
PON	Passive Optical Network	. . .
POP	Picture-Outside-Picture	. . .
	re: Multiple television pictures within one display tube	
POP	Point Of Presence	. . .
	Point at which a common carrier appears in a local access and transport area (LATA)	
POP	Polar Orbiting Platform	. . .
PORTAL	Private Offerings and Reciprocal Trading through Automated Linkages	NASDAQ
	Private securities exchange through an electronic stock market	
POS	Point Of Sale	. . .
POS	Program Option Select	IBM
POSE	Picture-Oriented Software Engineering	CSA
POSI	Promoting Conference for Open Systems Interconnection	POSI
POSIX	Portable Operating System Interface [standard]	IEEE
POST	Point-Of-Sale Terminal	. . .
POTS	Plain Old Telephone Service	AT&T
	General acronym for all types of analog telephone service	
POWCON	Polytechnic of Wales Conferencing [system]	Polytechnic of Wales
POWER	Performance Optimization with Enhanced RISC	IBM
	Second generation RISC architecture	
	sa *RISC, Reduced Instruction Set Computer*	

POWTEX	Polytechnic of Wales Teletex	Polytechnic of Wales
	General purpose information database videotex system	
PP	Push-Pull	. . .
	re: Electronic circuit design, usually audio or control circuits	
PPA	Parallel Port Adapter	. . .
PPA	Physical Page Address	. . .
PPC	Parallel Poll Configure	IEEE
	IEEE Standard 488 bus command; sa *IEEE*	
PPC	Parallel Protocol Controller	TI
PPDL	Postscript Page Description Language	Adobe Systems
PPDMS	Product and Process Document Management System	Boeing Computer Srvcs.
PPDS	Personal Printer Data Stream	IBM
PPDU	Presentation Protocol Data Unit	. . .
PPF	Plain Paper FAX	. . .
	sa *FAX, Facsimile*	
PPFA	Page Printer Formatting Aid	IBM
PPG	Partial Product Generator	. . .
PP*i*	Pyrophosphate, inorganic	. . .
	A compound important in biochemistry	
PPI	Plan Position Indicator	. . .
	The "pip" on a radar screen	
PPL	Process-to-Process Link	Walker Richer & Quinn
ppm	parts per million	. . .
PPM	Pit Position Modulation	. . .
	re: Optical disk data recording technology	
PPM	Pulse Position Modulation	. . .
	re: Disk access technology	
PPM	Pulses Per Minute	. . .
PPN	Processor Port Network	AT&T
	Element of Generic 3 telephone switching system	
PPOLL	Parallel Poll	IEEE
	IEEE Standard 488 bus command; sa *IEEE*	
PPP	Point-to-Point Protocol	IETF
pps	packets per second	. . .
	Alternate form: *PPS*	
pps	pulses per second	. . .
	Also expressed as Hertz (Hz)	

PPS	Packets Per Second	. . .
	Alternate form; see *pps*	
PPS	Precision Positioning Service	DoD
	A precision time/frequency service	
PPS	Programmable Power Supply	. . .
PPS	Pulses Per Second	. . .
PPSE	Parallel Programming Support Environment	OACIS
PPSFP	Parallel-Pattern Single-Fault Propagation	IBM
	A mathematical process used for simulating	
	faults in electronic circuit board testing	
PPT	Processing Program Table	IBM
PPT	Punched Paper Tape	. . .
PPTFE	Plasma-Polymerized Tetrafluoroethylene	. . .
PPU	Parallel Poll Unconfigure	IEEE
	IEEE Standard 488 bus command;	
	sa *IEEE*	
PPU	Primary Physical Unit	IBM
PQET	Print Quality Enhancement Technology	Lexmark
PQFP	Plastic Quad Flat Pack	. . .
	Dense integrated circuit mounting	
	technology with pins on on all four sides	
Pr	Praseodymium	. . .
	Atomic element number 59	
PR	Perpendicular Recording	. . .
	A magnetic recording technology	
	Also called *Vertical Recording*, *VR*	
PR/SM	Processor Resource/Systems Manager	IBM
	Hardware feature allowing definition of	
	multiple environments within a single	
	multi-processor machine	
PRA	Primary Rate Access	. . .
PRAM	Programmable Random Access Memory	. . .
PRB	Private Radio Bureau	. . .
PRBS	Pseudo-Random Bit Sequence	. . .
PRECAP	Preprocessor Electronic Circuit Analysis	. . .
	Program	
PREPnet	Pennsylvania Research and Economic	PREPnet
	Partnership Network	
PRF	Pulse Repetition Frequency	. . .
PRI	Primary Rate Interface	AT&T
	ISDN notation for 1.54 Mbit/sec aggregate	
	data rate	
	sa *BRI*, *Basic Rate Interface* and *ISDN*,	
	Integrated Services Digital Network	
PRK	Photo-Refractive Keratectomy	. . .
	Medical use of lasers for ophthalmological	
	rectification	

PRM	Performance Report Message	. . .
	A Facility Data Link (FDL) message	
Pro	Proline	. . .
	A compound important in biochemistry	
PROCLIB	Procedure Library	IBM
PROFS	Professional Office System	IBM
PROLOG	Programming Logic	IBM
	Artificial intelligence language	
PROM	Pockel's Read-Out Optical Modulator	. . .
	re: Light communications modulator	
PROM	Programmable Read Only Memory	. . .
PROMICE	Programmable Read Only Memory In-Circuit	Grammar
	Emulator	Engine
PROMIS	Problem-Oriented Medical Information	. . .
	System	
PROP	Programmable Operator	IBM
PRR	Pulse Repetition Rate	. . .
PRT	Personal Rapid Transit	Boeing
	Experimental computer-controlled	
	transportation device	
PRT	Platinum Resistance Thermometer	. . .
PRV	Peak Reverse Voltage	. . .
ps	picosecond	. . .
	10^{-12} second; alternate form: *psec*	
PS	Polarization Sensitivity	. . .
PS/1, 2	Personal System/1, 2	IBM
	Personal computer designation; also, *ad hoc*	
	standard for personal computer hardware	
	and software	
PSA	Parallel Signature Analyzer	. . .
	Process used in self-testing chips	
PSAF	Print Services Access Facility	IBM
PSB	Parallel System Bus	Intel
PSB	Program Specification Block	. . .
PSC	Pittsburgh Supercomputer Center	PSC
PSC	Polar Stratospheric Clouds	. . .
PSCN	Program Support Communications Network	NASA
PSCS	Packet-Switched Communication System	. . .
PSD	Position Sensing Detector	. . .
	re: Photo-optical device	
PSDN	Packet Switching Data Network	. . .
PSDS	Postal Source Data System	US Postal
		Service
PSDS	Public-Switched Data Service	BOC
PSE	Portable STREAMS Environment	Mentat
	A UNIX-related architecture;	
	sa *UNIX* and *STREAMS*,	

PSE	Project Support Environment	IBM
psec	picosecond	. . .
	10^{-12} second; alternate form: *ps*	
PSF	Point Spread Function	. . .
	Mathematical procedure frequently used for characterizing performance of lasers and other optical systems	
PSF	Pre-Select Filter	. . .
PSF	Print Services Facility	IBM
PSG	Programmable Sequence Generator	TI
psi	pounds per square inch	. . .
PSI	Packetnet System Interface	DEC
PSI	Pounds per Square Inch	. . .
	Alternate form; see *psi*	
psia	pounds per square inch, absolute	. . .
psig	pounds per square inch, guage	. . .
PSINet	Performance Systems International Network	PSI
PSK	Phase Shift Keying	. . .
PSMA	Phase-Synchronous Multiple-Access	. . .
PSN	Packet Switched Network	. . .
PSO	Programmable Storage Oscilloscope	Krenz
PSPDN	Packet-Switched Public Data Network	. . .
PSR	Primary Surveillance Radar	. . .
PSRR	Power Supply Rejection Ratio	. . .
	A measure of the quality of an amplifier or other electronic circuit	
PSS	Packet-Switched Service	AT&T
PSSC	Public Service Satellite Consortium	. . .
PSSD	Parallel/Serial Scan Design	. . .
PST	Pacific Standard Time	. . .
PST	Point Source Transmittance	. . .
	A measure of stray light in optical systems	
PSTN	Public Switched Telephone Network	CCITT
PSW	Program Status Word	IBM
Pt	Platinum	. . .
	Atomic element number 78	
PT	Paper Tape	. . .
	Usually used in the form *PPT, Punched Paper Tape*	
PTA	Percutaneous Transluminal Angioplasty	. . .
PTAT	Private Trans-Atlantic Telecommunications	PTAT Systems
PTAT-1	Private Trans-Atlantic 1	US Sprint
	Private Trans-Atlantic cable	
PTC	Positive Temperature Coefficient	. . .
PTCA	Percutaneous Transluminal Coronary Angioplasty	. . .

PTD	Parallel Transfer Disk (or Drive)	Fujitsu
PTDA	Per Task Data Area	Intel
PTDAS	Parallel Transfer Disk Array Subsystem	Storage Concepts
PTEC	Power Train Electronics Controller Electronic microprocessor for automotive power train control	Motorola/Ford
PTF	Phase Transfer Function Mathematical procedure frequently used for characterizing performance of lasers and other optical systems	. . .
PTF	Program Temporary Fix	IBM
PTF	Programmable Transversal Filter	Electronic Decisions
PTFE	Polytetrafluoroethylene A polymer commonly used in electronic circuit board substrates	. . .
PTH	Plated Through Hole Designation given to a conductive hole in an electronic circuit board Also designated by *LTH, Leaded Through Hole*	IBM
PTIP	Pluribus Terminal Interface Processor	DARPA
PTM	Pulse Time Modulation	. . .
PTO	Public Telecommunications Operator	. . .
PTP	Paper Thin Package re: Electronic circuit packaging technology	. . .
PTR	Pulse Time Reference re: Loran-C navigation and time/frequency standard reception sa *Loran-C, Long-Range Navigation-C*	. . .
PTS	Processor Transaction Server	. . .
PTSS	People's Timesharing System	LLL
PTT	Poste, Téléphone et Télécommunications [Ministry] French government agency	France
PTT	Post, Telephone and Telegraph Generic term used to designate any similar agency in any country	. . .
PTTI	Precise Time and Time Interval	. . .
Pu	Plutonium Atomic element number 94	. . .
PU	Physical Unit re: *SNA, Systems Network Architecture,* which see	IBM
PUC	Peripheral Unit Controller	. . .
PUC	Public Utility Commission	US Dept. of Commerce

PUCP	Physical Unit Control Point	IBM
	re: IBM's *Systems Network Architecture*, *SNA*	
PUMS	Physical Unit Management Services	IBM
PUP	Principal User Processing (or Processor)	. . .
	re: Radar station for weather data analysis	
PV	Photovoltaic	. . .
PV	Programmable Via	IBM
PV-WAVE	Precision Visuals Workstation Analysis and Visualization Environment	Precision Visuals
PVAX	Personal Virtual Address Extension	DEC
	Virtual Address Extension (VAX) for DEC's personal computer (PC)	
PVB	Polyvinyl Butyral	. . .
	A plastic bonding agent	
PVC	Permanent Virtual Circuit	OSI
PVC	Polyvinyl Chloride	. . .
PVD	Physical Vapor Deposition	. . .
PVD	Polymer Vapor Deposition	. . .
PVDF	Polyvinylidene Fluoride	. . .
	An organic compound important for its piezoelectric and pyroelectric properties; also used in fiberoptic cables	
PVR	Photovoltaic Relay	Int'l Rectifier
PWA	Posted Write Array	Zenith
	A system memory buffering technology	
PWB	Printed Wiring Board	. . .
	sa *PCB, Printed Circuit Board*	
PWM	Pit Width Modulation	. . .
	re: Optical data recording technology	
PWM	Pulse Width Modulation	. . .
PWT	Pressure Wind Tunnel	NASA
PZT	Plumbum (lead)-Zirconate-Titanate	. . .
	A pyroelectric detector material	

Q

Q	—Electric Charge (symbol)	. . .
	Expressed in units of *Coulombs, (C)*, which see	
Q	Quality [factor]	. . .
	re: Electronic circuit efficiency figure	
Q-Band	Q-Band	. . .
	Microwave frequency allocation of 36–46 GHz Now obsolete; see *QA-Band* through *QE-Band*	

Q.E.D.	Quod Erat Demontrandum Latin for "which was to be proved"	. . .
QA	Quality Assurance	. . .
QA-Band	QA-Band Microwave frequency allocation of 36–38 GHz	. . .
QAM	Quadrature Amplitude Modulation	. . .
QB-Band	QB-Band Microwave frequency allocation of 38–40 GHz	. . .
QBE	Query By Example	. . .
QBO	Quasi-Biennial Oscillation re: Earth science	. . .
QC	Quality Control	. . .
QC-Band	QC-Band Microwave frequency allocation of 40–42 GHz	. . .
QCD	Quantum Chromodynamics re: Physics; particle and force theory	. . .
QCIF	Quarter Common Intermediate Format re: Videophone image pixel representation containing 180 × 144 pixels; sa *CIF, Common Intermediate Format*	CCITT
QCPE	Quantum Chemistry Program Exchange	Indiana Univ.
QCSE	Quantum Confined Stark Effect	. . .
QD	Quick Disconnect	. . .
QD-Band	QD-Band Microwave frequency allocation of 42–44 GHz	. . .
QDL	Quenched Dye Laser	. . .
QE	Quantum Efficiency re: Radiation detector performance	. . .
QE-Band	QE-Band Microwave frequency allocation of 44–46 GHz	. . .
QED	Quantum Electrodynamics re: Physics; particle and force theory	. . .
QFA	Quick File Access	. . .
QFET	Quantum Field-Effect Transistor	. . .
QFP	Quad Flat Pack re: Surface mount device (SMD) with dense pin configuration	. . .
QIC	Quarter Inch Cartridge Tape data storage standard	. . .
QIO	Query Input/Output	. . .
QIO	Queued Input/Output	. . .

QISAM	Queued Indexed Sequential Access Method	IBM
QLLC	Qualified Logical Link Control	IBM
QLP	Query Language Processor	. . .
QLV	Quantized Linear Velocity re: Disk access technology	. . .
QMF	Query Management Facility	IBM
QNDE	Quantitative Non-Destructive Evaluation	Langley Research Ctr.
QOS	Quality of Service A set of parameters used to quantify network performance	. . .
QPL	Qualified Parts List Pertains to joint Army-Navy (JAN) specifications	DoD
QPSK	Quadrature Phase Shift Keying	. . .
QRS	Readability, Signal Strength, Tone Received radio signal quality appraisal system	ARRL
QRSS	Quasi-Random Signal Sequence	. . .
QRSS	Quasi-Random Signal Source	. . .
QRT	Quick Response Team A group of information systems professionals assembled as needed to quickly solve information systems problems	. . .
QS	Quiet Series re: Integrated circuit (IC) series with high signal-to-noise ratio (SNR)	Fairchild
QSAM	Quadrature Sideband Amplitude Modulation	. . .
QSAM	Queued Sequential Access Method	IBM
QSOP	Quality Small-Outline Package Subminiaturized intgrated circuit with 25- mil pin spacing; one-half the size of the *SOIC*, small outline integrated circuit	. . .
QSRS	Quasi-Stellar Radio Source Astronomy; now commonly known as *Quasars*	. . .
QTAM	Queued Telecommunications Access Method	IBM
QUEST	Quantized Electronic Structure	NSF
QUIC	QUIC Univ. of Cal. at San Francisco version of *KWIC, Keyword In Context*	Univ. of SF
QW	Quantum Well	. . .
QWERTY	—QWERTY Acronym used to designate the standard typewriter keyboard, as distinguished from the Dvorak keyboard	. . .

| QWIP | Quantum Well Infrared Photodetector | . . . |

R

R	Resistance	. . .
	Electrical resistance; expressed in units of *Ohms*; denoted by *omega* (Ω), the last letter of the Greek alphabet Named in honor of German physicist Georg Simon Ohm (1787–1854)	
R	Roentgen	. . .
	Unit of radiation intensity, ususally expressed in *Roentgens per hour* Named in honor of German physicist Wilhelm Konrad Roentgen (1845–1923)	
R	Rydberg [constant]	. . .
	1.0973731×10^7 per meter (m^{-1}) Named in honor of Swedish mathemetician and physicist Johannes Robert Rydberg (1845–1919)	
R&D	Research and Development	. . .
R/D	Resolver to Digital [converter]	. . .
R-S	Reset-Set	. . .
	re: Electronics; multivibrator (MV) circuit; "Flip-Flop" (FF)	
R/V	Research Vessel	WHOI
R/W	Read/Write	. . .
Ra	Radium	. . .
	Atomic element number 88	
RA	Right Ascension	. . .
	re: Astronomy; one of the coordinates used in stating the position of an astronomical body	
RAC	Reflective Array Compressor	. . .
	re: Surface acoustic wave (SAW) device fabrication	
RAC	Reliability Analysis Center	RAC
RAC	Remote Asynchronous Concentrator	. . .
RAC	Resolved Acceleration Control	. . .
	Mathematical theory	
RACE	Research and Development for Advanced Communications in Europe	. . .
RACF	Resource Access Control Facility	IBM
RACON	Radar Beacon	. . .
	A navigation aid	

rad	rad Unit of radiation dosage equal to 100 ergs per gram of the absorbing substance	. . .
rad	radian The angle subtended by an arc equal in length to the radius of the circle; 2π radians = 360°	. . .
RAD	Rapid Application Development	. . .
RAD	Repository and Application Development sa *AD/CYCLE, Application Development/ Cycle*	IBM
RADAR	Radio Detection and Ranging Now accepted as an English word: *radar*	. . .
RADIUS	Research and Development for Image Understanding Systems	DARPA
RADL	Robotic Applications Development Laboratory	NASA
RADS	Ruggedized Advanced Disk System	CDC
RAF	Remote Access Facility	Datability Software
RAID	Redundant Array of Inexpensive Disks A collection of small disk storage units with automated back-up to ensure against loss of data	. . .
RALA	Registered Automatic Line Adapter	. . .
RAM	Random Access Memory Memory chip that needs no refreshing to retain data Compare with *DRAM, Dynamic Random Access Memory*, which requires power to maintain data Also designated by *SRAM, Static Random Access Memory*	. . .
RAM	Relative Access Method	IBM
RAMAC	Random Access [storage] IBM's first disk mass storage device, c. 1955	IBM
RAMDAC	Random Access Memory Digital-to-Analog Converter Mixed analog and digital integrated circuit (IC) used in graphics processors (GPs)	Brooktree
RAPID	Reusable Ada Products for Information Systems Development	DoD
RAPPI	Random Access Plan Position Indicator	. . .
RARP	Reverse Address Resolution Protocol re: Local area network (LAN) support	. . .
RAS	Reliability, Availability, Serviceability	IBM
RAS	Row Address Select (or Strobe) Address selection method in memory controller	. . .

RASSR	Reliable Advanced Solid-State Radar	TI
RATO	Rocket-Assisted Take-Off	US Air Force
	A modular add-on unit used to provide additional thrust to aircraft during take-off; sa *JATO, Jet-Assisted Take-Off*	
RAVE	Real-time Audio/Video Environment	Microware Systems
RAW	Read After Write	...
Rb	Rubidium	...
	Atomic element number 37	
RBBS	Remote Bulletin Board Service	...
RBHC	Regional Bell Holding Company(-ies)	...
	sa *RBOC, Regional Bell Operating Company(-ies)*	
RBI	Remote Bus Isolator	...
RBM	Repository-Based Methodology	...
RBOC	Regional Bell Operating Company(-ies)	...
	sa *RBHC, Regional Bell Holding Company(-ies)*	
RBS	Rules-Based System	...
RBW	Resolution Bandwidth	...
	re: Spectrum analyzer performance specification	
RC	Return Code	...
	re: Error return code in a procedure	
RC	Resistance-Capacitance	...
	Frequently used in reference to the time-constant-determining components in analog (or linear) electronic timing circuits	
RCAS	Reserve Component Automation System	GSA
RCCB	Remote Controlled Circuit Breaker	...
RCF	Remote Console Facility	IBM
RCM	Remote Control Module	...
RCP	Remote Communications Processor	...
RCS	Radar Cross-Section	...
RCS	Radio Command System	...
RCS	Reaction Control System (or Subsystem)	IEEE
RCS	Reentry Control System	...
RCS	Remote Control System	...
RCTL	Resistor Capacitor Transistor Logic	...
	An integrated circuit (IC) logic family	
RD	Receive Data	...
	re: *RS-232-C* protocol, which see	
RD	Request Disconnect	IBM
	Synchronous data link control (SDLC) command	

RDA	Radar Data Acquisition	. . .
RDA	Remote Database Access	ANSI
	A database standard	
RDAT	Rotating [head] Digital Audio Tape	. . .
Rdb	Relational database	DEC
	Alternate form; see *RDB*	
RDB	Relational Database	. . .
RDBMS	Relational Data Base Management System	. . .
RDF	Recirculating Document Feeder	. . .
RDM	Remote Device Module	. . .
RDOS	Real-time Disk Operating System	Data General
RDS	Raster Display System	. . .
RDS	Remote Data Services	IBM
RDSS	Radio Determination Satellite Service	Geostar
RDT	Remote Data Transmitter	. . .
RDTL	Resistor Diode Transistor Logic	. . .
	An Integrated circuit (IC) logic family	
	developed c. 1950s	
RDVM	Remote Digital (or Data) Voice Multiplexer	AT&T
Re	Reynolds [number]	. . .
	re: Fluid dynamics	
Re	Rhenium	. . .
	Atomic element number 75	
REAC	Reeves Electronic Analog Computer	Reeves
	An analog computer based on	
	servomechanisms, c. 1950s	
REB	Remote Ethernet Bridge	RAD Network Devices
RECAP	Reformatter Electronic Circuit Analysis	. . .
	Program	
ReGIS	Remote Graphics Instruction Set	DEC
REJ	Reject	CCITT
	Command and command response in *X.25*	
	protocol, which see	
RELP	Residual-Excited Linear Predictive [coding]	. . .
	A hybrid (analog + digital) method of	
	compressing speech and other analog data	
REM	Ring Error Monitor	IBM
REN	Remote Enable	IEEE
	IEEE Standard 488 bus command;	
	sa *IEEE*	
REPO	Remote Emergency Power Off	. . .
RER	Reverse Explicit Route	IBM
RESET	Reset [virtual call]	CCITT
	X.25 protocol packet assembly/disassembly	
	(PAD) command	
	sa *X.25*	

RESQ	Research Queuing	. . .
RET	Resolution Enhancement Technique	H-P
	Technique for improving dot matrix printer quality	
RET	Return	. . .
	Alternate for *CR, Carriage Return*	
RETMA	Radio Electronics Television Manufacturers Association	RETMA
REWST	Reprogramming Electronic Warfare System Test	US Air Force
REXX	Restructured Extended Executor	IBM
REYES	Renders Everything You've Ever Seen	Pixar
	Software for implementation of image description language	
RF	Radio Frequency	. . .
RFA	Remote File Access	. . .
RFA	Record File Address	DEC
	Component of *DDCMP, Digital Data Communication Protocol*	
RFB	Recording For the Blind	. . .
RFC	Radio Frequency Choke	. . .
RFC	Request for Comment	Internet
	re: *TCP/IP, Transmission Control Protocol/ Internet Protocol*	
RFD	Refuse-Derived Fuel	. . .
	Community refuse used as fuel for generating electricity, heat, etc.	
RFI	Radio Frequency Interference	. . .
RFI	Request for Information	. . .
RFID	Radio Frequency Identification	. . .
RFIU	Radio Frequency Interface Unit	. . .
RFNM	Ready For Next Message	. . .
	Equivalent to the CCITT *ACK, Acknowledge*, which see	
RFOG	Resonator Fiberoptic Gyro	. . .
RFOT	Remote Fiber-Optic Terminal	. . .
RFP	Request for Proposal	. . .
RFS	Ready for Sending	. . .
RFS	Remote File Sharing	Wang
RFS	Remote File System	AT&T
RFT	Radio Frequency Terminal	. . .
RFT	Report Format Table	IBM
RGA	Regenerative Amplifier	. . .
RGB	Red/Green/Blue	. . .
	re: Television and computer color display monitors; the three primary color signals (actually, magenta, green, and cyan)	

RGIS	Remote Graphics Instruction Set	. . .
RGP	Raster Graphics Processor	. . .
Rh	Rhodium	. . .
	Atomic element number 45	
RH	Relative Humidity	. . .
RH	Request/Response Header	IBM
RHC	Radio High-density Circuit	. . .
RHC	Regional Holding Company	AT&T
RHC	Right-Hand Circular	. . .
	re: Polarization of electromagnetic radiation (EMR)	
RHCP	Right-Handed Circular Polarization	. . .
	re: Microwave (MW) transmission	
RHE	Raman Holographic Edge	. . .
	re: Image analysis	
RHEED	Reflectance High Energy Electron Diffraction	. . .
RHR	Radar Horizon Range	. . .
Rib	D-Ribose	. . .
	A compound important in biochemistry	
RIC	Remote Interactive Communications	Xerox
RIC	Repeater Interface Controller	National Semicond.
RIE	Reactive Ion Etch	. . .
	Dielectric etching process used in integrated circuit (IC) manufacturing	
RIF	Routing Information Field	. . .
	re: Field in the source routing transparent (SRT) algorithm for facilitating communications between dissimilar local area networks (LANs); sa RII, Routing Information Indicator	
RIFF	Resource Interchange File Format	IBM/Microsoft
	re: Multi-media applications interface/data format	
RIG	Raster Image Generator	. . .
RII	Routing Information Indicator	IEEE
	re: A bit within the routing information field (RIF)	
RIM	Radio Imaging Method	. . .
RIM	Real-time Interactive Map	Ames Res. Ctr.
RIM	Request Initialization Mode	IBM
	Synchronous data link control (SDLC) command	
RIM	Ring Interface Module	DCA
RIMS	Resource Information Management System	Octel Comm.

RIN	Relative Intensity Noise	. . .
	A measure of quality in fiber-optic	
	communications	
RIP	Raster Image Processor	. . .
RIP	Routing Information Protocol	. . .
RIPE	Robot-Independent Programming	. . .
	Environment	
RIS	Radiological Information System	. . .
RIS	Renaissance Infinite Storage	Epoch Systems
RISC	Reduced Instruction Set Computer	UC-Berkeley
	sa *CISC* and *MISC* (two definitions) for	
	related information	
RISLU	Reduced Instruction Set [computer] Logical	. . .
	Unit	
RJ-11	RJ-11	AT&T
	Generic designation given to modular	
	telephone connector with four (RJ-11-4) or	
	six (RJ-11-6) conductors	
RJ-45	RJ-45	AT&T
	Designation given to modular telephone	
	connector with eight conductors	
RJE	Remote Job Entry	IBM
RK	Radial Keratotomy	. . .
	Corneal surgery, currently being done by	
	laser sculpting	
RLA	Raytheon Linear Array	Raytheon
RLG	Research Libraries Group	Stanford Univ.
RLG	Ring Laser Gyro(scope)	. . .
RLIN	Research Libraries Information Network	RLIN
RLL	Run Length Limited	. . .
	Microcomputer hard disk encoding	
	technology	
RLN	Remote LAN Node	Intercomputer
		Comm.
	sa *LAN, Local Area Network*	
RLS	Recursive Least Squares	. . .
	Statistical procedure	
RMATS	Remote Maintenance and Testing Service	AT&T
RMC*	Read Modify Cache [signal]	. . .
	Note: "*" indicates that a signal (called	
	"active high") must be present at the circuit	
	terminal in order for the described function	
	to be activated.	
RME	Relay Mirror Experiment	SDIO/Ball
RMF	Reduced Magnetic Field	NEC
	re: Cathode ray tube (CRT) display	
	construction	

RMF	Resource Management Facility	
RMF	Resource Measurement Facility	IBM
RMON	Remote Monitor(-ing)	. . .
RMOS	Refractory Metal Oxide Semiconductor	. . .
rms	root mean square	. . .
	Mathematics: The square root of the sum of the squares of the the amplitudes of a set of variables. Electronics: A measure of an alternating current (AC) waveform equal to the square root of the mean of the squares of the of the amplitudes of the signal	
	Alternately designated by *RMS*	
RMS	Record Management Services	DEC
RMS	Resource Management System	. . .
RMS	Root Mean Square	. . .
	Alternate form; see *rms*	
RMTS	Remote Mode Transfer Switch	. . .
Rn	Radon	. . .
	Atomic element number 86	
RN	Record Number	IBM
RNA	Ribonucleic Acid	. . .
	Cell substance associated with control of cell chemistry	
RNase	Ribonuclease	. . .
	A compound important in biochemistry	
RNC	Reflective Null Corrector	. . .
	re: Optical mirror testing	
RNET	Republic Network	Republic Telcom Sys.
RNID	Record Number Identifier	IBM
RNR	Receive Not Ready	CCITT
	X.25 protocol command and command response;	
	sa *X.25*	
RNS	Residue Number System	. . .
RO	Receive Only	. . .
ROCS	Resource-Oriented Computer System	US Dept. of Interior
ROHSI	Rogers High-Speed Interconnection Program	. . .
	Effort to develop next generation interconnect products	
ROI	Region of Interest	. . .
	Portion of a raster-scanned area to be manipulated	
ROM	Read Only Memory	. . .
ROMP	Ring Opening Metathesis Polymerization	. . .
ROS	Remote Operation Service	. . .

ROSE	Remote Operation Service Element	OSI
	Subset of *TCAP*, *Transaction Capabilities Application*	
ROSES	Receive-Only Ship Earth Station	INMARSAT
ROTHR	Relocatable Over-the-Horizon Radar	US Navy/ Raytheon
ROTL	Remote Office Test Line	IBM
ROW	Resonant Optical Waveguide	. . .
RPC	Remote Power Controller	. . .
RPC	Remote Procedure Call	. . .
RPC	Rotary Power Conditioner	. . .
	Motor-generator used in uninterruptible power supplies (UPS)	
RPE	Rectangular Pulse Excitation	. . .
RPE	Remote PABX Exchange	Northern Telecom
	sa *PABX*, *Private Automatic Branch Exchange* and *PBX*, *Private Branch Exchange*	
RPE	Remote Procedure Error	CCITT
	X.25 protocol packet assembly/disassembly (PAD) service signal	
	sa *X.25*	
RPG	Radar Product Generation	. . .
	re: Mathematical analysis utilizing radar signals as input	
RPG	Report Program Generator	. . .
rpm	revolutions per minute	. . .
RPM	Remote Processing Module	Republic Technology
RPM	Repeater Performance Monitor	. . .
RPOA	Recognized Private Operating Agency	. . .
	Used in reference to X.25 protocol selection of a transit network (when more than one such network exists)	
	sa *X.25*	
RPQ	Request Price Quotation	. . .
RPS	Ring Parameter Server	IBM
RPS/CMI	Real-time Programming System/ Communications Monitor	IBM
RQ	Respiratory Quotient	. . .
	re: Physiology	
RQBE	Relational Query By Example	. . .
RQM	Real-time Quality Measurement	ATA
RR	Receive Ready	DoD
	Command and command response in *X.25* protocol, which see	

RRDS	Relative Record Data Set	. . .
RS	Record Separator	CCITT
	Information separator 2 (IS_2) under CCITT	
	Recommendation V.3;	
	sa *CCITT*, *V.3* and *ISn*	
RS-*nnn*	Recommended Standard *nnn*	EIA
	Communications standards recommended	
	by the Electronics Industry Association	
	(EIA) A few of the more commonly	
	encountered standards are listed.	
RS-232-C	—(Data terminal interface standard)	. . .
RS-422	—(Data terminal interface standard)	. . .
RS-423	—(Data terminal interface standard)	. . .
RS-449	—(Data terminal interface standard)	. . .
RSA	Rural Service Area	FCC
	re: Cellular telephone access	
RSCS	Remote Spooling Communication Subsystem	IBM
RSDM	Rapid Systems Development Methodology	Rapid Systems Dev't.
RSE	Removeable Storage Element	. . .
	re: Computer memory, usually rotating disk	
RSEC	Radio Spectrum Engineering Criteria	. . .
RSEXEC	Resource Sharing Executive [system]	DoD
	ARPANET distributed data base system;	
	sa *ARPANET*	
RSI	Repetitive Strain Injury	. . .
	A painful malady of the wrist, common in	
	the data entry field	
	sa *CTS*, *Carpal Tunnel Syndrome*	
RSM	Remote Switch Module	AT&T
RSM	Remote System Manager	DEC
RST	Readability, Strength, Tone	ARRL
	Ham radio signal quality rating designations	
RSTS	Resource Sharing Timesharing System	DEC
RSTS/E	Resource Sharing Timesharing System/ Extended	DEC
RSX	Realtime [resource] Sharing Executive	DEC
RT	Real-Time	. . .
RT	Run-Time	IBM
RTAC	Real-Time Advisory Control	Mitech
RTAP	Real-Time Applications Platform	H-P
RTAS	Rapid Telephone Access System	Sudbury Systems
	Digitized voice dictation of medical reports	
RTB	Remote Token Bridge	. . .
RTC	Real-Time Clock	. . .

RTD	Resistance Temperature Detector	. . .
RTE	Run-Time Evaluator	Cullinet Software
RTEID	Real-Time Executive Interface Definition	Motorola
RTF	Remote Tape Facility	DEC
RTI	Remote Terminal Interface	. . .
RTIC	Real-Time Interface Coprocessor	IBM
RTIS	Radar Test Instrumentation System	Lockheed Aero.
RTL	Register Transfer Level A chip-level simulation and modeling system	. . .
RTL	Resistor Transistor Logic An integrated circuit (IC) logic family c. 1950s	. . .
RTL	Run-Time Library	DEC
RTM	Response Time Monitor	. . .
RTMP	Routing Table Maintenance (or Management) Protocol	. . .
RTOS	Real-Time Operating System	. . .
RTP	Rapid Thermal Processing re: Vapor deposition of ultra-fine layers in electronic integrated circuit wafer production	. . .
RTP	Real-Time Processor	. . .
RTR	Real-Time Reliable Pertaining to capability of operating system to act in "real time," as opposed to recorded or simulated time	. . .
RTS	Real-Time System	. . .
RTS	Register Transfer Scan	. . .
RTS	Reliable Transfer Service	. . .
RTS	Remote Terminal Stores	. . .
RTS	Request To Send	. . .
RTSI	Real-Time System Integration	. . .
RTU	Remote Terminal Unit	Amtrak
RTU	Remote Transmission Unit	. . .
RTU	Real-Time UNIX Extended UNIX (possibly with hardware) to approach real-time response; sa *UNIX*	. . .
RTV	Real-Time Video	. . .
RTV	Room Temperature Vulcanizing	Dow Corning
RTX	Real-Time Executive	. . .
Ru	Ruthenium Atomic element number 44	. . .
RU	Remote Unit	. . .

RU	Request Unit	IBM
RU	Response Unit	IBM
RUN	Running	DEC
	Digital network architecture (DNA) message	
RVDT	Rotational Velocity/Displacement Transducer	. . .
	(or Transmitter)	
RVI	Remote Visual Inspection	Olympus
RVI	Reverse Interrupt	. . .
	Bisync equivalent to *X-OFF*, which see	
RWR	Radar Warning Receiver	. . .
Rx	Receive (or Receiver)	. . .
RZ	Return to Zero	IBM
	A method of encoding magnetic tape whereby the flux changes in both directions for a corresponding binary "one"	

S

s	second	. . .
	Unit of time; also unit of angular measure	
S	S [interface]	. . .
	Four-wire connection installed at customer premises	
S	Schottky	. . .
	Name applied to various effects noted in electronic circuits attributed to the behavior of certain electronic charge carriers. Also, used in names of electronic circuit devices which take advantage of this fact in fabrication of high-speed devices. Named in honor of Swiss physicist Walter Schottky (1886–1976), discoverer of the principle.	
S	Siemen	. . .
	Unit of conductance and admittance; expressed in units of *mhos*; reciprocal of resistance: 1 mho = $(1 \text{ ohm})^{-1}$ sa *X, admittance*	
S	Sulfur	. . .
	Atomic element number 16	
S	Supervisory (format of X.25 control field)	CCITT
	re: Format of X.25 control field; sa *X.25*	
S-Band	S-Band	. . .
	High-frequency radio allocation of 2.0–4.0 GHz	
S/D	Synchro-to-Digital [converter]	. . .

S/H	Sample and Hold Also designated by *S&H);* sa SHA, *Sample and Hold Amplifier*	. . .
S/N	Signal to Noise [ratio] Sometimes designated by *SNR*	. . .
S-SEED	Symmetric Self Electro-optic Effect Device High speed (1 billion operations/second) optical switch	AT&T
SA	Source Address Field in IEEE 802.5 token ring data communications specification sa *IEEE, Institute of Electrical and Electronics Engineers*	IEEE
SA/MS	Special Access/Management System	. . .
SA-RT	Structured Architect-Real Time	Meta
SAA	Systems Application Architecture	IBM
SAAM	Simulation, Analysis, And Modelling	. . .
SABM	Set Asynchronous Balanced Mode Command in *X.25* protocol, which see	CCITT
SABME	Set Asynchronous Balanced Mode Extended	OSI
SABRE	Semi-Automatic Business-Related Environment	IBM
SAC	Set Address (space) Control	IBM
SAC	Slanted Array Compressor re: Surface acoustic wave (SAW) device fabrication	. . .
SAC	Strategic Air Command	US Air Force
SACS	Secure Access Control System	AT&T
SAD	Silicon Avalanche Diode	. . .
SADC	Sampling Analog-to-Digital Converter	. . .
SADF	Semi-Automatic Document Feeder	. . .
SAF	System Administration Facility	Novell
Safenet	Survivable Adaptable Fiberoptic-Embedded Network	US Navy
SAFER	Split Access Flexible Egress Routing	AT&T
SAFIRE	Spectroscopy of the Atmosphere using Far Infra-Red Emission	NASA
SAGE	Semi-Automatic Ground Environment First computerized air defense system (c. 1958)	US Air Force
SAGE	Stratospheric Aerosol and Gas Experiment	NASA
SAM	Sample and Analysis Management	Beckman
SAM	Scanning Acoustic Microscope	Sonotek
SAM	Security Access Monitor	DEC
SAM	Semi-Autonomous Mobility	. . .
SAM	Sequential Access Method	IBM

SAM	Serial (or Sequential) Access Memory	. . .
SAM	Stratospheric Aerosol Measurement	. . .
SAMMS	Standard Automated Materiel Management System	US Army
SAMON	SNA Applications Monitor sa *SNA, Systems Network Architecture*	IBM
SAMOS	Silicon-Aluminum Metal Oxide Semiconductor	IBM
SAMS	Storage Automation Management System	Sterling Software
SAMS	Student Aid Management System	Sigma Systems
SAO	Smithsonian Astrophysical Observatory	NASA
SAP	Service Access Point	. . .
SAP	Service Advertising Protocol	. . .
SAPI	Service Access Point Identifier	. . .
SAR	Stand Alone Restore	Innovation Data Proc.
SAR	Synthetic Aperture (or Array) Radar	. . .
SAR	Successive Approximation Register re: Analog-to-digital (A/D) conversion circuitry	. . .
SARM	Set Asynchronous Response Mode Command in *X.25* protocol, which see	CCITT
SARME	Set Asynchronous Response Mode Extended	OSI
SARMIS	Search and Rescue Management Information System	US Coast Guard
SARSCAT	Synthetic Aperture Radar Scatterometer	. . .
SAS	Service Activation System	Bellcore
SAS	Single Attachment Station	. . .
SAS	Statistical Analysis System	SAS Institute
SASE	Special Application Service Elements	. . .
SatLAN	Satellite Local Area Network	Vitalink
SATO	Self-Aligned Thick Oxide A semiconductor fabrication process	TI
SAW	Software Analysis Workstation	Cadre
SAW	Surface Acoustic Wave	. . .
Sb	Stibium Symbol for *antimony*, atomic element number 51	. . .
SB	Subnegotiation Begin TELNET command; sa *TELNET, Telecommunications Network*	DoD
SBB	Store Back Buffer	IBM
SBC	Single-Board Computer	. . .
SBC	Sub-Band Coding	. . .

SBD	Schottky Barrier Diode Semiconductor material with no stored charge used in fabrication of high-speed integrated circuits (ICs)	. . .
SBI	Synchronous Backplane Interconnect	DEC
SBIR	Small-Business Innovative Research	US Government
SBIS	Sustaining Base Information Services	US Army
SBL	Scanned Beam Laminography	. . .
SBNR	Signed Binary Number Representation	. . .
SBR	Space-Based Radar	. . .
SBS	Satellite Business Systems	. . .
SBS	Silicon Bilateral Switch Asymmetrical alternating current (AC) controlling device	. . .
SBS	Stimulated Brillouin Scattering re: Laser technology; light scattering by sound waves in in a solid or in a liquid	. . .
SBU	System Bus Unit	NCR
Sc	Scandium Atomic element number 21	. . .
SC	Suppressed Carrier	. . .
SC	Switched Capacitor re: Technique used in analog-to-digital converters	. . .
SC	Secondary Channel	. . .
SC	Short Circuit	. . .
SCA	Security, Control, and Auditing [system]	Computer Associates
SCA	Source Code Analyzer	DEC
SCADA	Supervisory Control and Data Aquisition	. . .
SCAI	Switch Computer-Automated Interface	MCI
SCAM	Scheduling Content-Addressable Memory	. . .
SCAN	Switched Circuit Automatic Network	AT&T
SCAT	Symbolic Code Assembly Translator Assembler language for IBM 7090-series computers (c. 1960)	IBM
SCATRAN	Symbolic Code Assembly Translator FORTRAN-like language for IBM 7090- series computers (c. 1960); sa *FORTRAN, Formula Translator*	Reeves, R., (OSU)
SCBA	Self-Contained Breathing Apparatus	. . .
SCC	Separation Control Character	CCITT
SCC	Serial Communications Controller (or Channel)	Motorola

SCC	Specialized Common Carrier CCITT Recomm. V.24	. . .
SCDL	Short-Cavity Dye Laser	. . .
SCF	Switched Capacitor Filter	. . .
SCG	Secondary Command Group re: IEEE Standard 488; sa *IEEE*	IEEE
SCH	Separate Carrier Heterostructure re: Laser structure	. . .
SCHG	Super-Corrected Holographic Grating	. . .
SCI	Serial Communications Interface	. . .
SCI	Source Code Input	ATI
SCILIB	Science Library	. . .
SCINET	Secure Compartmented Information Network A component of the Defense Data Network (DDN)	DoD
SCL	Screen Control Language	DEC
SCM	Software-Configuration Management	. . .
SCM	Station Configuration Management re: Fiber-distributed data interface (FDDI) standard	. . .
SCODL	Scan Conversion Object Definition Language	Matrix Imaging Sys.
SCOPE	Scientific Committee on Problems of the Environment	SCOPE
SCOPE	Supervisory Control of Program Execution	CDC
SCP	Secondary Communications Processor	Merit Network
SCP	Service Control Point	. . .
SCP	Signal Control Point	. . .
SCP	System Control Program	IBM
SCPC	Single Channel Per Carrier Very small aperture satellite (VSAT) access technique	. . .
SCPI	Standard Commands for Programmable Instrumentation re: IEEE Standard 488; sa *IEEE*	IEEE
SCR	Silicon-Controlled Rectifier	. . .
SCS	Shared Communications Service	. . .
SCS	Silicon-Controlled Switch	. . .
SCS	SNA Character String sa *SNA, Systems Network Architecture*	IBM
SCS	Society for Computer Simulation	SCS
SCS	Soil Conservation Service	USDA
SCS	System Communications Services	. . .

SCSI	Small Computer System Interface
	   High-level interface for optical storage
	   devices
		. . .

SCSR	Single-Channel Signalling Rate	. . .
SCT	Suppressed Carrier Transmission	. . .
SCU	Storage Control Unit	IBM
SCU	System Control Unit	DEC
SCUBA	Self-Contained Underwater Breathing Apparatus	. . .
SCUG	Smart Card Users Group	SCAT Conference
SCW	Space Charge Waves	. . .

SD	Send Data
	   Command in fiber-distributed data interface
	   (FDDI) standard
		. . .

SD	Start Delimiter
	   Field in IEEE 802.5 token ring data
	   communications specification
	   sa *IEEE, Institute of Electrical and*
	   Electronic Engineers
		. . .

SDA	Signal Design and Analysis	. . .
SDA	Software Disk Array	. . .
SDBN	Software-Defined Broadband Network	AT&T

SDC	Selected Device Clear
	   IEEE Standard 488 bus command;
	   sa *IEEE*
		IEEE

SDC	Synchro-to-Digital Converter	. . .

SDD-*n*	System for Distributed Databases ($n=1, 2,$
	   . . .)
	   Worldwide distributed database system
		. . .

SDDN	Software-Defined Data Network	AT&T
SDDS	Structured Description Data Set	IBM
SDF	Screen Definition Facility	IBM
SDF	Software Distribution Facility	IBM

SDH	Synchronous Digital Hierarchy
	   European data rate standard; equivalent to
	   US STS-3
	   sa *STM*-n and *STS*-n
		. . .

SDI	Standard Disk Interconnect	DEC

SDI	Strategic Defense Initiative
	   Large-scale computer project (in part)
	   Popularly known as "Star Wars"
		DoD

SDI	Switched Digital [service] International re: Data communication services	AT&T

SDIF	SGML Document Interchange Format
	   sa *SGML, Standard Generalized Markup*
	   Language
		. . .

SDIO	Stragic Defense Initiative Organization	SDIO
SDIP	Shrink Dual In-Line Package	. . .
	A miniaturized version of the dual in-line package (DIP) electronic integrated circuit (IC)	
SDIS	Switched Digital Integrated Service	AT&T
SDIS	Structured Description Index [data] Set	IBM
SDK	Software Development Kit	Microsoft
SDL	Specification and Description Language	CCITT
SDLC	Synchronous Data Link Control	IBM
	Communications protocol	
SDLC	Systems Development Life Cycle	. . .
SDLDS	Structured Description Log Data Set	IBM
SDM	Sub-rate Data Multiplexing	. . .
SDN	Software-Defined Network	AT&T
SDNI	Software-Defined Network International	AT&T
SDNS	Software-Defined Network Services	AT&T
SDP	Service Delivery Point	GSA
	Termination point within the Federal Telecommunications System (FTS)	
SDS	Software Development System	AT&T
SDS	Switched Data Service	AT&T
SDSC	San Diego Supercomputer Center	SDSC
SDSF	System Display and Search Facility	IBM
SDSI	Shared Data Set Integrity	SMM
	Data management system for Virtual Storage 1 (VS-1) and Multiple Virtual Systems (MVS)	
SDU	Service Data Unit	AT&T
SDU	Synchronous Data Unit	AT&T
SDV	Scientific Data Visualization	Hussey, K.
Se	Selenium.	. . .
	Atomic element number 34	
SE	Service Element	. . .
	re: ISO OSI seven-layer standard	
	sa *ISO, International Standards Organization* and *OSI, Open Systems Interconnection*	
SE	Shield Effectiveness	. . .
	Measure of performance of electromagnetic shielding	
SE	Subnegotiation End	DoD
	TELNET command;	
	sa *TELNET, Telecommunications Network*	
SEA	System Extension Assist	Amdahl
SEAM	Software Enhancement and Maintenance	Beckman

sec	secant	. . .
	Trigonometric function	
sec	second	. . .
	Mean solar second, unit of time; alternate form: *s*	
SEC	Secondary [address]	IEEE
	IEEE Standard 488 bus command; sa *IEEE*	
SEC	Secondary Electron Conduction	. . .
SECAM	Séquence à Mémoire	. . .
	(French) A video transmission standard	
sech	secant, hyperbolic	. . .
	Trigonometric function	
sech⁻¹	secant, inverse hyperbolic	. . .
	Trigonometric function; "angle whose hyperbolic secant is. . ."	
SEE	Simultaneous Engineering Environment	. . .
SEE	Software Engineering Environment	. . .
SEED	Self-Excited Electro-Optic Device	AT&T
SEED	Software Engineering Environment Development	III, Taiwan
SEI	Software Engineering Institute	NREN
SEI	Space Exploration Initiative	NASA
SEL	Surface-Emitting Laser	. . .
SELDS	Sealed Enclosure Leak Detection Survey	. . .
SEM	Scanning Electron Microscope	. . .
SEM	Standard Electronics Module	NAC
SEMCIP	Shipboard Electromagnetic Compatability Improvement Program	US Navy
SEMS	Seafloor Earthquake Measurement System	SNL
Ser	Serine	. . .
	A compound important in biochemistry	
SES	Severely Errored Seconds	. . .
SES	Ship Earth Station	US Navy
SES	Strategic Engineering Support	Novell
SET	Set [parameters]	CCITT
	X.25 protocol packet assembly/disassembly (PAD) command sa *X.25*	
SETA	South Eastern Telecommunications Association	SETA
SETI	Search for Extraterrestrial Intelligence	. . .
SEU	Single-Event Upset	. . .
	Disturbance of integrated circuit (IC) function due to radiation	
SF	Superframe Format	. . .

SFB	Silicon Fusion Bonding	. . .
	re: Wafer electronic circuit technology	
SFC	Supercritical Fluid Chromatography	. . .
SFD	Self-Frequency Doubling	. . .
	re: Laser optical crystals	
SFD	Start Frame Delimiter	IEEE
	Field in IEEE 802.3 Ethernet data	
	communications specification	
	sa *IEEE, Institute of Electrical and*	
	Electronics Engineers	
SFDR	Spurious-Free Dynamic Range	. . .
SFH	Simple Forwarding Header	. . .
	re: Electronic mail	
SFM	Scanning Force Microscope	. . .
SFM	Sum Frequency Mixer (or Mixing)	. . .
SFMS	Supercomputer Facilities Management	. . .
	Services	
SFS	Start of Frame Sequence	FDDI
SFT	System Fault Tolerant	. . .
SFUN	Special Functions [library]	. . .
SG	Signal-Ground	. . .
	re: Test lead arrangement in testing	
	microelectronic devices	
SG	Stochastic Gradient	. . .
	Statistical entity	
SGML	Standard Generalized Markup Language	. . .
SGS	Stereoscopic Graphics System	Tektronix
SGSIT	Surface Gate Static Induction Transistor	GTE
SGVS	Self-Guided Vehicle System	Caterpillar
SHA	Sample and Hold Amplifier	. . .
	sa *S/A* and *S&H)*	
SHARP	Self-Healing Alternate Route Protection	US West
	re: Automatic alternate path selection in	
	fiber networks	
SHARP	Spacecraft Health Automated Reasoning	NASA
	Prototype	
SHF	Super High Frequency	. . .
	3 to 30 GHz	
SHG	Second Harmonic Generation	. . .
SHNS	Self Healing Network Services	US West
	re: Automatic alternate path selection in	
	fiber networks	
SHOP	Sequential Heuristic Optimization	. . .
	Programming	
Shoran	Short range navigation	. . .
	sa *Loran-C, Long range navigation-C*	

SHPi	Super High Pi Process for manufacturing high speed npn semiconductor devices; sa *npn*	Tektronix
SHR	Superheterodyne Receiver	. . .
SHS	Smart Hydrogen Sensor	NASA
Si	Silicon Atomic element number 14	. . .
SI	Shift In A component of the binary code in CCITT Recommendation V.3 sa *CCITT* and *V.3*	CCITT
SI	Storage Interconnect	DEC
SI	Système International (French) International System [of units]	BIPM
SI	Systems Integration	. . .
SIA	Semiconductor Industry Association	SIA
SIC	Switchgear Interface Controller	. . .
SiCB	Silicon Circuit Board A high-density circuit board technology sa *MBT, Multilayer Bonding Technique, MCM-C, Multichip Module–Ceramic, MCM-D, Multichip Module–Deposited, MCM-L, Multichip Module–Laminate, VIL, Vertical In-Line*	. . .
SICBM	Small Intercontinental Ballistic Bissile	DoD
SIG	Special Interest Group	. . .
SIGGraph	Special Interest Group in Computer Graphics	ACM
SIGI	System of Interactive Guidance and Information	Educational Testing Service
SIGUCC	Special Interest Group for University and College Computing	ACM
SILEX	Semiconductor-Laser Intersatellite Link Experiment	Matra-Marconi
SIM	Set Initialization Mode re: *SDLC*, which see	IBM
SIM	Stepper Image Monitor re: Integrated circuit wafer production and inspection	Optical Associates
SIM	Strategic Information Management	. . .
SIMBAD	Set of Identifications, Measurements and Bibliography for Astronautical Data	Harvard Univ.

SIMD	Single-Instruction Multiple-Data [processor] re: Computer architecture; also designated by *SMD*	. . .
SIMM	Single In-Line Memory Module Integrated circuit packaging technology	. . .
SIMOX	Silicon-Implanted Oxide Radiation resistant transistor (gate) isolation in ICs	. . .
SIMS	Secondary Ion Mass Spectrometry	. . .
SIMS	Space Information Management System	US Navy
sin	sine Trigonometric function	. . .
$\sin^{-1}$	—arc sine Trigonometric function; inverse sine: "angle whose sine is . . ."	. . .
SINAD	Signal-to-Noise-And-Distortion	. . .
SINDA	Systems-Improved Numerical Differencing Analyzer	NASA
SINET	Schlumberger Information Network	Schlumberger
sinh	sine, hyperbolic Trigonometric function	. . .
$\sinh^{-1}$	sine, inverse hyperbolic Trigonometric function; "angle whose hyperbolic sine is . . ."	. . .
SINPO	Signal strength, Interference, Noise, Propagation disturbance, Overall merit A method of rating reception of radio signals where factors range from 5 (best) to 1 (poorest)	. . .
SIO	Serial Input/Output	. . .
SIO	Start Input/Output	IBM
SIO	Systems Interconnect Operation	Intel
SIP	Single In-line Package (or Plastic) re: packaging of electronic components; sa *DIP*, *Dual In-line Package (or Plastic)*	. . .
SIP	SMDS Interface Protocol sa *SMDS*, *Switched Multi-Megabit Data Service*	. . .
SIP	SMDS Internet Protocol re: T3 communications service; sa *T3* and *SMDS*, *Switched Multi-Megabit Data Service*	Internet
SIPMOS	Single In-line Package Metal Oxide Semiconductor Composite acronym: *SIP* + *MOS*	Siemens
SIR	Shuttle Imaging Radar	Bell Aerospace

SIR	Surface Insulation Resistance	. . .
SIRTF	Space Infrared Telescope Facility	NASA
	Part of NASA's *Great Observatory Program,*	
	GOP	
	sa *NASA*	
SIS	Strategic Information System	. . .
SIS	Student Information System	SCT
SIS	Superconductor/Insulator/Superconductor	JPL/NASA
	re: Solid-state (SS) fabrication technology	
SISD	Single-Instruction Single-Data [processor]	. . .
	re: Computer architecture	
SIT	Silicon-Intensified Tube	. . .
	re: Active photorecording device (camera)	
	for streak image recording	
SIT	Static Induction Transistor	GTE
SIT	System Initialization Table	IBM
SIU	System Interface Unit	. . .
SKIMP	Simultaneous Kinetic Imaging of Multiple	S. Morris et al.
	Photophores	
Skynet	Sky Network	AT&T
	AT&T satellite service	
SLA	Serial Link Adapter	IBM
SLA	Stereo Lithography Apparatus	3-D Systems
SLAC	Stanford Linear Accelerator Complex	Stanford Univ.
SLAM	Scanning Laser Acoustic Microscope	. . .
SLAM	Simulation Language for Alternative Modeling	. . .
SLAR	Side-Looking Airborne Radar	US Coast
		Guard
SLB	Single-Layer Board	. . .
	re: Single-layer printed circuit boards (PCBs)	
SLC	Stanford Linear Collider	Stanford Univ.
SLC	Surface Laminar Circuit	IBM
	re: Dense circuit packaging technology	
SLD	Standard Longitude Difference	. . .
	Difference between local time and	
	Greenwich Mean Time (GMT)	
SLD	Super-Luminescent Diode	. . .
	A solid-state (SS) incoherent light source	
SLDM	Synchronous Long-Distance Modem	. . .
SLED	Surface Light-Emitting Diode	. . .
	A solid-state (SS) incoherent light source	
SLIC	Subscriber Line Interface Circuit	. . .
SLIP	Serial Line Internet Protocol	. . .
	Internet protocol (IP) via RS-232-C	
	protocol;	
	sa *RS-232-C*	

SLM	Single Longitudinal Mode [oscillator]	. . .
	A method of producing stable oscillations in laser diodes for fiber-optic communications	
SLM	Scanning Laser Microscope	Tavaglione, D.
SLM	Spacial Light Modulation(-or)	. . .
SLO	Swept Local Oscillator	. . .
SLP	Single-Link Procedure	CCITT
	X.75 protocol circuit description; sa *X.25*	
SLR	Single-Lens Reflex [camera]	. . .
SLS	Stabilized Light Source	. . .
	re: Optical standards	
SLS	Station Logic Switch	. . .
SLS	Strained Layer Superlattice	. . .
	re: Crystal structure	
SLSE	Software Lifecycle Support Environment	DoD
SLT	Solid-Logic Technology	. . .
	re: Solid-state (SS) electronic logic circuitry	
Sm	Samarium	. . .
	Atomic element number 62	
SM	Session Manager	IBM
SM	Surface Mount	. . .
	sa *SMT, Surface Mount Technology*	
SMA	Sub-Miniature A [connector]	. . .
	A commonly used miniature radio frequency (RF) connector	
SMAE	System Management Application Entity	. . .
SMAP	System Management Application Process	. . .
SMART	Sony Multi-Assembly Robot Technology	Sony
SMB	Server Message Block	IBM
SMB	Structured Message Block	. . .
SMB	Sub-Miniature B [connector]	. . .
	A commonly used miniature RF (radio frequency) connector	
SMC	Sub-Miniature C [connector]	. . .
	A commonly used miniature RF (radio frequency) connector	
SMD	Single instruction/Multiple Data	. . .
	Also designated by *SIMD*, which see	
SMD	Standard Military Drawing	DESC
SMD	Storage Module Drive (or Device)	. . .
SMD	Surface Mount Device	. . .
	Integrated circuit (IC) or other electronic device that is attached to a printed circuit board (PCB) without using plug-in sockets or connectors	
	sa *SMT, Surface Mount Technology*	

SMDI	Simplified Message Desk Interface	. . .
SMDR	Station Message Detail Recording	AT&T
SMDS	Switched Multi-megabit Data Service	Bellcore
SMEX	Small Explorer [program]	NASA
	Part of NASA's *Great Observatory Program,* *GOP,* which see	
SMF	Single-Mode Fiber	. . .
SMF	Systems Management Facility	IBM
SMG	Screen Management Guidelines	DEC
SMI	Structure of Management Information	. . .
SMI	System Management Interrupt	. . .
SMIS	Specific Management Information-passing Service	
SMM	System Management Mode	Intel
SMP	Shared Memory Processor	. . .
SMP	Symmetrical Multi-Processing	H-P
SMP	System Modification Program	IBM
SMP/E	System Modification Program, Extended	IBM
SMPS	Switch Mode Power Supply	. . .
SMR	Specialized Mobile Radio	Millicom
SMS	Service Management System	. . .
SMS	Site Management Station	DEC
SMS	Storage Management Services	Novell
SMS	Systems Managed Storage	IBM
SMSCRC	Standard Multiuser Small-Computer Requirements Contract	GSA
SMT	Standard Mean Time	. . .
SMT	Station Management re: Fiber-distributed data interface (FDDI) standard	. . .
SMT	Storage Management Task	Masstor
SMT	Surface Mount Technology Surface mounting of components as opposed to socket mounting; sa *LGA, Land Grid Array, PGA, Pin Grid Grid Array* and *SMD, Surface Mount Device*	. . .
SMTCON	Surface Mount Technology Conference [and Exposition]	SMTCON
SMTP	Simple Mail Transfer Protocol	. . .
Sn	Stannum Symbol for *tin,* atomic element number 50	. . .
SNA	Systems Network Architecture	IBM
SNAC	SNA Network Access Controller sa *SNA, Systems Network Architecture*	. . .
SNADS	Systems Network Architecture Distributed Services	IBM

SNAFS	Systems Network Architecture File Services	. . .
SNAP	Sub-Network Address Protocol	. . .
SNE/FTF	Strategic Network Environment/File Transfer Facility	. . .
SNI	Subscriber Network Interface	. . .
SNI	SNA Network Interconnection sa *SNA, Systems Network Architecture*	IBM
SNI	Systems Network Interconnection	. . .
SNL	Sandia National Laboratory	SNL
SNMP	Simple Network Management Protocol	. . .
SNMP	Simple Network Monitoring Protocol	. . .
SNOBOL	—String-Oriented Symbolic Language	. . .
SNR	Signal-to-Noise Ratio Variant of *S/N*	. . .
SNRM	Set Normal Response Mode	OSI
SNRME	Set Normal Response Mode, Extended	OSI
SO	Shift Out A component of the binary code in CCITT Recommendation V.3 sa *CCITT* and *V.3*	CCITT
SO	Small Outline re: integrated circuit (IC) chip physical configuration	. . .
SOA	Semiconductor Optical Amplifier	Hitachi
SOAP	Symbolic Optimum Assembly Program	IBM
SOAPY	Symbolic Optimum Assembly Program-Y SOAP for an IBM 650 without the "alphabetic feature" sa *SOAP, Symbolic Optimum Assembly Program*	Henderson, John, MPRL
SOC	Services Oversight Center A monitoring system whereby the General Services Administration ensures Federal Telecommunications System (FTS) standards	GSA
SODA	Small Optical Design and Analysis	Don Small Optics
SOEMI	Serial Original Equipment Manufacturer (OEM) Interface	IBM
SOFIA	Stratospheric Observatory for Inra-Red Astronomy Part of NASA's *Great Observatory Program, GOP*, which see	NASA
SOG	Sapphire on Garnet re: Integrated circuit substrate	. . .

SOH	Start Of Header Transmission control 1 (TC₁) under CCITT Recommendation V.3; sa *CCITT*, *V.3* and *TC*ₙ	CCITT
SOI	Silicon-On-Insulator Semiconductor wafer technology with high breakdown voltage	. . .
SOI	Standard Operator Interface Software using standard icons, indicators, etc., for coordinate measuring machines (CMMs)	Automation Software
SOIC	Small-Outline Integrated Circuit	. . .
SOICS	Special Operations Improved Cryptographic System	ITT
SOJ	Stand-Off Jammer A radar jamming technique	Hughes
SOLP	Small-Outline Large-Package	. . .
SOLT	Short-Open Load-Through Vector network analyzer calibration methodology	. . .
SOM	Satellite Office Microfilm	. . .
SOM	Start of Message	. . .
SONAR	Sound Navigation and Ranging Now accepted as an English word: *sonar*	. . .
Sonet	Synchronous Optical Network Variant of *SONET*	. . .
SONET	Synchronous Optical Network Also designated by *Sonet*	US/CCITT
SOOT	Significantly Out Of Tolerance	. . .
SOR	Synchrotron Orbital Radiation	. . .
SOS	Silicon On Sapphire Substrate for advanced integrated circuits (ICs)	H-P
SOS	Special Ordered Sets Processing algorithm in *MPSX*, which see	IBM
SP	Single Pole [switch]	. . .
SP	Space A component of the binary code in CCITT Recommendation V.3 sa *CCITT* and *V.3*	CCITT
SP	System Product	IBM
SPAG	Standards Promotion and Applications Group European network standards organization	SPAG
SPAN	Space Physics Analysis Network	NASA
SPAN	System Performance Analyzer	. . .

SPARC	Scalable Processor Architecture	. . .
SPARC	Standards Planning and Requirements Committee	ANSI
SPC	SCSI Protocol Controller sa *SCSI, Small Computer Systems Interface*	Fujitsu
SPC	Statistical Process Control	. . .
SPC	Stored Program Control	. . .
SPCS	Service Point Command Service	IBM
SPD	Serial Poll Disable IEEE Standard 488 bus command; sa *IEEE*	IEEE
SPDT	Single-Pole Double-Throw [switch] A switch to select one of two circuits	. . .
SPDU	Session Protocol Data Unit	. . .
SPE	Serial Poll Enable IEEE Standard 488 bus command; sa *IEEE*	IEEE
SPE	Synchronous Payload Envelope Part of the synchronous optical network (SONET) data transmission signal	. . .
SPEC	Systems Performance Evaluation Cooperative	H-P et al.
SPF	Shortest Path First	. . .
SPI	Single Program Initiator	IBM
SPICE	Simulation Program with Integrated Circuit Emphasis	. . .
SPID	Service Profile Identifier re: *ISDN, Integrated Services Digital Network*	AT&T
SPIE	Society of Photo-optical Instrumentation Engineers	SPIE
SPIKE	Science Planning Interactive Knowledge Environment [system]	NASA
SPIRES	Stanford Public Information Retrieval System	Stanford Univ.
SPL	Sound Pressure Level Expressed in units of *decibels, dB* with respect to a reference level	. . .
SPL	Structured Programming Language	. . .
SPL	Student Programming Language Algol 60 subset of *PL/I*, which see	Stanford Univ.
SPM	Scanning Probe Microscope (-scopy)	. . .
SPM	Self-Phase Modulation re: Laser technology	. . .
SPM	Statistical Packet Multiplexing re: High-speed telecommunications technology	. . .
SPM	Systems Performance Monitor	Cray Research

SPMUX	Sperry Multiplexer	Sperry
SP*n*T	Single-Pole *n*-Throw [switch]	. . .
	Single-circuit switch with *n* circuit positions	
SPOOL	Simultaneous Peripheral Operation on Line	. . .
SPP	Sequenced Packet Protocol	. . .
SPP	Serial Pattern Processor	. . .
SPR	Statistical Pattern Recognition	. . .
SPREAD	Supercomputer Project Research Experiment for Access and Development	Stanford Univ.
SPS	Samples Per Second	. . .
SPS	Standard Positioning Service	. . .
	A precision time/frequency service	
SPS	Standby Power Supply (or System)	. . .
	Compare with *UPS, Uninterruptible Power Supply*	
SPS	Symbolic Programming System	. . .
SPSS	Statistical Package for the Social Sciences	
SPST	Single-Pole Single-Throw	. . .
	A simple single-circuit on/off switch	
SPT	Symbolic Programming Tape	Honeywell
SPU	System Processing Unit	Ztel
SPUDT	Single-Phase Uni-Drectional Transducer	. . .
SPW	Signal Processing WorkSystem	Comdisco
SPWG	Site Security Policy Handbook Working Group	NREN
SPX	Sequenced Packet Exchange	Novell
SP3T	Single-Pole Triple-Throw [switch]	. . .
	Single-circuit switch with three positions sa *SPnT, DPnT* and *nPnT*	
SQA	Software Quality Assurance	. . .
SQE	Signal Quality Error	. . .
SQF	Subjective Quality Factor	*Popular Photography*
	A means of rating lenses for center and edge performance	
SQL	Structured Query Language	. . .
SQL/DS	Structured Query Language/Data System	IBM
SQMS	Single Queue Multiple Server	. . .
SQUID	Superconductive Quantum Interference Device	Westinghouse
SQW	Single Quantum Well	. . .
	re: Laser technology	
sr	steradian	. . .
	Unit of solid angle measure	
Sr	Strontium	. . .
	Atomic element number 38	

SR	Slew Rate	. . .
	re: Servo mechanisms, operational amplifier	
	specifications, mechanical plotter head	
	movements, etc.	
SR-TB	Source-Routing Transparent Bridge	. . .
	Ethernet token ring bridge;	
	sa *Ethernet*	
SRA	Selective Routing Arrangement	AT&T
SRA	Source Routing Accelerator	. . .
SRAM	Static Random Access Memory	. . .
	Memory chip that needs no refreshing to	
	retain data Compare with *DRAM*	
	sa *DRAM* for electronic converse	
SRB	Scheduler Request Block	IBM
SRB	Single Route Broadcast	. . .
SRB	Solid Rocket Booster	. . .
SRC	Stored Response Chain	IBM
	A series of instructions or responses to be	
	executed in response to a system inquiry	
SRC	Supercomputer Research Center	. . .
SRD	Step Recovery Diode	. . .
SRDM	Sub-Rate Data Multiplexer	AT&T
	Also designated by *SDM, Sub-rate Data*	
	Multiplexing	
SREJ	Selective Reject	OSI
SRF	Self-Resonance Frequency	. . .
SRIC	Switching-Regulator Integrated Circuit	. . .
	Integrated circuit (IC) chips containing both	
	a switching regulator and a power switch	
SRM	Shared Resource Manager	H-P
SRM	Short-Range Modem	RAD
SRM	Standard Reference Material	NIST
SRM	Storage and Resource Management [system]	Computer
		Associates
SRM	System Reference Manual	DEC
SRM	Systems Resources Manager	IBM
SRMU	Subrate Data Multiplexer	BOC
SRN	Software Release Notice	DARPA
SRP	Signal Relay Point	Northern
		Telecom
SRPI	Server-Requester Programming Interface	IBM
SRQ	Service Request	IEEE
	IEEE Standard 488 bus command;	
	sa *IEEE*	
SRS	Stimulated Raman Scattering	. . .
	re: laser technology; light scattering by	
	sound waves in a solid or a liquid	

SRT	Silicon Resistance Thermometer	. . .
SRT	Source Routing-Transparent	IBM
	A data transmission standard	
SRT	Specular Reflectance and Transmittance	Optronic Laboratories
SRT	Sweeney Robertson Tocher	. . .
	A division logic used in computer integrated circuit (IC) central processing unit (CPU) chips	
SRT	System Recovery Table	IBM
SRTB	Source Routing Transparent Bridge	IBM
SS	Sampled Servo	. . .
SS	Satellite Switching	. . .
SS	Signal-Signal	. . .
	re: Test lead arrangement in testing microelectronic devices	
SS	Solid-State	. . .
SSA	Source Spectral Analysis	Optronic Laboratories
SSB	Single Sideband [modulation]	. . .
SSBLT	Source Synchronous Block Transfer	. . .
	A technique used to increase the transfer rate of data across a computer bus	
SSC	Superconductor Super Collider	DoE
SSCC	Special Service Common Carrier	. . .
SSCP	System Services Control Point	IBM
SSD	Solid-State DASD	. . .
	sa *DASD, Direct Access Storage Device*	
SSD	Solid-State Disk	. . .
	Synonym for *Solid State DASD*	
	sa *DASD, Direct Access Storage Device*	
SSD	Solid-state Storage Device	Cray Research
	Synonym for *Direct Access DASD*	
	sa *DASD, Direct Access Storage Device*	
SSEC	Selective Sequence Electronic Calculator	IBM
	IBM's precursor to high-speed computers (c. 1947)	
SSI	Small-Scale Integration	. . .
	IC technology developed c. 1960 containing <1000 gates	
SSI	Synchronous Serial Interface	. . .
SSMA	Spread Spectrum Multiple Access	. . .
	CDMA in which all carriers occupy the entire bandwidth of a transmitted signal; usually connected with satellite communications; sa *CDMA, Code Division Multiple Access*	

SSME	Space Shuttle Main Engine	NASA
SSMP	Shared Symmetric Multiprocessor	. . .
SS*n*	Signalling System *n* (*n*=5, 7, . . .) Telecommunications control systems	AT&T
SSOP	Shrink Small Outline Package re: Miniaturized integrated circuit (IC) design (with 50-mil pin spacing)	TI
SSP	Scientific Subroutine Package	IBM
SSP	Service Switching Point	CCITT
SSP	System Support Program	IBM
SSPA	Solid-State Phased Array re: Radar antenna technology	TI
SSPM	Solid-State Photosensitive Material	. . .
SSR	Secondary Surveillance Radar	. . .
SSR	Solid-State Relay	. . .
SSRL	Stanford [University] Synchrotron Research Laboratory A "third generation" synchrotron	Stanford Univ.
SSS	Solid-State Storage sa *SSD, Solid-State DASD, Solid-State Disk,* and *Solid-State Storage Device,* and *DASD,* *Direct Access Storage Device*	. . .
SST	Spread Spectrum Technology (or Transmission)	. . .
SST	Super Sonic Transport	. . .
SST	Suspended Substrate Technology	Reactel
SSTO	Single Stage To Orbit re: Space rocket technology in which a single rocket motor is sufficient to put the payload into orbit	NASA
SSTV	Slow Scan Tele-Video (or Television)	. . .
SS7	Signalling System Seven	CCITT
ST	Stream Protocol Packet-switching protocol used for voice/ video traffic	. . .
ST	Subminiature "T" [connector]	. . .
ST-LCD	Super Twist Liquid Crystal Display High-contrast liquid crystal display (LCD)	. . .
STA	Spanning Tree Algorithm	. . .
STAIRS	Storage And Information Retrieval System	IBM
STAM	Shared Tape (and disk) Allocation Manager	SMM
STAMIS	Standard Army Management Information System	US Army
STARS	Surveillance Target Attack System Advanced high-resolution airborne radar system	US Air Force

STAT	Status [request] X.25 packet assembly/disassembly (PAD) command; sa *X.25*	CCITT
STATMON	Status Monitor	IBM
STB	Strobe	. . .
STC	Science and Technology Center	NSF
STC	Society for Technical Communications	STC
STC	Society of Telecommunications Consultants	STC
STDADS	Space Telescope Data Archival and Distribution Service	NASA
STDM	Statistical Time Division Multiplexer	. . .
STDMA	Slotted Time Division Multiple Access Local area network (LAN) access protocol for fixed-length packets	. . .
STE	Signalling Terminal X.75 protocol network node; sa *X.25*	CCITT
STEN	Strobe Enable	. . .
STEP	Standard for Exchange of Product [model] Data	ISO
STEP	Systematic Test and Evaluation Process	SQE
STERM*	Synchronous Termination [signal] Note: "*" indicates that a signal (called "active high") must be present at the circuit terminal in order for the described function to be activated.	. . .
STFF	Schmitt Trigger Flip-Flop Electronic multivibrator (MV) circuit with Schmitt trigger signal input conditioning	. . .
STI	Standard Tape Interconnect	DEC
STIS	Science and Technology Information System	NSF
STL	Schottky Transistor Logic re: High-speed integrated circuit (IC) technology sa *S, Schottky*	. . .
STM	Scanning Tunneling Microscope	. . .
STM	Self-Test Module	. . .
STM	Single Transverse Mode re: Laser operational mode	. . .
STM	SONET Transmission Manager High-speed communications switch; sa *SONET*	Adaptive
STM	Synchronous Transfer Mode	. . .

STM-*n*	Synchronous Transfer Mode, level *n*	. . .
	High-speed data transfer standard	
	n=1 ⟹ 155.52 Mbps Theoretically, other	
	modes can be developed	
	sa *SDH, Synchronous Digital Hierarchy*;	
	STM-n, *Synchronous Transfer Mode*-n; and	
	STS-n, *Synchronous Transport Signal*-n	
STN	Scientific and Technical Network	. . .
STN	Super-Twisted Nematic [display]	. . .
	A form of liquid crystal display (LCD)	
STOCC	Space Telescope Operations Control Center	NASA
STOKEN	Space Token	IBM
STOL	Short Takeoff and Landing	. . .
	re: Aircraft	
STP	Shielded Twisted Pair	. . .
	re: Local area network (LAN) cabling	
STP	Signal (or Service) Transfer Point	AT&T
STP	Spanning Tree Protocol	Vitalink
STP	Standard Temperature and Pressure	
	Refers to one standard atmosphere of	
	pressure (760 mm Hg) and zero degrees	
	Centigrade (C)	
STRAM	Self-Timed Random Access Memory	Fujitsu
STRESS	Structural Engineering System Solver	. . .
STRIDE	Strategically Tiered Regionally Integrated Data	GSA
	Environment	
STRUDL	Structural Design Language	. . .
STS	Synchronous Transport Signal	. . .
STS-*n*	Synchronous Transport Signal, Level *n*	. . .
	Synchronous optical network (SONET) data	
	communications signal *n*=1 ⟹ 51.84 Mbps	
	n=2 ⟹ 103.68 Mbps . . . etc. in 51.84 Mbps	
	multiples	
	sa *SDM, Sub-rate Data Multiplexing* and	
	STM-n, *Synchronous Transfer Mode*-n	
STScI	Space Telescope Science Institute	STScI
STSX	Synchronous Transport Signal Cross-Connect	CCITT
STTL	Schottky Transistor-Transistor Logic	. . .
	re: High-speed integrated circuit (IC)	
	technology	
	sa *S, Schottky*	
STU	Secure Telephone Unit	DoD
STX	Start of Text	CCITT
	Transmission control 2 (TC$_2$) under CCITT	
	Recommendation V.3;	
	sa *CCITT, V.3* and *TC*$_n$	

SUB	Substitute Character	CCITT
	A component of the binary code in CCITT Recommendation V.3	
	sa *CCITT* and *V.3*	
SUBS	Single-User Benchmark Set	DEC
SUNET	Swedish University Network	SUNET
SUPER!	Supercomputing by University People for Education and Research	SUPER!
SURANet	Southeastern Universities Research Association Network	SURA
SURE	Semi-Markov Unreliability Range Evaluation	NASA
SUS	Silicon Unilateral Switch	. . .
SUSP	System Use Sharing Protocol	Rock Ridge Group
SVC	Supervisor Call	IBM
SVC	Switched Virtual Circuit	. . .
SVD	Singular Value Decomposition	. . .
	A mathematical computation used in signal processing technology	
SVGA	Super Video Graphics Array	. . .
SVID	System V Interface Definition	AT&T
SVP	Surge Voltage Protector	. . .
SVS	Single Virtual Storage	IBM
SVS	Switched Voice Service	AT&T
SW	Short Wave	. . .
	re: Radio transmissions above approximately 1600 kHz	
SWAS	Submillimeter Wave Astronomy Satellite	NASA
	Part of NASA's *Great Observatory Program*, *GOP*	
	sa *NASA*	
SWAT	Stock Watch Automated Tracking	NASD
SWIFT	Society for Worldwide Interbank Financial Telecommunication	SWIFT
SWIR	Short-Wave Infrared	. . .
	Equivalent to near infrared (NIR)	
SWL	Short-Wave Listener	. . .
SWP	Software Write Protect	. . .
SWPS	Strategic War Planning System	US Air Force
SWR	Standing Wave Ratio	. . .
SYMAP	Synagraphic Mapping [system]	Dougenik & Sheehan
SYN	Synchronous Idle	CCITT
	Transmission control 9 (TC_9) under CCITT Recommendation V.3;	
	sa *CCITT*, *V.3* and *TC_n*	

| SYSGEN | System Generation | IBM |
| SYSIN | System Input | IBM |

T

t	time	. . .
T	Tera	. . .
	Prefix for 10^{12}	
T	Temperature	. . .
	In scientific literature, expressed in units of degrees Celsius, symbol: °C	
	sa *C, Celsius*	
T	Thymine	. . .
	A compound important in biochemistry; a component of *DNA*, which see	
T/H	Track and Hold	. . .
	Also designated by *T&H)*	
T&H	Track and Hold	. . .
	Also designated by *T/H*	
T-NDS	T1 Network Diagnostic System	Larse
T-R	Transmit-Receive [tube]	. . .
	Designation given to a device in shared-antenna radar systems, which is used for protection of receiving equipment during transmission of radar signals also designated by *ATR, Anti-Transmit-Receive*	
T/S	Terminal Server	. . .
T-0	Telecommunications Level 0	. . .
	Alternate form; see *T0*	
T-1	Transmission [link] 1	. . .
	Alternate form; see *T1*	
T-3	Transmission [link] 3	. . .
	Alternate form; see *T3*	
Ta	Tantalum	. . .
	Atomic element number 73	
TA	Technology Assessment	. . .
TA	Terminal Adapter	CCITT
TAB	Tape-Automated Bonding	. . .
TABS	Telemetry Asynchronous Block Serial [protocol]	. . .
TAC	Tactical Advanced Computer	US Navy
TAC	Telecommunications Associations Council	TAC
TAC	The Application Connection	Lotus
	Micro-to-Mainframe link	
TACCS	Tactical Army Combat [service support] Computer System	US Army

TACE	Traffic Analysis and Control Extension	Vitalink
TACS	Telebit Asynchronous Communications Server	Telebit
TAD	Talk Address Device	IEEE
	IEEE Standard 488 bus command;	
	sa *IEEE*	
TAE	Transportable Applications Environment	NASA
TAF	Terminal Access Facility	IBM
TAG	Talk Address Group	IEEE
	re: IEEE Standard 488;	
	sa *IEEE*	
TAM	Terminal Activity Monitor	DEC
TAMMIS	Theater Army Medical Management	US Army
	Information System	
tan	tangent	. . .
	Trigonometric function	
tan^{-1}	—arctangent	. . .
	Trigonometric function; inverse tangent:	
	"angle whose tangent is . . ."	
tanh	tangent, hyperbolic	. . .
	Trigonometric function	
tanh^{-1}	tangent, inverse hyperbolic	. . .
	Trigonometric function: "angle whose	
	hyperbolic tangent is . . ."	
TAP	Test Access Port	. . .
TAR	Test Accuracy Ratio	. . .
TASI	Time Assignment Speech Interpolation	. . .
TAT	Trans-Atlantic Telecommunications	. . .
TAT-X	Trans-Atlantic Telecommunications [cable]	British Telecom/MTI
TAXIR	Taxonic Information Retrieval	. . .
	Biological specimen data retrieval system	Rogers, David
TAZ	Transient Absorption Zener [diode]	. . .
Tb	Terbium	. . .
	Atomic element number 65	
TB	Terabyte	. . .
	10^{12} bytes	
TBBS	The Bread Board System	. . .
	Host program for bulletin boards	
TBC	Twin Beam Contact	AMP
	re: Electronic circuit connector design with	
	two rows of connectors	
TBE	Time Base Error	. . .
	A measure of tape recorder performance	
TBGG	Two Boundary Grid Generation	. . .

Tc	Technetium	. . .
	Atomic element number 43	
TC	Temperature Compensated (or Compensation)	. . .
TC	Transmission Control	CCITT
TCA	Task Control Architecture	CMU
TCA	Task Control Area	IBM
TCA	Tele-Communications Association	TCA
TCA	Transconductance Amplifier	. . .
TCAM	Telecommunications Access Method	IBM
TCAP	Transaction Capabilities Application	AT&T
	Applications protocol implementation of	
	CCITT SS7, which see	
TCAS	Traffic Alert and Collision Avoidance	. . .
	System	
TCB	Thread Control Block	IBM
TCB	Trusted Computing Base	DoD/AT&T
TCC	Technology Coordination Center	NREN
TCC	TeleCommunications Closet	. . .
TCCC	Technical Committee for Computer	IEEE
	Communications	
TCCC	Tower Control Computer Complex	. . .
	re: Analysis of aircraft radar data	
TCDF	T Cumulative Distribution Function	. . .
	re: Statistical analysis	
TCE	Thermal Coefficient of Expansion	. . .
TCK	Test Clock	. . .
TCM	Thermal Conduction Module	. . .
	Junction of dissimilar metals which absorb	
	heat when an electric current is passed	
	through it; Peltier device	
TCM	Time Compression Multiplexing	. . .
TC_n	Transmission Control n ($n=1, 2, 3, \ldots, 10$)	CCITT
	The CCITT designated characters *ACK*,	
	DLE, ENQ, EOT, ETB, ETX, NAK, SOH,	
	STX and *SYN*, which see	
TCP	Transmission Control Protocol	. . .
TCP/IP	Transmission Control Protocol/Internet	Internet
	Protocol	
TCT	Take Control—Transfer	IEEE
	IEEE Standard 488 bus command;	
	sa *IEEE*	
TCT	Task Control Table	IBM
TCU	Transmission Control Unit	. . .
TCXO	Temperature-Compensated Crystal	. . .
	Oscillator	

TD	Transmit Data	. . .
	re: *RS-232-C* protocol, which see	
TD	Tunnel Diode	. . .
TDBI	Test During Burn-In	. . .
TDBS	Text [architecture] Database System	Paralog
TDC	Tape Data Controller	. . .
TDCAM	Table-Driven Computer Access Method	IBM
	re: Time share system (TSS) network	
TDCC	Transportation Data Coordinating Committee	EDIA
	re: Data transmission standards	
TDD	Telecommunications Device for the Deaf	AT&T
TDE	Time Displacement Error	. . .
	A measure of tape recorder performance	
TDE	Total Dynamic Error	. . .
	A measure of performance quality of electronic circuits, especially in sample/hold (S/H) devices	
TDF	Transborder Data Flow	. . .
TDHS	Time-Domain Harmonic Scaling	. . .
	re: Voice compression technology	
TDI	Test Data In	. . .
TDI	Time Delay and Integration	. . .
TDL	Test and Diagnostic Language	. . .
TDM	Time Division Multiplexing	. . .
TDMA	Time Division Multiple Access	. . .
TDO	Test Data Out	. . .
TDOS	Tape and Disk Operating System	IBM
TDP	Thymidine Diphosphate	. . .
	A compound important in biochemistry	
TDR	Thermal Delay Relay	. . .
TDR	Time Delay Relay	. . .
TDR	Time Domain Reflectometer (or Reflectometry)	. . .
TDRS	Tracking and Data Relay Satellite	NASA
TDRSS	Tracking and Data Realy Satellite System	NASA
TDS	Terrestrial Data (or Digital) Service	. . .
TDS	Test Development Software	. . .
TDWR	Terminal Doppler Weather Radar	. . .
Te	Tellurium	. . .
	Atomic element number 52	
TE	Terminal Equipment	CCITT
TE	Thermoelectric	. . .
TE	Tracking Error	. . .
	re: Computer disk drive actuator positioning accuracy	

TE	Transverse Electric [mode] re: Wave propagation in fiber-optic communications	
TEC	Transparent Electrical Conductor	. . .
TECO	Text Editor and Corrector	DEC
TECS	Treasury Enforcement Control System	US Customs
TEDI	Text Editor	Cray Research
TEE	Transesophageal Echocardiography Ultrasound imaging technology	. . .
TEF	Thermodynamic Electret Film	. . .
Teflon	Tetrafluorocarbon	DuPont
TEI	Terminal Endpoint Identifier	. . .
TEL	Terminal Emulation Language	Metafile
TEL-A-GRAF	TEL-A-GRAF Computer graphics software package	. . .
telco	telephone company Generic term for any telephone/ telecommunications company	. . .
Telecom	Telecom French satellite communications system	Telecom
Telex	Teleprinter Exchange	. . .
TELNET	Telecommunications Network Used as a noun to describe the network and as a verb to describe the file transfer process over the network; not to be confused with *Telenet*, a proprietary telecommunications network	. . .
TELOPS	Telemetry On-Line Processing System	IBM
TEM	Transmission Electron Microscope	. . .
TEM	Transverse Electromagnetic [wave] re: wave mechanics within a microwave solid-state (SS) device	. . .
TEM	Transverse Electromagnetic Mode re: Wave propagation in fiber-optic communications	. . .
TEM	Tunneling Electron Microscope	. . .
TEMPEST	—TEMPEST A term used in reference to the compromise of information from computer or communications devices or in the transmission of such information	. . .
TEO	Technical Electronic Office	Data General
TEP	Transverse Electric Polarization	. . .
TER	Total External Reflectance	. . .
teraops	tera operations per second re: Computer central processing unit (CPU) speed; 10^{12} operations per second	. . .

TES	Terminal Emulation Server	Hudson Laboratories
TeV	Tera electron-Volts 10^{12} electron volts Sometimes designated by *TEV*	. . .
Tex	Tex [programming language]	Knuth, Donald
TE1	Terminal Endpoint Type 1 re: Directly connected Integrated Services Digital Network (ISDN) devices	AT&T
TE1	Terminal Equipment [new]	CCITT
TE2	Terminal Equipment 2	CCITT
TE2	Terminal Endpoint Type 2 Non-ISDN-supported devices (RS-232-C, V.24, Ethernet, etc.) sa *ISDN, Integrated Services Digital Network, RS-232-C* and *V.24*	AT&T
TFE	Tetrafluoroethylene Teflon	. . .
TFEL	Thin-Film Electro-Luminescent [display]	. . .
TFIS	Timeline Financial Information System	Timeline
TFR	Tightly Folded Resonator re: Laser design	. . .
TFT	Thin-Film Transistor Technology commonly used in flat color displays	. . .
TFTP	Trivial File Transfer Protocol	. . .
TFTR	Tokamak Fusion Test Reactor A toroidal plasma device	. . .
TGA	Thermogravimetric Analysis	. . .
Th	Thorium Atomic element number 90	. . .
TH	Time-Hopped Re: Covert message detection; sa *FH, Frequency-Hopped* and *PN, Pseudonoise* for related acronyms	. . .
TH	Thymine A compound important in biochemistry	. . .
THAM	Tris(hydroxymethyl)aminomethane	. . .
THD	Total Harmonic Distortion	. . .
THE	Threshold Excision Frequency domain representation of a spread spectrum signal	. . .
THEnet	Texas Higher Education Network	TX Dept. of Higher Ed.
THF	Tetrahydrofuran	. . .

THF	Tremendously High Frequency 300 to 3000 GHz	. . .
THG	Third Harmonic Generation Laser process to produce higher harmonic wavelengths	. . .
THOR	Tandy High-Density Optical Recording	Tandy/R-S
Thr	Threonine A compound important in biochemistry	. . .
THT	Token Holding Timer re: Token ring local area network (LAN) technology	. . .
THz	Tera Hertz 10^{12} Hertz	. . .
Ti	Titanium Atomic element number 22	. . .
TI	Test Indicator	. . .
TIA	Telecommunications Industry Association	TIA
TIA	Telephone Interface Adapter	. . .
TIA	Time Interval Analyzer	. . .
TIA	Transimpedance Amplifier	. . .
TIC	Time Interval Counter	. . .
TIC	Token-Ring Interface Coupler	IBM
TICR	Transmit Interrupt Control Register	. . .
TIF	The Information Facility	IBM
TIFF	Tagged Image File Format	. . .
TIG	Tungsten/Inert Gas re: Welding technology	. . .
TIGA	Texas Instruments Graphics Architecture	TI
TIGER	Topologically-Integrated Geographic Encoding and Referencing	US Census Bureau
TIM	TCP/IP Integration Module	VXM Technologies
	sa *TCP/IP, Transmission Control Protocol/ Internet Protocol*	
TIM	Terminal Inactivity Monitor	DEC
TIME	Tandem Integrated Manufacturing Environment	Tandem Computers
TIMS	Text Information Management System	. . .
TIMS	Thermal Infrared Multispectral Scanner	. . .
TIP	Terminal Interface Processor	. . .
TIRS	The Integrated Reasoning Shell	IBM
TiW	Titanium-Wolfram (tungsten) Semiconductor fuse material	. . .
TK	Tool Kit Microcomputer software	. . .

Tl	Thallium	. . .
	Atomic element number 81	
TLB	Translation Look-aside Buffer	Signetics
TLC	Thin-Layer Chromatography	. . .
TLI	Transport Layer Interface	. . .
TLM	Transmission Line Matrix	. . .
	Mathematical analysis of multi-dimensional electromagnetic problems	
TLMA	Telematic Access Unit	CCITT
TLU	Table Look-Up	. . .
TLV	Threshold Limit Value	ACGIH
	re: Toxic chemical or other hazard exposure	
TL1	Transport Language 1	Bellcore
Tm	Thulium	. . .
	Atomic element number 69	
TM	Telemetry	. . .
TM	Thematic Mapper	Hughes
TM	Transverse Magnetic [mode]	. . .
	re: Wave propagation in fiber-optic communications	
TMA	Telecommunications Managers Association	TMA
TMC	Tape Management Catalog	IBM
TMEP	Tymnet Modified Emulator Program	Comm-Pro
	Pertains to software for the IBM 3705 Communications Controller	
TMF	Transaction Monitoring Facility	Tandem Computers
TMG	Test Message Generator	. . .
TMIS	Telecommunications Management Information System	US Dept of Commerce
TMN	Telecommunications Management Network	. . .
TMOS	Telecommunications Management and Operations Support	Ericsson
TMP	Terminal Monitor Program	IBM
TMP	Thymidine Monophosphate	. . .
	A compound important in biochemistry	
TMP	Transverse Magnetic Polarization	. . .
TMS	Tape Monitoring System	. . .
TMS	Telemanagement System	. . .
TMS	Test Management System	Tektronix
TMS	Test Mode Select	. . .
TMS	Transport Management System	General DataComm
TMSCP	Tape Mass Storage Control Protocol	DEC
TMSL	Test and Measurement System Language	H-P
TMSS	Time-Multiplexed Space Switch	. . .

TMTV	Time-Multiplexed Television	. . .
TMV	Tobacco Mosaic Virus	. . .
	A virus important to understanding bichemical functions	
Tn	Transmission Type n	AT&T
	Transmission line services: $n=0$ &rArr 57.6 kbps $n=1$ &rArr 1.544 Mbps $n=3$ &rArr 44.736 Mbps	
TN	Twisted Nematic [LCD]	. . .
	Technology for increased contrast in liquid crystal displays (LCDs)	
TNAS	TELCON Network Administration System	. . .
TNC	Threaded Neill-Concelman [connector]	. . .
	Threaded version of the ubiquitous *BNC*, *Baby N Connector*, which see	
TNDS	Total Network Data System	Larse/Telenex
TNM	Transmission Network Manager	IBM
TNT	Trinitrotoluene	. . .
TOC	Table Of Contents	. . .
TOC	Time Of Coicidence	. . .
	re: Loran-C navigation and time/frequency standard reception sa *Loran-C, Long range navigation-C*	
TOF	Time Of Flight	. . .
	re: Subatomic particles in nuclear and electron physics	
TOP	Technical and Office Protocol	
TOS	Tape Operating System	RCA
TOTS	Tower Operator Training System	FAA
TP	Teleprocessing	. . .
TP	Terminal Packet	CCITT
TP	Thermopile	. . .
	Multi-layered thermocouple for producing higher voltage than would be possible with a single thermocouple	
TP	Transaction Processing	. . .
TP	Transaction Protocol	OSI
TP	Transmission Priority	IBM
TPA	Telephone Pioneers of America	TPA
	Organization of past telephone engineers and technicians	
TPAD	Terminal Packet Assembler/Disassembler	. . .
TPC	—Fiber-Optic Cable	. . .
TPCM	Third-Party Computer Maintenance	. . .
TPD	Two-Page Display	. . .

TPDDI	Twisted Pair Distributed Data Interface	. . .
	Equivalent to the fiber-distributed data interface (FDDI) 100 MHz standard, only over twisted pair (TP) instead of fiber-optic (FO) cable	
TPDU	Transport Protocol Data Unit	. . .
TPE	Twisted Pair Ethernet	Intel
TPEX	Twisted Pair Ethernet Transceiver	Adv. Micro Devices
tpi	tracks per inch	. . .
	re: Disk drive magnetic recording density	
TPI	Tool-Path Image	. . .
TPI	Transport Provider Interface	. . .
	re: Computer numeric control (CNC) machining	
TPI	Twisted Pair Interface	. . .
TPM	Total Passivation Module	. . .
TPO	Transaction Processing Option	Oracle
TPON	Telephony over a Passive Optical Network	. . .
TPP	Thiamine Pyrophosphate	. . .
	A compound important in biochemistry	
TPS	Thermal Protection System	. . .
TPS	Transactions Per Second	. . .
TPU	Text Processing Utility	DEC
TQC	Total Quality Control	. . .
	re: Quality control in *fine pitch technology*, *FPT*, which see	
TQM	Total Quality Management	. . .
	re: Software development	
TR	Technical Reference	Bellcore
TR	Terminal Ready	. . .
TR	Token Ring	. . .
	A networking technology	
TR-LSC	Time-Resolved Liquid Scintillation Counting	. . .
TRACER	Tropospheric Radiometer for Atmospheric Chemistry and Environmental Research	NASA
TRAMAR	Tropical Rain Mapping Radar	. . .
TRANSET	Transportation Network Set	. . .
TransLAN	Transparent Local Area Network	Vitalink
TRAPS	Telemetry-Radar Acquisition and Processing System	NASA
TRC	Token Ring Controller	Toshiba
TRF	Tuned Radio Frequency	. . .
TRIP	Transcontinental ISDN Project	COS
	sa *ISDN, Integrated Services Digital Network*	

Triac	Triode AC [switch]	GE
	A bi-directional triode thyristor; a solid-state (SS) alternating current (AC) control device	
TRL	Through-Reflect-Line	. . .
	Vector network analyzer calibration methodology	
TRM	Transmission Resource Manager	NET
	re: *IDNX, Integrated Digital Network Exchange*	
TRN	Token Ring Network	. . .
tRNA	transfer Ribonucleic Acid	. . .
	sa *RNA, Ribonucleic Acid*	
TROLI	Token-Ring Optimized LAN Interface	. . .
	sa *LAN, Local Area Network*	
Trp	Tryptophan	. . .
	A compound important in biochemistry	
TRS	Turbo Reflow Solder [system]	. . .
TRT	Token Rotation Timer	FDDI
	re: Token ring technology	
TRU	Tape Restore Unit	GigaTrend
	Proprietary backup/recovery system	
TRV	Triple Redundant Voting	August Systems
	Triple redundant fault-tolerant system	
TSA	Technical Support Alliance	. . .
TSAP	Transport Service Access Point	. . .
TSB	Transfer Services Bridge	Wollongong Group
TSCA	Terminal Simulator Communications Area	IBM
TSCL	Traffic Signal Control Link	US West Comm.
	City-wide Computer control of traffic signals	
TSD	Through/Short/Delay	. . .
	A method of describing characteristics of an electronic circuit or device	
TSD	Transmission System Dependent	IEEE
	re: IEEE Standard 802.6 on metropolitan area networks (MANs)	
	sa *IEEE, Institute of Electrical and Electronic Engineers*	
TSDB	Threat Systems Data Base	DoD
TSI	Test System Interface	Tektronix
TSI	Time Slot Interchange	Ericsson
TSL	Tri-State Logic	. . .
	Solid-state (SS) logic in which inactive outputs can be placed in a high-impedance (Hi-Z) state	

TSM	Terminal Server Manager	DEC
TSM	Time-Sharing Modulation	. . .
TSM	Time-Sharing Monitor	IBM
TSNS	Telecommunications Services, Network Support	IBM
TSO	Time-Sharing Option	IBM
TSOP	Thin Small-Outline Package	Mitsubishi
	High-density electronic circuit chip packaging technology in which the package is virtually identical in size to the chip itself	
TSP	Technical Support Package	NASA
TSP	Terminal Simulator Panel	IBM
TSR	Telecommunications Service Request	DARPA
TSR	Terminal Surveillance Radar	. . .
TSR	Terminate and Stay Resident	. . .
TSS	Task State Segment	Intel
TSS	Time-Share System	IBM
TSS	Time-Sharing System	. . .
TSS	Top Secret Security [system]	. . .
TSSOP	Thin-Scaled Small Outline Package	TI
	re: Integrated circuit (IC) packaging technology	
	sa *TSOP, Thin Small Outline Package*	
TST	Temporary Storage Table	IBM
TST	Transparent Spanning Tree	IEEE
	An Ethernet algorithm	
TSTN	Triple Supertwist Nematic [display]	. . .
	Color liquid crystal display (LCD) technology	
TT	Touch Tone	AT&T
	sa *DTMF, Dual Tone Multiple Frequency*	
TTC&M	Tracking, Telemetry, Control and Monitoring	. . .
TTI	Transmitter Terminal Identification	. . .
TTL	Through The Lens	. . .
	re: Exposure control, field-of-view (FOV) control, etc., in single-lens reflex (SLR) photography	
TTL	Transistor-Transistor Logic	. . .
	Integrated circuit (IC) technology developed c. 1960s	
TTP	Telephone Twisted Pair	. . .
TTP	Thymidine Triphosphate	. . .
	A compound important in biochemistry	
TTR	Timed Token Rotation	. . .
TTRT	Target Token Rotation Time	. . .
	re: Fiber-distributed data interface (FDDI) standard	

TTY	Teletypewriter	. . .
TU	Technology Utilization	NASA
TUO	Technology Utilization Officer	NASA
TUP	Technology Utilization Program	NASA
TUP	Telephone User Part	. . .
TUR	Test Uncertainty Ratio	. . .
TVC	Thermal Voltage Conversion(-ter)	. . .
TVD	Thrust Vector Deflector	Johnson Space Center

re: Attitude control rocket engines on satellites

TVI	Television Interference	. . .
TVM	Transistor Voltmeter	. . .

Solid-state (SS) equivalent to the *VTVM*, *Vacuum Tube Voltmeter*

TVRO	Television Receive Only	. . .

A satellite earth station (receive only)

TVS	Transient Voltage Suppressor	. . .
TVSS	Transient Voltage Surge Suppressor	. . .
TVV	Token Validation Value	. . .

re: Data encryption technology

TW	Terawatt	. . .

10^{12} watts (*W*)

TWA	Transaction Work Area	IBM
TWT	Traveling Wave Tube	. . .
TWX	Teletypewriter Exchange	Western Union

A communications network of teletypwriters (TTYs), but also used to designate *Teletypewriter Exchange [terminal]*

Tx	Transmit (or Transmitter)	. . .
Tyr	Tyrosine	. . .

A compound important in biochemistry

T0	Telecommunications Level 0	AT&T

A digital cable service, but also used to refer to the T1 bandwidth of 57.6 kbits/sec Also designated by *T-0*

T1	Transmission [link] 1	. . .

A digital cable service, but also used to refer to the T1 bandwidth of 1.544 Mbits/sec Also designated by *T-1*

T1.606	—T1.606	ANSI

Frame-relay service description standard

T1.617	—T1.617	ANSI

Frame-relay signalling access description (proposed)

| T1.618 | —T1.618
Frame-relay core standard description
(proposed) | ANSI |
| T3 | Transmission [link] 3
A digital cable service, but also used to refer
to the T3 bandwidth of 44.736 Mbits/sec
Also designated by *T-3* | . . . |

U

u	—micro Prefix for 10^{-6} Note: "u" is a print substitution for the Greek letter *mu* (μ).	. . .
U	U [interface] Two-wire device that connects customer premises with local telephone lines	. . .
U	Unnumbered Format of X.25 protocol control field; sa *X.25*	CCITT
U	Uracil A compound important in biochemistry	. . .
U	Uranium Atomic element number 92	. . .
uA	microampere 10^{-6} Ampere Note: "u" is a print substitution for the Greek letter *mu* (μ).	. . .
UA	Unnumbered Acknowledgement	CCITT
UA	User Agent X.25 protocol command; sa *X.25*	. . .
UAE	Unrecoverable Application Error	Microsoft
UAE	User Agent Entity	. . .
UAI	User Application Interface	. . .
UARS	Upper Atmosphere Research Satellite	NASA
UART	Universal Asynchronous Receiver/Transmitter	. . .
UAT	Unaligned Address Transfer re: Virtual memory extended (VME) bus data transfer	. . .
UAV	Unmanned Air Vehicle	. . .
UCA	Utility Communications Architecture	EPRI
UCAR	University Corporation for Atmospheric Research	NSF
UCD	Uniform Call Distribution	. . .

UCG	Universal Command Group re: IEEE Standard 488; sa *IEEE*	IEEE
UCIC	Universal Counter Integrated Circuit	H-P
UCS	Universal Character Set	. . .
UD	Ultra-Low Dispersion re: Optical glass	. . .
UDD	User-Defined Disassembler	Arium
UDF	User Danger Factor	DEC
UDF	User-Defined Function	. . .
UDI	Universal Development Interface	. . .
UDL	Universal Data Link	Telcom
UDL/I	Unified Description Language for ICs Japanese very large scale integration (VLSI) design-language standard; sa *IC, Integrated Circuit*	Japan
UDMH	Unsymmetrical dymethylhydrazine A liquid rocket fuel	. . .
UDMS	User Data Management System	Interactive Software
UDP	Universal Data Protocol	. . .
UDP	UNIX Datagram Protocol UNIX transport protocol	. . .
UDP	Uridine Diphosphate A compound important in biochemistry	. . .
UDP	User Datagram Protocol	. . .
UDS	User-Defined Sequence	. . .
ufd	microfarad 10^{-6} farad Note: "u" is a print substitution for the Greek letter *mu* (μ).	. . .
UFD	User Identification Code	. . .
UFO	Unidentified Flying Object	. . .
UGA	University of Georgia SURANet node name; sa *SURANet*	. . .
UHD	Ultra-High Density re: Electronic connector design	. . .
UHECL	Ultra-High-Speed Emitter Coupled Logic	Fujitsu
UHF	Ultra-High Frequency 300 to 3000 MHz	. . .
UHS	Universal Helical Scan re: Video magnetic tape recording technology	. . .
UHV	Ultra-High Vacuum	. . .

uHz	microhertz 10^{-6} Hertz Note: "u" is a print substitution for the Greek letter *mu* (μ).	. . .
UI	UNIX International	UI
UI	User Interface	. . .
UIC	Unreferenced Internal Count	IBM
UIC	User Identification Code	DEC
UIL	User Interface Language	. . .
UIS	Universal Information Service	AT&T
UJT	Unijunction Transistor	. . .
UL	Underwriters Laboratories	UL
ULANA	Unified Local Area Network Architecture	US Air Force
ULC	Universal Launch Cable re: Fiber-optic testing	Fotec
ULE	Ultra-Low Expansion re: Glass used in manufacture of telescope mirrors and other optical devices whose high sensitivity to thermal expansion would be detrimental to performance	Corning Glass
ULSI	Ultra-Large-Scale Integration Integrated circuit technology containing in excess of 300,000 gates and upwards of 500 leads per chip	. . .
UM	User Module	. . .
UMB	Upper Memory Block That occupying memory above 640 K in microcomputers; also known as "high DOS" sa *k* (factor of 1024) and *DOS, Disk Operating System*	. . .
UMIDS	Uniform Microcomputer Dispersing System	US Navy
UMP	Uridine Monophosphate A compound important in biochemistry	. . .
UNC	Universal Noiseless Coder	JPL/NASA
UNI	User Network Interface	. . .
UNICOS	UNIX Cray Operating System	Cray Research
UNIDATS	Unified Data Transmission Service	. . .
Univac	Universal automatic computer Eckert and Mauchly's first commercial computer (1946); also (later) the name of Eckert and Mauchly's company, later purchased by Remington-Rand	Eckert & Mauchly
UNIX	UNIX [operating system]	AT&T

UNL	Unlisten	IEEE
	IEEE Standard 488 bus command;	
	sa *IEEE*	
UNMA	Unified Network Management Architecture	AT&T
UNT	Untalk	IEEE
	IEEE Standard 488 bus command;	
	sa *IEEE*	
UOS	Universal Operations Systems	. . .
UPC	Universal Price Code	. . .
UPI	Universal Peripheral Interface	Nat'l. Semi-conductor
UPS	Uninterruptible Power Supply (or System)	. . .
	Compare with *SPS*, *Standby Power Supply*	
URD	Unit Record Device	DEC
UREP	UNIX RSCS Emulation Program	DEC
	sa *RSCS*, *Remote Spooling Communications Subsystem*	
URR	Ultra-Reliable Radar	. . .
US	Underscore	. . .
US	Unit Separator	CCITT
	Information separator 1 (IS_1) under CCITT Recommendation V.3;	
	sa *CCITT*, *V.3* and *IS_n*	
USAN	University Satellite Network	NCAR
USART	Universal Synchronous/Asynchronous Receiver/Transmitter	. . .
USASCII	USA ASCII	
	Archaic; see *ASCII*	
USB	Upper Sideband	. . .
USC	Undershoot Corrector	. . .
	Electronic circuitry to improve frequency response on switching at high speeds	
USC	Universal Serial Controller	Zilog
USN	Universal Services Node	. . .
USNO	United States Naval Observatory	US Navy
USOP	Ultra-Small-Outline Package	. . .
	Compact packaging technology of high density electronic integrated circuit (IC) chips	
USR	Unsatisfactory Service Report	DARPA
USRT	Universal Synchronous Receiver/Transmitter	. . .
USVR	User Security Verification Routine	IBM
UT	Universal Time	. . .
UTC	Universal Time Coordinated	NBS
	Commonly referred to as "coordinated universal time" or "universal time code"	
UTC	Utilities Telecommunications Council	. . .

UTM	Universal Transverse Mercator	US Army
	A grid mapping system	
UTP	Unshielded Twisted Pair	...
	re: Local area network (LAN) cabling;	
	common "twisted pair" telephone cabling	
UTP	Uridine Triphosphate	...
	A compound important in biochemistry	
UTS	Universal Terminal Syste m	Sperry
UTS	Universal Timesharing System	Amdahl
UTV	User Targeted Voice	BBN
UUCP	UNIX to UNIX Copy Protocol	AT&T
UUT	Unit Under Test	...
	sa *DUT, Device Under Test* and *LUT, Logic Under Test*	
UV	Ultraviolet	...
	Invisible radiation with wavelength less than 400 nm	
UV	Undervoltage	...
UVB	Ultraviolet Band	...
UVD	Undervoltage Detector	...
UVEPROM	Ultraviolet Eraseable Programmable Read Only Memory	...
	sa *EEPROM, Electrically Eraseable Programmable Read Only Memory* and *EPROM, Eraseable Programmable Read Only Memory*	
UVL	Undervoltage Lockout	...
	Alternate form; see UVLO	
UVLO	Undervoltage Lock-Out	...

V

V	Vanadium	...
	Atomic element number 23	
V	Volt	...
	Unit of electromotive force	
	Named in honor of Italian physicist Alessandro Volta (1745–1827)	
V	Voltage	...
	Electric potential; expressed in units of *Volts, V*	
VA	Volt-Ampere	...
	sa *V, Volt* and *A, Ampere*	
V-Band	V-Band	...
	Extremely high frequency (EHF) radio allocation of 46–56 GHz	

V.nn	—CCITT data communications recommendations A few of the more commonly encountered standards are listed	CCITT
V(S)	Variable (Send) State variable in *X.25* protocol, which see	CCITT
V/STOL	Vertical/Short Takeoff and Landing re: Aircraft	. . .
VCTV	Viewer-controlled Cable Television	AT&T
V.3	—V.3 A CCITT recommendation concerning the interpretation of codes for data transmission; sa *CCITT*	CCITT
V.21	V.21 300 baud duplex modem standard	CCITT
V.22	V.22 1.2 kbps duplex modem standard	CCITT
V.22bis	—V.22bis (secondary) 2.4 kbps duplex dial-up modem standard	CCITT
V.24	—V.24 CITT counterpart of EIA RS-449 sa *CCITT, Consultative Committee for International Telephone and Telegraph* and *EIA, Electronics Industry Association*	CCITT
V.25	—V.25 Automatic originate/answer equipment standard	CCITT
V.26	—V.26 2.4 kbps modem standard for four-wire telephone circuits	CCITT
V.26bis	—V.26bis (secondary) 1.2 and 2.4 kbps modem standard	CCITT
V.26ter	—V.26ter (tertiary) 2.4 kbps full duplex modem standard with echo cancel	CCITT
V.27	—V.27 4.8 kbps modem standard with manual equalization	CCITT
V.27bis	—V.27bis (secondary) 2.4 and 4.8 kbps modem standard with automatic equalization	CCITT
V.27ter	—V.27ter (tertiary) 2.4 and 4.8 kbps modem standard	CCITT
V.28	—V.28 CCITT counterpart to *RS-232C*, which see	CCITT

V.29	—V.29 9.6 kbps modem standard	CCITT
V.32	—V.32 9.6 kbps full duplex modem standard	CCITT
VA	Volt-Ampere	. . .
VAC	Value-Added Carrier	. . .
VAC	VME-Bus Address Controller	VTC
VAC	Volts Alternating Current	. . .
VAD	Value-Added Dealer (or Distributor)	. . .
VAD	Velocity Azimuth Display re: Weather analysis and prediction technology	. . .
VADS	Verdix Ada Development System sa *Ada*	Verdix
VAI	Value-Added Installer	. . .
Val	Valine A compound important in biochemistry	. . .
VAN	Value-Added Network	. . .
VANA	Vector-Automated Network Analyzer	. . .
VAP	Value-Added Platform	Unisys
VAP	Value-Added Process re: Data communications network monitoring technology	. . .
VAPC	Vector-Adaptive Predictive Coding	. . .
VAR	Voice-Actuated Recorder	. . .
VAR	Value-Added Reseller	. . .
VAS	Voice-Actuated System Audio tape recording control by means of voice	. . .
VASGH	VHDL Analysis and Standards Group sa *VHDL*	IEEE
VAST	Virtual Archival Storage Technology	. . .
VAT	Virtual Address Translator	IBM
VAT	Voice Actuated Typewriter	. . .
VAWS	Vector Arbitrary Waveform Synthesizer	H-P
VAX	Virtual Address Extension	DEC
VAXBI	Virtual Address Extension (VAX) Backplane Interconnect	DEC
VAXft	Virtual Address Extension (VAX), fault tolerant	DEC
VAXSIM	Virtual Address Extension (VAX) System Integrity Monitor	DEC
VBC	VSB Bus Controller sa *VSB, VME Subsystem Bus* and *VME,* *Virtual Memory Extended*	. . .

VBI	VAX Bus Interface	DEC
	sa *VAX, Virtual Address Extension*	
VBI	Vertical Blanking Interval	. . .
	re: Television raster scanning interval	
VBL	Vertical Block Line	. . .
	Computer bubble memory technology	
VBN	Virtual Backbone Network	. . .
VBN	Virtual Block Number	DEC
VC	Virtual Call (service)	. . .
VCA	Voltage-Controlled Amplifier	. . .
VCCS	Voltage-Controlled Current Source	. . .
VCDRO	Voltage-Controlled Dielectric Resonator Oscillator	. . .
	sa *DRO, Dielectric Resonator Oscillator*	
VCF	Voltage-Controlled Frequency	. . .
VCHP	Variable Conductance Heat Pipe	Tanzer, H.
VCM	Voice Coil Motor	. . .
	Computer disk memory read head/arm positioning technology, so-called due to its similarity to loudspeaker voice coils	
VCO	Variable-Coupled Oscillator	. . .
VCO	Voltage-Controlled Oscillator	. . .
VCP	Vista Communications Card	Datability Software
VCP	Vitalink Communications Protocol	Vitalink
VCP	Voltage-Controlled Potentiometer	. . .
VCPI	Virtual Control Program Interface	Intel
VCR	Video Cassette Recorder	. . .
VCS	VAXcluster Console System	DEC
	sa *VAX, Virtual Address Extension*	
VCS	Virtual Circuit Switch	AT&T
VCS	VMS Command Substitution	. . .
	sa *VMS, Virtual Memory System*	
VCSE	Vertical Cavity Surface-Emitter [laser]	. . .
	re: Semiconductor laser	
VCSEL	Vertical Cavity Surface-Emitting Laser	. . .
VCTCXO	Voltage-Controlled Temperature-Compensated Crystal Oscillator	. . .
VCU	VAX Calendar Utility	DEC
	sa *VAX, Virtual Address Extension*	
VCVS	Voltage-Controlled Voltage Source	. . .
VCX	Virtual Channel Executive	. . .
VCXO	Voltage-Controlled Crystal Oscillator	. . .
VD	Vacuum Deposition	. . .
VD	Vertical Drive	. . .
	re: Video camera vertical deflection circuitry	

VDA	Visual Data Analysis	. . .
VDC	Volts Direct Current	. . .
VDFM	Virtual Disk File Manager	Epoch Systems
VDI	Video Display Interface	. . .
VDI	Virtual Device Interface	. . .
VDL	Visible Diode Laser	. . .
	Diode laser that emits light in the visible spectrum	
VDM	Virtual Device Metafile	. . .
	A graphics acronym, now generally replaced by *CGM*, *Computer Graphics Metafile*	
VDM	Voice-Data Manager	NCR
VDM	Voice-Data Multiplexer	. . .
VDT	Video Display (or Data) Terminal	. . .
VDU	Video Data Unit	. . .
VE	Virtual Environment	CDC
VEPC	Voice-Excited Predictive Coding	. . .
VESA	Video Electronics Standards Association	VISA
VEX	Video Extension to X-Windows	. . .
VF	Vector Facility	IBM
VF	Vertical Form	. . .
	Printer forms (Z-fold, roll)	
VF	Voice Frequency	. . .
	300 to 3000 Hz	
VFC	Voltage-to-Frequency Converter	. . .
VFD	Vacuum Fluorescent Display	. . .
VFE	VME-to-VME Futurebus Extended	Force Computers
	sa *VME*, *Virtual Memory Extended*	
VFEA	VME Futurebus Extended Architecture	IEEE
	sa *VME*, *Virtual Memory Extended*	
VFU	Vertical Forms Unit	DEC
	re: Any printer, but generally refers to mainframe devices	
VG	Voice Grade	. . .
	re: Communication line quality	
VGA	Video Graphics Array	. . .
VGPL	Voice Grade Private Line	AT&T
	re: Ordinary (unconditioned) telephone circuit	
VH	Vertical-Horizontal	Held, D.N., JPL
	re: Imaging data from transmitted and received radar signals	
VHD	Very High Density	. . .
	re: Data storage	

VHDF	Very High Density Floppy [diskette]	. . .
VHDL	VHSIC Hardware Description Language	. . .
	sa *VHSIC, Very High-Speed Integrated Circuit*	
VHF	Very High Frequency	. . .
	30 to 300 MHz	
VHS	Video Helical Scan [format]	. . .
	Video tape recording format	
VHSIC	Very-High-Speed Integrated Circuit	Hughes
VIA	VAX Information Architecture	DEC
	sa *VAX, Virtual Address Extension*	
VIA	Videotex Industries Association	. . .
VIC	VME-Bus Interface Controller	VTC
	sa *VME, Virtual Memory Extended*	
VIDA	VAX IBM Data Access	DEC
	sa *VAX, Virtual Address Extension*	
VIDEOTEX	Video Text	. . .
	Generic name for information retrieval system accessed via cable television (CATV)	
VIEW	Virtual Interface Environment Workstation	NASA
	Head-mounted stereoscopic display system	
VIEWDATA	View Data	. . .
	Information retrieval system	
VIFF	Visualization and Image File Format	. . .
VIIS	Vessel Identification Information System	US Coast Guard
VIL	Vertical In-Line	. . .
	re: Electronic circuit chip packaging for increased circuit density; see also the following: *MBT, Multilayer Bonding Technique, MCM-C, Multichip Module— Ceramic, MCM-D, Multichip Module— Deposited, MCM-L, Multichip Module— Laminate, SiCB, Silicon Circuit Board* and *VIL, Vertical In-Line*	
VIM	Vendor Independant Messaging	. . .
VINES	Virtual Network System	. . .
VIS	Visible Infrared Spectrum	. . .
VIS	Voice Information Services	. . .
VISCA	Video Systems Control Architecture	Sony
VISSTA	Vehicle for Implementation of Standards and Specifications through Technological Assistance	DoD
VITA	VME International Trade Association	. . .
	sa *VME, Virtual Memory Extended*	

VLA	Very Large Area	. . .
	re: Ion implantation in wafer substrates	
VLBA	Very Long Baseline Array	NASA
	re: Radio telescopes	
VLBI	Very Long Baseline Interferometry	NASA
VLCBX	Very Large Computer Branch Exchange	Rolm
VLD	Visible Laser Diode	. . .
VLDS	Very Large Data Store	Honeywell
VLF	Very Low Frequency	. . .
	3 to 30 kHz	
VLF	Virtual Lookaside Facility	IBM
VLIW	Very Long Instruction Word	PRL/Signetics
	A computer hardware architecture	
VLL	Virtual Lightning Library	Micro Technology
VLM	Virtual Library Manager	Micro Technology
VLS	Virtual LAN Server	. . .
	sa *LAN, Local Area Network*	
VLSI	Very Large Scale Integration	. . .
	Integrated circuit technology containing in excess of 10^5 gates	
VLSIC	Very Large Scale Integrated Circuit	. . .
	sa *VLSI, Very Large Scale Integration*	
VLSM	Voltage Level Sensitivity Measurement	Cadic
VLSW	Virtual Line Switching	Comm-Pro
	Pertains to software for the IBM 3705 Communications Controller	
VLT	Very Large Telescope	. . .
VM	Virtual Machine	IBM
VM	Voice Mail	. . .
VM-Assist	Virtual Machine Assist	IBM
VM/ESA	Virtual Machine/Enterprise Systems Architecture	IBM
VM/IS	Virtual Machine/Integrated System	IBM
VM/SP	Virtual Machine/System Product	. . .
VM/XA	Virtual Machine/Extended Architechture	. . .
VMARK	Vector Marking [facility]	Cray Research
VMB	Voice Mail Box	. . .
VMD	Video Model Deformation	Langley Research Ctr.
VME	Virtual Memory Extended	. . .
VMEbus	Virtual Memory Extended bus	Motorola
VMM	Variable Mission Manufacturing	. . .
VMM	Vector Matrix Multiplication	. . .
VMS	Virtual Memory System	DEC

VMTP	Virtual Message Transport Protocol	DoD
VMX	Voice Message Exchange	. . .
	Voice store-and-forward communications system	
VNA	Vector Network Analyzer	H-P
VNESSA	Voyager Neptune Encounter Science Support Activity	NASA
Vnet	Virtual network	. . .
	Also designated by *VNET*	
VNET	Virtual Network	MCI
	Also designated by *Vnet*	
VNM	Virtual Network Model	Cabletron Systems
VOA	Voice of America	VOA
	Radio network	
VOC	Volatile Organic Compound	. . .
VOD	Video On Demand	. . .
VOM	Volt-Ohm-Milliameter	. . .
VOR	Very-High-Frequency Omnidirectional Range	NIST
VOT	Voice-Operated Typewriter	. . .
VOTS	VAX OSI Transport Services	DEC
	sa *VAX, Virtual Address Extension* and *OSI, Open Systems Interconnection*	
vox	voice	. . .
VP	Virtual Program	IBM
VPA	VAX Performance Advisor	DEC
	sa *VAX, Virtual Address Extension*	
VPDN	Virtual Private Data Network	. . .
VPDS	Virtual Private Data Services	MCI
VPI	Virtual Path Interconnect	. . .
	re: Network switching methodology	
VPL	Virtual Private Line	. . .
VPM	Virtual Protocol Machine	. . .
VPN	Virtual Private Network	MCI
VPPA	Variable Plasma Pulse Arc	. . .
	A welding technology	
VPPA	Variable Polarity Plasma Arc	NASA
	A welding technology	
VPS	Vacuum Plasma System	. . .
VPS	Vapor Phase Soldering	. . .
VPS	Virtual Print Spool	. . .
VPS	Voice Processing Station	. . .
VPS	VTAM Printer Support	IBM
	sa *VTAM, Virtual Telecommunications Access Method*	
VPWM	Variable Pulse Width Modulation	. . .

VQFP	Very Fine Pitch Quad Flatpack	. . .
VQL	Variable Quantization Level	Aydin
	Proprietary voice quantizing algorithm	
VR	Vertical Recording	. . .
	A magnetic recording technology	
	Also called *PR, Perpendicular Recording*	
VR	Virtual Reality	NASA
	Computer simulation of an artificial	
	environment	
	sa *HUD, Head Up Display*	
VR	Virtual Route	IBM
VR	Voltage Regulator	. . .
VRA	Virtual Route Analyzer	IBM
VRAM	Video Random Access Memory	. . .
VRC	Vertical Redundancy Check	. . .
	A method of checking received data for	
	accuracy	
	sa *CRC, Cyclic Redundancy Check* and	
	LRC, Longitudinal Redundancy Check	
VRM	Variable Reflectivity Mirror	. . .
VRM	Version Release Modification	IBM
VRM	Virtual Resource Manager	. . .
VRTX	Virtual Real-Time Executive	. . .
VRU	Voice Response Unit	. . .
VS	Virtual Storage	IBM
VS-1	Virtual Storage One	IBM
VSAM	Virtual Storage Access Method	IBM
VSAT	Very Small Aperture [satellite] Terminal	. . .
VSB	Vestigial Side-Band	. . .
	re: Telecommunications transmission	
VSB	VME Subsystem Bus	. . .
	sa *VME, Virtual Memory Extended*	
VSC	Virtual Storage Constraint	. . .
VSC	Virtual System Control	. . .
VSCR	Virtual Storage Constraint Releif	IBM
VSCS	Virtual SNA Console Support	IBM
	sa *SNA, Systems Network Architecture*	
VSCS	Virtual System Console Support	IBM
VSCS	Voice Switching and Control System	FAA
VSE	Virtual Storage Extended	IBM
VSLAN	Very Secure Local Area Network	. . .
	A 100% encrypted local area network (LAN)	
VSMF	Visual Search Microfilm File	NASA
VSOP	Very-Small-Outline Package	. . .
	High-density electronic circuit packaging	
	technology	

VSP	Video Signal Processor	. . .
VSWR	Voltage Standing Wave Ratio	. . .
VT	Vertical Tabulation	CCITT
	Format effector 3 (FE$_3$); a component of the binary code in CCITT Recommendation V.3;	
	sa *FE$_n$, Format Effector* n, *CCITT* and *V.3*	
VT	Virtual Terminal	. . .
VT	Virtual Tributary	. . .
	Basic element of information in the synchronous payload envelope (SPE) of the synchronous optical network (SONET) data communication standard (DCS)	
VTAM	Virtual Telecommunications Access Method	IBM
VTAME	Virtual Telecommunications Access Method Entry	IBM
VTC	Video Tele-Conferencing	. . .
VTCC	Video Terminal Cluster Controller	DEC
VTIP	VHDL Tool Integration Platform	CLSI
	sa *VHDL, VHSIC Hardware Description Language,* and *VHSIC, Very-High-Speed Integrated Circuit*	
VTLS	Virginia Tech Library System	Virginia Tech.
VTNS	Virtual Telecommunications Network Service	AT&T
VTO	Voltage-Tuned Oscillator	. . .
VTOC	Visual Table Of Contents	. . .
	re: structured design	
VTOC	Volume Table Of Contents	IBM
VTOL	Vertical Take-Off and Landing [aircraft]	. . .
VTP	Virtual Terminal Protocol	OSI
VTR	Video Tape Recorder	. . .
VTRC	VME Token Ring Controller	Data General
	sa *VME, Virtual Memory Extended*	
VTS	Video Transmission Service	AT&T
VTVM	Vacuum Tube Voltmeter	. . .
VTVOM	Vacuum Tube Volt-Ohm-Milliameter	. . .
VTX	Videotex [system]	DEC
VU	Volume Unit	. . .
	A measure of power level in audio circuits; expressed in *decibels, dB*	
VUE	Visual User Environment	. . .
VUIT	Visual User Interface Tool	DEC
VUP	VAX Units of Performance	DEC
	One VUP = Performance of one VAX-11/780	
	sa *VAX, Virtual Address Extension*	

VUV	Visible Ultraviolet	. . .
VV	Vertical-Vertical	Held, D.N., JPL
	re: Imaging data from transmitted and received radar signals	
	sa *HH, Horizontal-Horizontal* and *VH, Vertical-Horizontal*	
VVA	Voltage Variable Attenuator	. . .
	re: Microwave passband attenuator	
VVCR	VSAM Volume Control Record	IBM
	sa *VSAM, Virtual Sequential Access Method*	
VVDS	VSAM Volume Data Set	IBM
	sa *VSAM, Virtual Sequential Access Method*	
VVR	VSAM Volume Record	IBM
	re: IBM's *Integrated Catalog Facility, ICF*	
	sa *VSAM, Virtual Sequential Access Method*	
VWT	Virtual Worlds Technology	. . .
VXI	VMEbus Extension for Instrumentation	IEEE
	sa *VME, Virtual Memory Extended*	

W

W	Watt	. . .
	Unit of energy	
	Named in honor of Scottish inventor James Watt (1736–1819)	
W	Wolfram	. . .
	Symbol for *tungsten*, atomic element number 74	
W	Work	. . .
	Expressed in units of *Joules, J*	
W-DCS	Wideband Digital Cross-Connect Signal	CCITT
W-ISDN	Wideband Integrated Services Digital Network	. . .
WAAN	Wide Area AppleTalk Network	Apple
WABCR	Wide Area Bar Code Reader	. . .
	re: US Postal Service use of a bar code reader for sorting mail	
WAN	Wide Area Network	. . .
WANK	Worms Against Nuclear Killers	. . .
	A computer "worm" propagated by a group of the same name	
WANKed	Worms Against Nuclear Killers (past tense)	. . .
	Term used to describe a system which has been invaded by the *WANK* worm, which see	
WAPA	Western Area Power Administration	DoE

WARC	World Administrative Radio Conference	WARC
WATBOL	Waterloo Business-Oriented Language	Univ. of Waterloo
WATR	Western Aeronautical Test Range	NASA
WATS	Wide Area Telephone Service	AT&T
WATTC	World Telephone and Telegraph Conference	WATTC
WAWS	Washington Area Wideband System	DoD
Wb	Weber	. . .
	Unit of magnetic flux	
	Named in honor of German physicist Ernst Heinrich Weber (1804–1891)	
WCS	Writeable Control Store	. . .
WDM	Wavelength Division Multiplexing	. . .
	re: Fiber-optic communications	
WDMA	Wave Division Multiple Access	. . .
	re: Fiber-optic communication	
WE	Write Enable	. . .
WEX	Wavelength Extender	Spectra-Physics
WFC	Wide Field (or Field-of-view) Camera	. . .
	re: Fiber-optic communications, photography	
WFIS	Wildlife and Fisheries Information System	Bureau of Land Mgt.
WFOV	Wide Field-Of-View	. . .
	re: Optical system coverage	
WHIP	Wafer Hybrid Interconnection Packaging	Mosaic Sys
WHOI	Woods Hole Oceanographic Institute	WHOI
WIDF	Weighted Integrate and Dump Filter	Sadr, Ramin, JPL
WIIS	Wang Integrated Image System	Wang
WIN	Wireless In-building Network	. . .
WIN	Wireless Information Network	. . .
WIN	Wollongong Integrated Network	Wollongong Group
WIN	Worldwide Intelligent Network	. . .
WINCS	WMCCS Intercomputer Network Communications System	DoD
	A component of the Defense Data Network (DDN)	
	sa *WMCCS, Worldwide Military Command and Control System*	
WIPS	Word Image Processing System	. . .
WISC	Writeable Instruction Set Chip (or Computer)	Int'l. Meta Systems
WISS	Workstation-Independent Segment Storage	. . .
WIT	Women in Telecommunications	. . .

WITS	Washington Interagency Telecommunications System	WITS
WLCT	Washington Legislative Council on Telecommunications	. . .
WMCCS	Worldwide Military Command and Control System	DoD
WOCE	World Ocean Circulation Experiment	NSF
WORM	Write Once Read Many re: Read only optical disk storage	. . .
WP	Word Processor	. . .
WPG	WordPerfect Graphics re: File format standard	WordPerfect
wpm	words per minute	. . .
WPS	Wideband Packet Switch	. . .
WPS	Word Processing System	. . .
WRP	Weighted Random Pattern A mathematical application used in electronic circuit board testing	IBM
WS	Waveguide Slab re: Microwave substrate dielectric constant measurement	. . .
WSI	Wafer Scale Integration Very large (12.5 cm diam.) substrate integrated circuit	. . .
WSR	Weather Surveillance Radar	. . .
WSTA	Wall Street Telecommunications Association	WSTA
WTO	Write To Operator	. . .
WTOR	Write To Operator with Reply	IBM
WTTY	World Trade Teletypewriter	. . .
WVDC	Working Volts Direct Current re: Voltage stress rating of capacitors, etc.	. . .
WVNET	West Virginia Network for Educational Telecomputing	WVNET
WWMCCS	Worldwide Military Command and Control System	US Armed Forces
WYLBUR	—WYLBUR A text editor; sa *ORVILLE*	OBS
WYPIWYF	What You Print Is What You FAX sa *FAX*, *Facsimile*	. . .
WYSBYGI	What You See Before You Get It	Bradley, G.
WYSIWYG	What You See Is What You Get	. . .

X

X	—10 Roman numeral designation	. . .

X	—Admittance Symbol; alternating current (AC) equivalent of direct current (DC) *conductance*; sa *S, Siemens*	
X	Hexadecimal A prefix indicating that the two characters following are in hexadecimal notation; for example, X4D is the hexadecimal notation for *Z* (capital Z) sa *H, Hexadecimal*	. . .
X	—X-Windows [software] A proprietary computer display window system	Microsoft
X-Band	—X-Band Microwave frequency allocation of 8.0 to 12.0 GHz	. . .
X-Bar	Crossbar Originally (c. 1946) an electro-mechanical telephone switching device, now used to describe a solid-state (SS) device with similar capability	. . .
X-MPxy	Experimental Multi-Processor xy where x = number of processors (1 digit) y = number of 64-bit megawords of storage (1 or 2 digits)	Cray Research
X.nn	—CCITT data communications recommendations A few of the more commonly encountered standards are listed	CCITT
X-OFF	—X-OFF "Flow control" in asynchronous (ASYNC) communications sa *RVI, Reverse Interrupt* for binary synchronous (Bisync) analog	. . .
X/Open	—X/Open A consortium of 13 computer vendors organized to support UNIX standards (Europe, 1988)	X/Open
X.PC	—X.PC Error-Correcting protocol	. . .
X.25	—X.25 Packet-switching protocol	. . .
X.26	—X.26 CCITT counterpart of EIA RS-423	. . .
X.27	—X.27 CCITT counterpart of EIA RS-422	. . .

X.400	—X.400	OSI
	Directories services standard	
X.500	—X.500	OSI
	Directories services standard	
XAIDS	Extended Aircraft Interrogation and Display	NASA
	System	
XBC	External Bus Controller	. . .
XCL	Executive Command Language	Cadic
XCONN	Cross-Connection	. . .
XDOS	UNIX Disk Operating System	Hunter
	Disk operating system (DOS) under UNIX	
XDP	X-Ray Density Probe	. . .
XDR	External Data Representation	Sun
		Microsystems
Xe	Xenon	. . .
	Atomic element number 54	
XER	Exception Register	IBM
XESS	X-Windows Engineering and Scientific	AIS
	Spreadsheet	
Xfer	Transfer	. . .
XGA	Extended Graphics Array	IBM
XHR	Extra-High Resolution	. . .
XHV	Extreme High Vacuum	. . .
XI	X.25 Interface	IBM
	SNA-to-X.25 interface/gateway;	
	sa *SNA*, *Systems Network Architecture* and	
	X.25	
XID	Exchange Identification	OSI
XIOP	(Block Multiplexer) Input/Output Processor	Cray Research
XIP	Execute In Place	. . .
	IEEE specification in which execution may	
	take place directly within a memory card;	
	sa *EXIP*, *LXIP* and *IEEE*	
XM	Expanded Menory	. . .
XM-P	Experimental Multi-Processor	Cray Research
XMAS	Extended Mission Apollo Simulation	. . .
XMFR	Transformer	. . .
XMI	Extended Memory Interconnect	DEC
XMIT	Transmit	. . .
XMS	Extended Memory Services	IBM
Xmt	Transmit	. . .
Xmtr	Transmitter	. . .
	Also designated by *XMTR*	
XMTR	Transmitter	. . .
	Also designated by *Xmtr*	

XNREN	X-400 National Research and Education Network	NSF
XNS	Xerox Network System (or Services)	Xerox
XO	Crystal Oscillator	. . .
XODUS	X-based Output and Display Utility for Simulators	Bower, J.
XOR	Exclusive OR [circuit or logic gate] Electronic circuit which exhibits the Boolean XOR logic function	. . .
XP	Expandable (or Expansion) Processor	IBM
XPDR	Transponder	. . .
XPIC	Cross-Polarization Interference Canceller	. . .
XPS	X-ray Photo-electron Spectrometry	. . .
XQP	Extended QIO Processing sa *QIO, Queued Input/Output*	DEC
XREF	Cross-Reference	. . .
XRF	Extended Recovery Facility Enhancement of MVS/EA, IMS/VS, ACF/VTAM, ACF/NCP sa individual entries	IBM
XSA	Extended Storage Architecture	StorageTek
XSI	X/Open System Interface sa *X/Open*	. . .
Xtal	Crystal re: Piezoelectric crystals used in electronics	
XTE	X-Ray Timing Explorer Part of NASA's *Great Observatory Program, GOP*, which see sa *NASA*	NASA
XTEN	Xerox Telecommunications Network	Xerox
XTI	X/Open Transport Interface sa *X/Open*	X/Open
XMTR	Transmitter	. . .
XTP	Xpress Transfer Protocol	Silicon Graphics
XTPA	Extended Transaction Processing Architecture	Unisys
Xtr	Transmitter Alternate form; see *XMTR*	. . .
XTR	Transmitter Alternate form; see *XMTR*	. . .
XU	X-ray Unit A unit of length equal to 10^{-11} cm	. . .
XUI	X-Windows User Interface re: X-Window standard interface	DEC
XUNET	Experimental University Network	. . .
XUV	Extreme Ultraviolet	. . .

XYL	Ex-Young Lady Amateur radio operators' expression for "wife"	ARRL

Y

Y	—Admittance (symbol) Expressed in units of *Siemens* Named in honor of German/British inventor Sir William Siemens (1823–1883)	. . .
Y	Yttrium Atomic element number 39 Named after Ytterby, Sweden, site of a quarry from which the ore was first obtained	. . .
YAC	Yeast Artificial Chromosome Hybrid human (or other) DNA and yeast DNA used for genetic research; sa *DNA, Deoxyribonucleic Acid*	. . .
YAG	Yttrium-Aluminum-Garnet Laser crystal material	. . .
Yb	Ytterbium Atomic element number 70 Named after Ytterby, Sweden, site of a quarry from which the ore was first obtained	. . .
YBCO	Yttrium Barium Copper Oxygen ($YBa_2Cu_3O_{7-x}$) re: Bolometer fabrication; superconducting thin film	. . .
YIG	Yttrium-Iron-Garnet Farady-rotating magneto-optic material	. . .
YLF	Yttrium Lithium Fluoride Laser crystal	. . .
YP	Yellow Pages A reference dataset in remote procedure call (RPC) environment	. . .
YSZ	Yttria-Stabilized Zircona re: Low thermallly conductive substrate used in bolometry	. . .
YTF	YIG (Yttrium-Iron-Garnet) Tuned Filter Optical laser filter technology	. . .

Z

Z	—Impedance Expressed in units of *Ohms*, &Omega Unit named in honor of German physicist Georg Simon Ohm (1787–1854)	. . .

Z	Z [-fold] re: Printer paper; so-named after the physical appearance of the folded paper; compare with *roll* paper	. . .
ZA	Zero-Adjusted	. . .
ZBR	Zone Bit Recording	Seagate
ZBTSI	Zero Byte Time Slot Interchange	AT&T
ZD	Zero Defect	. . .
ZDP	Zinc Dialkyldithiophosphate Lubricant/anti-oxidant	. . .
ZDR	Zoned Data Recording Computer memory disk recording technique that results in approximately linear recording density Compare with *CDR*, *constant density recording*	. . .
ZGS	Zero Gradient Synchrotron	. . .
ZIF	Zero Insertion Force Integrated circuit (IC) socket designed to accept integrated circuits (ICs) with no vertical pressure	. . .
ZIP	Zigzag In-line Package Packaging technology for densely organized electronic integrated circuit (IC) chips	. . .
ZIP	Zone Information Protocol	US Postal Service
ZMR	Zone-Melt Recrystallization Radiation-resistant transistor (gate) isolation in integrated circuits (ICs)	. . .
Zn	Zinc Atomic element number 30	. . .
Zr	Zirconium Atomic element number 40	. . .
ZSL	Zero Slot LAN sa *LAN, Local Area Network*	. . .
ZTC	Zero Temperature Coefficient	. . .
ZUM	Zoned Usage Messaging re: Charging algorithm for mileage-sensative phone calling	. . .

Numerical

0TLP	Zero Transmission Level Point	. . .
10Base-F	10Base-Fiber Fiber-optic based Ethernet local area network (LAN) standard	IEEE

10Base-T	10Base-Twisted [Pair] 10 MHz data rate Ethernet-over-twisted-pair standard utilizing two twisted pairs	IEEE
10BT	10Base-Twisted [pair] Alternate designation for *10Base-T*, which see	. . .
1553	—1553 Derived from MIL-STD-1553 A data bus used in all major US military aircraft	US
2B1Q	Two binary, one quaternary A digital signal processing (DSP) algorithm for 160 kbps transmission of data over a poor-quality twisted pair	Bellcore
3B2T	Three Binary, Two Tertiary Communications transmission standard designed to maximize error-free usable bandwidth in a two-wire loop	. . .
3-D	Three-Dimensional Also designated by *3D*	. . .
3D	Three-Dimensional Also designated by *3-D*	. . .
3GL	Third Generation Language	. . .
3PG	3-Phosphoglycerate A compound important in biochemistry	. . .
4B3T	Four Binary, Three Tertiary Communications transmission standard designed to maximize error-free usable bandwidth in a two-wire loop	. . .
4fs	4X [oversampled digital] filter sampling re: Digital audio recording (DAR) technology sa n*fs* for the generic form	. . .
4GL	Fourth Generation Language	. . .
5ESS	Five Electronic Signalling System	AT&T
8-DPSK	Octal Differential Phase Shift Keying	. . .
8fs	8 (times oversampled digital) filter sampling re: Digital audio recording (DAR) technology sa n*fs* for the generic form	. . .

Appendix A: Sources

AAC	Account-A-Call Corp.
ACE	Advanced Computer Environments
ACM	Association for Computing Machinery
Acorn	Acorn Data Systems, Inc.
ACUTA	Association of College and University Telecommunications Administrators
Adaptive	Adaptive Corporation
ADCU	Association of Data Communications Users
ADDS	Applied Digital Data Systems, Inc.
Adobe Systems	Adobe Systems, Inc.
ADR	Applied Data Research
Adv. Micro Dev't.	Advanced Micro Development Corp.
Adv. Micro Devices	Advanced Micro Devices
Adv. TV Test Center	Advanced Television Test Center
AEA	American Electronics Association
AEC	Atomic Energy Commission (Now the Nuclear Regulatory Commission)
AFIPS	American Federation of Information Processing Societies
AFRTS	American Forces Radio and Television Service
AFSCC	Air Force Super Computer Center (USAF)
Agronin, M.L., JPL	Agronin, M.L., Jet Propulsion Laboratory (Individual)
AGS	AGS Management Systems, Inc.
AGS/NYNEX	— (See individual entries)
AI	AI Corp.

AIIM	Association for Information and Image Management
AIS	Applied Information Systems, Inc.
Alabama	Alabama, State of
Alacrity Systems	Alacrity Systems, Inc.
Alantec	Alantec (A LAN Technology Company)
Alcatel	Alcatel
Altera	Altera Corporation
AMD	Advanced Micro Devices, Inc.
Amdahl	Amdahl Corp.
Amer. Air.	American Airlines
AMA	American Medical Association
Amer. Mgt. Assoc.	American Management Association
Amer. Phys. Soc.	American Physical Society
American Express	American Express
American Mgt Systems	American Management Systems, Inc. (AMS)
Ameritech	Ameritech Corp.
Ameritech/Bellcore	— (See individual entries)
Ames Research Center	Ames Research Center
AMP	AMP, Inc.
Ampex	Ampex Corp.
AMS	American Management Systems, Inc.
Analogic	Analogic Corp.
ANDIP	American National Dictionary for Information Processing
Andyne Computing	Andyne Computing, Ltd.
Ansa Software	Ansa Software
ANSI	American National Standards Institute
ANU	Australian National University
APOMA	American Precision Optics Manufacturers Association
Apple Computer	Apple Computer, Inc.
Apple/IBM	— (See individual entries)
Applitek	Applitek Corp.
APS	American Physical Society
Aptix	Aptix Corp.
ARC	Automation Research Consultants
Ardire	Ardire, — (Individual)
Ardire, Stratigakis, Hayduk	— (See individual entries)
Arium	Arium Corp.
ARL	Association of Research Libraries
ARMA	American Records Management Association
ARRL	American Radio Relay League
ASA	American Standards Association
ASDL	Advanced Sensor Development Laboratory (NASA)
ASI	American Standards Institute

AST Research	AST Research, Inc.
ASTD	American Society for Training and Development
ASTE	American Society of Test Engineers
ASTIA	Armed Services Technical Information Agency
ASTM	American Society for Testing and Materials
AT&T	American Telephone and Telegraph Corp.
AT&T/Sprint	— (See individual entries)
ATA	Automated Technology Associates
ATAC	Advanced Technology Advisory Committee (NASA)
ATI	ATI, Inc.
ATTC	Advanced Television Test Center
Augat	Augat Alcoswitch
August Systems	August Systems, Inc.
AURA	Association of Universities for Research in Astronomy
Automation Software	Automation Software
AVC	American Valuation Consultants
Avion	Avion Corp.
Aydin	Aydin Controls
Azix	Azix
Dahmani, B. et al.	Dahmani, B. (Individual)
B&B	Boole & Babbage
Ball	Ball Corp.
BARRNet	Bay Area Regional Research Network
BBN	Bolt, Baranek and Neumann, Inc.
BBN/ARPA	— (See individual entries)
BBUG	Boole & Babbage Users Group
Beckman	Beckman Instruments, Inc.
Bell Aerospace	Bell Aerospace
Bell Atlantic	Bell Atlantic
Bell Canada	Bell of Canada
Bell Labs	Bell Laboratories, Inc.
Bell System	Bell System (US)
Bell-Northern	Bell-Northern Research
Bellcore	Bell Communications Research
Bendata	Bendata Management Systems, Inc.
Bendix Research Labs	Bendix Research Laboratories
Bently Nevada	Bently Nevada Corp.
Beryl Bellman	Beryl Bellman
BIH	Bureau Internationale l'Heure (French, International Bureau of Time, Paris, France)
Bio-Optronics	Bio-Optronics
BitWise Designs	BitWise Designs
Bloom, F.	Bloom, Floyd (Individual)
Bloom, F. & Young, W.	— (See individual entries)
BMS	BMS Computer, Inc.

BMW	Bavarian Motor Works
BNL	Brookhaven National Laboratory (Associated Universities, Inc.)
BOC	Bell Operating Companies
Boeing	Boing Aircraft Corporation
Boeing Computer Srvcs.	Boeing Computer Services
Bond, John	Bond, John (Individual)
Boole & Babbage	Boole & Babbage, Inc.
Borland	Borland International
Bower, J.	Bower, J. (Individual)
Bowers, Derek	Bowers, Derek (Individual)
Box Hill	Box Hill
Boyle	Boyle, — (Individual)
Bradley, G.	Bradley, George (Individual)
Braegen	Braegen Associates
Breault Research Org.	Breault Research Organization
Bridge	Bridge Communications, Inc.
British Telecom	British Telecom
British Telecom/MTI	— (See individual entries)
Brooktree	Brooktree Corp.
BRS	BRS Information Technologies
Brunauer	Brunauer, — (Individual)
Brunauer, Emmet and Teller	— (See individual entries)
Bruyn-Ward	Bruyn-Ward
Bull HN Info. Sys.	Bull HN Information Systems, Inc.
Bureau of Land Mgt.	US Bureau of Land Management
Burroughs	Burroughs Corp.
Byte Magazine	*Byte Magazine* (McGraw-Hill, Publ.)
C.T.I.S.	Cahners Technical Information Service
CA	Computer Associates International, Inc.
Cabletron Systems	Cabletron Systems, Inc.
CACI	CACI International
Cadic	Cadic
Cadkey	Cadkey, Inc.
Cadre	Cadre Technologies, Inc.
CAE Plus	CAE Plus Inc.
Caltech/MIT	Calif. Inst. of Tech./Mass. Inst. of Tech.
Cambridge College	Cambridge College of Open Studies (USA)
Cambridge Instruments	Cambridge Instruments
Cambridge/Oxford	— (See individual entries)
Canada	Canada (Country)
Canon	Canon USA, Inc.
CARL	Colorado Alliance of Research Libraries
CARTS	Capacitor and Resistor Technology Symposium
CAST	Center for Advancd Studies in Telecommunications

Caterpillar	Caterpillar Corporation
CBEMA	Computer and Business Equipment Manufacturers Association
CBTA	Canadian Business Telecomm Alliance
CCIR	International Radio Consultative Committee
CCITT	Consultataive Committee on Telephony and Telegraphy
CCT	Comité Cosultatif de Thermometrie (French, International Consutative Committee on Thermometry)
CDC	Centers for Disease Control
CDC	Control Data Corp.
CEC	Consolidated Electrodynamics Corporation
CECOM	Communications and Electronics Command (US Army)
CEPT	Conference of European Postal & Telecommunications
CERC	Concurrent Engineering Research Center (WVU)
CFCC	Central Florida Community College
CFS	CFS, Inc.
Chen	Chen, — (Individual)
Cherry	Cherry Semiconductor Corp.
CHI/COR	CHI/COR Information Management
Chipcom	Chipcom Corp.
Chips & Technologies	Chips & Technologies, Inc.
Ciarcia	Steve Ciarcia (Individual)
CICA	Chicago Industrial Communications Association
CICC	Custom Integrated Circuits Conference
Cincom Systems	Cincom Systems, Inc.
CIPM	Comité Internationale des Poids et Measures (French, International Committee of Weights and Measures)
Cisco Systems	Cisco Systems, Inc.
CLEO	Conference on Lasers and Electro-Optics
CMD	Consultants for Management Decisions
CMU	Carnegie-Mellon University
CMU/Bell of PA	— (See individual entries)
Coastcom	Coastcom, Inc.
Codenoll Tech.	Codenoll Technology, Inc.
Codenoll Tech./GM	— (See individual entries)
Cohen, G., Info. Bldrs.	Cohen, G., Information Builders (Individual)
Colorado Data Sys.	Colorado Data Systems
Columbia Univ.	Columbia University
Comdisco	Comdisco Systems, Inc.
Comm-Pro	Comm-Pro Associates
Compaq	Compaq Computer Corp.

CompuAdd	CompuAdd Corp.
Computer Associates	Computer Associates International, Inc.
Computer Automation	Computer Automation
Computer-X	Computer-X
Compuware	Compuware Corp.
Concelman	Concelman, — (Individual)
Concord Data Systems	Concord Data Systems
Concurrent Technologies	Concurrent Technologies, Inc.
Contel	Contel Business Systems
Core International	Core International
Cornell Univ.	Cornell University
Corning Glass	Corning Glass Works
COS	Corporation for Open Systems
COSI	Center of Science and Industry
CoTRA	Computer Threat Research Association
CPEM	Conference on Precision Electronic Measurements
CPSR	Computer Professionals for Social Responsibility
Cray Research	Cray Research Corp.
Crosspoint	Crosspoint
CSA	Computer System Advisors, Inc.
CSC	The Computer Software Co.
CSG	Cambridge Systems Group, Inc.
CSMC	Communications Services Management Council
CTIA	Cellular Telecommunications Industry Association
CTIS	Cahners Technical Information Service
CTS	CTS Corp.
Culbert	Culbert, —, Johnson Space Center (Individual)
Cullinet Software	Cullinet Software, Inc.
CVIA	Computer Virus Industry Association
CyberOptics	CyberOptics
Cylink	Cylink Corp.
D.O. Industries	D.O. Industries, Inc.
DAC	Design Automation Conference
Dahmani, D.	Dahmani, D. (Individual)
DARPA	Defense Advanced Reasearch Projects Administration (US Department of Defense)
Dartmouth Univ.	Dartmouth University
Data General	Data General Corp.
Data I/O	Data I/O Corp.
Data/Ware Development	Data/Ware Development, Inc.
Datability Software	Datability Software Systems
Datachron	Datachron
DataEase Int'l.	DataEase International, Inc.
Datalogix	Datalogix International
Datapoint	Datapoint Corp.
David Sarnoff Res.	David Sarnoff Research

DCA	Digital Communications Associates
DEC	Digital Equipment Corp.
DEC/Atherton	– (See individual entries)
DEC et al.	Digital Equipment Corp.
Decco	Defense Commercial Communications Office
Defense Logistics Agy.	US Defense Logistics Agency
Destiny Technology	Destiny Technology Corp.
DICE	DARPA Initiative in Concurrent Engineering (US Department of Defense)
Digital Pathways	Digital Pathways, Inc.
Digital Research	Digital Research
DIN	Deutches Institut für Normung (German, German Institute for Standards)
DMA	Defense Mapping Agency (US Department of Defense)
DoD	United States Department of Defense
DoD/AT&T	– (See individual entries)
DoE	United States Department of Energy
Dome	Dome Imaging Systems, Inc.
Don Small Optics	Don Small Optics
Dougenik & Sheehan	Dougenik & Sheehan
Dow Corning	Dow Corning Glass Works
DP-Tek	DP-Tek, Inc.
DR	Digital Research
DSB	Defense Science Board (DoD)
DSP Development	DSP Development Corp.
DSS	Dylaker Software Systems, Inc.
Dun & Bradstreet	Dun & Bradstreet
DuPont	E.I. DuPont de Nemours & Co.
DuPont Pixel Systems	DuPont Pixel Systems
Duquesne Systems	Duquesne Systems, Inc.
E & S Computer	Evans & Southerland Computer
Echelon	Echelon Systems, Inc.
Eckert	Eckert, J. Presper (Individual)
Eckert & Mauchly	– (See individual entries)
ECMA	European Computer Manufacturers Association
EDIA	Electronics Data Industry Association
EDS	Electronic Data Systems Corp.
Educational Testing Service	Educational Testing Service (ETS)
EIA	Electronics Industries Associates
EIAJ	Electronics Industry Association of Japan
Electronic Data Sys.	Electronic Data Systems Corp. (EDS).
Electronic Decisions	Electronic Decisions Inc.
Elgar	Elgar Corp.
Emmett	Emmett, – (Individual)

EMPF	Electronics Manufacturing Productivity Facility (US Navy)
ENTELEC	Energy Telecommunications and Electrical Association
Enzyme Commission	Enzyme Commission
EPA	Environmental Protection Agency (US)
Epoch Systems	Epoch Systems
EPRI	Electric Power Research Institute
EPS	European Physical Society
Equinox	Equinox Data Systems
ERIM	—
ESA	European Space Agency
ESnet	Energy Services Network
ESNIB	European Science News Information Bulletin
ESO	European Southern Observer
ETCOM	European Testing for Certification of Office and Manufacture
ETSI	European Telecommunications Standards Institute
European Community	European Community
EWOS	European Workshop on Open Systems
EXOS	EXOS, Inc.
FAA	Federal Aviation Administration (US)
FACT	Federation of Automated Coding Technologies
Fairchild	Fairchild Electronics
Fairchild Space	Fairchild Space Electronics, Inc.
FARNET	Federation of American Research Networks
FBI	Federal Bureau of Investigation
FCC	Federal Communications Commission (US)
FCLA	Florida Center for Library Automation
FCRDC	Frederick Cancer Research & Development Center
Feher, K.	Feher, K. (Individual)
Fluke	John Fluke Corp.
Focal Point	Focal Point, Inc.
Force Computers	Force Computers, Inc.
Ford	Ford Motor Company
FortuNet	FortuNet, Inc.
Fotec	Fiber Optic Technologies, Inc.
Frame Technology	Frame Technology Corp.
France	France (country)
France Telecom	France Telecom
Frequency Electronics	Frequency Electronics, Inc.
Fritz, J., WVU	Fritz, Jeffrey, West Virginia University (Individual)
FSI	Foresight Systems, Inc.
Fujitsu	Fujitsu Microelectronics, Inc.
GBA	GBA International
GDR	German Democratic Republic
GE	General Electric Co.

GE/Honeywell	— (See individual entries)
General DataComm	General DataComm
General Motors	General Motors Corp.
General Radio	General Radio (Now Genrad)
General Telephone	General Telephone
Genrad	Genrad (Formerly General Radio)
GeoSpectra	GeoSpectra Corp.
Geostar	Geostar, Inc.
Geoworks	Geoworks, Inc.
Gibson Optics	Gibson Optics
GigaTrend	GigaTrend, Inc.
GM	General Motors Corp.
GMIS	Government Management Information Services
Goal	Goal Systems, Inc.
Goddard Space Flt. Ctr.	Goddard Space Flight Center
Gould Electronics	Gould Electronics
GPO	Government Printing Office (US)
Grammar Engine	Grammar Engine
Greyhawk Systems	Greyhawk Systems
Grumman	Grumman Corp.
Grumman Data Systems	Grumman Data Systems
GSA	General Services Administration (US)
GSS	Graphic Software Systems, Inc.
GTE	General Telephone and Electronics
H-P	Hewlett-Packard
H-P/Sony	— (See individual entries)
H-P/Sun Microsystems	— (See individual entries)
Harris Semiconductor	Harris Semiconductor, Inc.
Harvard Univ.	Harvard University
Hawaii	Hawaii, State of
Hayduk	Hayduk, — (Individual)
Hayes	Hayes Microcomputer Products
Hearst	Hearst Publications, Inc.
Held, D. N.	Held, D. N., Jet Propolsion Laboratory (Individual)
Henderson, John, MPRL	Henderson, John, Military Physics Research Laboratory (Individual)
Hitachi	Hitachi Electronics
HNC	HNC, Inc.
Honda, T.	Honda, T., Tokyo Institute of Technology (Individual)
Honeywell	Honeywell Data Systems
Honeywell/Intel	— (See individual entries)
Honeywell, IBM	— (See individual entries)
Hong Kong	Hong Kong
Hudson Laboratories	Hudson Laboratories
Hughes	Hughes Aircraft/Industrial Prods.

Hunter	—
Hussey, K.	Hussey, K. (Individual)
Hutchinson, T.	Hutchinson, Thomas (Individual)
IAS	Institute for Advanced Study
IBM	International Business Machines, Inc.
IBM/Microsoft	— (See individual entries)
IBM/MPRL	— (See individual entries)
IBM/Univ. of Wash.	— (See individual entries)
IBM/3Com	— (See individual entries)
IBM,TSC	— (See individual entries)
ICA	International Communications Association
ICSTI	International Centre for Scientific and Technical Information
ICT	In-Circuit Test
ICTP	International Center for Theoretical Physics
IDA	Institute for Defense Analysis
IE	Innovative Engineering
IEC	International Electrotechnical Commission
IEEE	Institute of Electrical and Electronics Engineers
IETF	Internet Engineering Task Force
IFIP	International Federation for Information Processing
IICIT	International Institute of Connector and Interconnection Technology
IIE	Institute of Industrial Engineers
III, Taiwan	—
IIT	Integrated Information Technology, Inc.
Illinois Capacitor	Illinois Capacitor Corp.
ILRC	International Laser Radar Conference
ILTA	International Laser Therapy Association
Imaging Technology	Imaging Technology, Inc.
IMSL	International Mathematical and Statistical Libraries
Indiana Univ.	
Infinity	Infinity Systems, Inc.
Infinity Photo-Opt.	Infinity Photo-Optical Co.
Infonet	Infonet
Informatics	Informatics, Inc.
Information Bldrs.	Information Builders, Inc.
Innovation Data Proc.	Innovation Data Processing
Innovation Software	Innovation Software
Int'l. Meta Systems	International Meta Systems
Int'l. Rectifier	International Rectifier
Intel	Intel Corp.
Intellicorp	Intellicorp
INTELSAT	International Telecommunications Satellite Corp.
Interactive Software	Interactive Software
Interactive Systems	Interactive Systems, Inc.

Intercomputer Comm.	Intercomputer Communications Corp.
Intergraph	Intergraph Corp.
Interlan	Interlan
Internet	Internet (National Science Foundation)
INTUG	International Telecommunications Users Group
IPNS Forum	Alcatel N.V., Siemens AG, et al.
IPPG	Integrated Police Planning Group
IQEC	International Quantum Electronics Conference
ISA	Insurance Systems of North America
ISD	—
ISHM	International Society for Hybrid Microelectronics
ISI	Integrated Solutions, Inc.
ISO	International Standards Organization
ISSCC	International Solid State Circuits Conference
ISTE	International Society of Technology in Education
ITT	International Telephone and Telecommunications Corp.
IUPAC	International Union of Pure and Applied Chemistry
IUPAP	International Union of Pure and Applied Physics
Iwatsu America	Iwatsu America
JAERI	Japan Atomic Energy Research Institute
Japan	Japan
JBM Electronics	JBM Electronics
JFK Space Ctr.	John Fitzgerald Kennedy Space Center (NASA)
JMITI	Japanese Ministry of International Trade & Industry
Johns Hopkins Univ.	The Johns Hopkins University
Johnson	Johnson Systems, Inc.
Johnson Space Center	John Space Center
Joing Electronics	Joing Electronics, Inc.
JPL	Jet Propulsion Laboratory
JSI	Johnson Systems International
JTAG	Joint Test Action Group
JvNC	John von Neumann National Supercomputer Center
Kato, M.	Kato, M., Tokyo Institute of Technology (Individual)
Keithly	Keithly Instruments, Inc.
Kent State University	Kent State University
Kilby	Kilby, — (Individual)
KnowledgeWare	KnowledgeWare, Inc.
Knuth, Donald	Knuth, Donald (Individual)
Kodak	Eastman Kodak Company
Kofax	Kofax Image Products, Inc.
Koh-I-Noor	Koh-I-Noor, Inc.
Krenz	Krenz Electronics
Lambda Electronics	Lambda Electronics, Inc.
Land Rover Parts	Land Rover Parts, Ltd.

Langley Research Ctr.	Langley Research Center (US Department of Defense)
LANL	Los Alamos National Laboratory (US Department of Defense)
Larse	—
Larse/Telenex	— (See individual entries)
Laser Technology	Laser Technology
LBL	Lawrence Berkeley Laboratory
Lempel	Lempel (Individual)
Lempel, Ziv, Welch	— (See individual entries)
Lexmark	Lexmark International
LLNL	Lawrence Livermore National Laboratory (US Department of Defense)
Lockheed Aero.	Lockheed Aerospace
Lopez	Lopez, —, Johnson Space Center (Individual)
Lotus	Lotus Development Corp.
Lotus/IBM/Apple	— (See individual entries)
Lotus/Intel/Microsoft	— (See individual entries)
LURE	Laboratoire pour l'Utilisation du Rayonnment Electromagnetique (French, Laboratory for the Utilzation of Electromagnetic Radiation)
M/A-Com	M/A-Com
Marble Computer	Marble Computer Corp.
Mass. Gen. Hosp	Massachusetts General Hospital
Masstor	—
Matra-Marconi	Matra-Marconi Space
Matrix Imaging Sys.	Matrix Imaging Systems
Mauchly	Mauchly, John W. (Individual)
Max Planck	Max Planck Institute
McCarthy, John	McCarthy, John, Stanford University (Individual)
MCET	Massachusetts Corporation for Educational Telecommunications
MCS	Management and Computer Services
Memorex	Memorex Corp.
Mentat	—
Mentor Graphics	Mentor Graphics
Merit Network	Merit Network; University of Michigan
Meta	—
Metafile	Metafile Information Systems, Inc.
METRAN	Managed European Transmission Network
Metro. Fiber Sys.	Metropolitan Fiber Systems
MGA	Mitchell & Ganthier Associates
Micom	Micom Communications Corp.
Micro Linear	Micro Linear Corp.
Micro Technology	Micro Technology, Inc.
Microrim	Microrim, Inc.

Microsoft	Microsoft Corp.
Microstar Labs	Microstar Laboratories
Microtest	Microtest Inc.
Microware Systems	Microware Systems
Mietec Alcatel	Mietec Alcatel, Brussels, Belguim
Millicom	Millicom Radio Telephone Co.
Mincom	Mincom Ltd.
Mini-Circuits	Mini-Circuits
MIT	Massachusetts Institute of Technology
Mitech	Mitech Corp.
Mitsubishi	Mitsubishi America
MMA	Microcomputers Managers Association
Molecular Design	Molecular Design, Ltd.
Monolithic Mem.	Monolithic Memories, Inc.
Morino	Morino Associates
Morris, S. et al.	Morris, S. (Individual)
Mosaic Sys.	Mosaic Systems
Motorola	Motorola, Inc.
Motorola/Ford	— (See individual entries)
MPEG	Motion Picture Experts Group
MPRL	Military Physics Research Laboratory, The University of Texas
MRNet	Minnesota Regional Network
MSA	Management Science America
MTC	Midwestern Telecommunications Association
MTTA	Multi Tenant Telecommunications Association
Multiflow	—
N.V. Philips	N.V. Philips
NAB	National Association of Broadcasters
NAC	Naval Avionics Center
NAEB	North American EDIFACT Board
NAG	National Algorithms Group
NAIS	National Association for Information Systems
NANPA	North American Numbering Plan Administration
NARA	National Archives and Records Administration
NARTE	National Association of Radio and Telecommunications Engineers
NARUC	National Association of Regulatory Utilities Commissioners
NASA	National Aeronautics and Space Administration (US)
NASD	National Association of Securities Dealers
NASIS	National Association for State Information Systems
NASTD	National Association of State Telecommunications Directors
Nat'l. Astro. Observ.	National Astronomical Observatory, Japan

Nat'l. Semiconductor	National Semiconductor, Inc.
NATA	North American Telecommunications Association
National Instruments	National Instruments
National Semicond.	National Semiconductor
NBS	National Bureau of Standards (See NIST)
NCAR	National Center for Atmospheric Research
NCBN	National Carriers Buyers Network
NCC	National Computer Conference
NCGA	National Computer Graphics Association
NCI	National Cancer Institute
NCI/FCRDC	— (See individual entries)
NCR	National Cash Register
NCR Comten	NCR Comten (A subsidiary of NCR)
NCS	National Communications System
NCSA	National Center for Supercomputer Applications
NCSA	National Computer Security Association
NCSL	National Council of Standards Laboratories
nCUBE	nCUBE
NCUG	National Centrex Users Group
NEARnet	New England Academic and Research network
NEC	Nippon Electronics Corp., NEC America
Neill	Neill, — (Individual)
Neill and Concelman	— (See individual entries)
NELC	Naval Electronics Laboratory Center (US Navy)
NEMA	National Electrical Manufacturers Association
NET	Network Equipment Technologies, Inc.
NETA	New England Telecommunications Association
Network-1	Network-1, Inc.
NeXT	NeXT Computer Corp.
Nikon	Nippon Kogaku
Nippon Tel. & Tel.	Nippon Telegraph & Telephone (Japan)
NIS	National Information Systems, Inc.
NISO	National Information Standards Organization
NIST	National Institute of Standards and Technology (Formerly, NBS, National Bureau of Standards)
NNSC	National Science Foundation Network Service Center
NOAA	National Oceanic and Atmospheric Association
NOAO	National Optical Astronomy Observatory (Association of Universities for Research in Astronomy)
Northern Telecom	Northern Telecom, Inc.
NOSC	Naval Ocean Systems Center (US Navy)
Novell	Novell, Inc.
Novell/Apple	— (See individual entries)
Noyce	Noyce, — (Individual)

Noyce & Kilby	– (See individual entries)
NPR	National Public Radio
NPT, UK	–
NRC	Nuclear Regulatory Commission
NRI	National Research Institute
NRN	National Research Network
NSC	Network Steering Committee
NSF	National Science Foundation
NSTL	National Software Testing Laboratory (US)
NTIA	National Telecommunications and Information Agency
NTIS	National Technical Information Service
NTN	National Telecommunications Network
NTT	Nippon Telephone and Telegraph
NWC	Naval Weapons Center (US Navy)
NY Times	New York Times, Inc.
NYNEX	NYNEX Communications
NYU	New York University
O'Neill Comm.	O'Neill Communications
OACIS	Oregon Advanced Computing Institute
OBS	On-Line Business Systems, Inc.
OCLC	On-Line College Library Corp. (Formerly Ohio College Library Center)
Octel Comm.	Octel Communications Corp.
Odetics	Odetics
Ohmi/Shibata	Tadahiro Ohmi/Tadashi Shibata
OITDA	Optoelectronic Industry Technology Development Association
Olympus	Olympus Optical Co.
OMB	Object Management Group
OMG	OMG Consortium
On-Line	On-Line Data Systems, Inc.
Optical Associates	Optical Associates
Optipro	Optipro, Inc.
Optotech	Optotech Corp.
Oracle	Oracle Corp.
Orbit Semiconductor	Orbit Semiconductor
ORNL	Oak Ridge National Laboratory (Associated Universities, Inc.)
OSA	Optical Society of America
OSA	Optical Society of America
OSC	Oxford Software Corp.
OSHA	Occupational Safety and Health Administration
Outlook Technology	–
Oxford	Oxford University
P-W	Price-Waterhouse

Pacific Bell	Pacific Bell
Page Studio Graphics	Page Studio Graphics
Palette	Palette Systems, Inc.
Pansophic	Pansophic Systems, Inc.
Paradyne	Paradyne Corp.
Parallel	Parallel Resources, Inc.
Paralog	Paralog
PBS	Public Broadcasting System
PCSI	Pacific Communications Sciences, Inc.
Philips Telecom	Philips Telecom
PictureTel	PictureTel
Pilot Executive Softw	Pilot Executive Software
Pirelli	Pirelli Armstrong Tire Corp.
Planck, Max	Planck, Max (Individual)
PlanPrint	—
Podolsky/Morehouse	—
Polytechnic of Wales	Polytechnic of Wales
Polytechnic Univ.	Polytechnic University
Popular Photography	*Popular Photography* (Hachette Magazines, Inc.)
POSI	Promoting Conference for Operating Systems Interconnection
PRC	Plastic Reel Corporation of America
Precision Visuals	Precision Visuals, Inc.
PREPnet	Pennsylvania Research and Economic Partnership network
Price, John	Price, John (Individual)
Prime	Prime Computer Corp.
PRL	Philips Research Laboratories (Div. of Signetics Corp.)
PRL/Signetics	— (See individual entries)
Prog. Intell.	Programmed Intelligence Corp.
PSC	Pittsburgh Supercomputer Center
PSI	Performance Systems International
PTAT Systems	Private Trans-Atlantic Telecommunications Systems
PTO	Patent and Trademark Office (US)
QStar	QStar Technologies, Inc.
RAC	Reliability Analysis Center
Racal-Milgo	Racal-Milgo
Racal-Vadic	Racal-Vadic
RAD	RAD Data Communications, Ltd.
RAD Network Devices	RAD Network Devices
Ramtron	Ramtron Corp.
Rand	Rand Corp.
Rapid Systems Dev't.	Rapid Systems Development, Inc.
Raytheon	Raytheon Co.
RCA	Radio Corp. of America

Reactel	—
Reader's Digest	Reader's Digest Association, Inc.
Reeves	Reeves Electrodynamics Corp.
Reeves, R., (OSU)	Reeves, Roy, The Ohio State University (Individual)
Rensselear P.I.	Rensselear Polytechnic Institute
Republic Technology	Republic Technology Corp.
Republic Telcom Sys.	Republic Telcom Systems Corp.
RETMA	Radio Electronics Television Manufacturers Association
Riley	Riley, —, Johnson Space Center (Individual)
Riley, Culbert, Lopez	— (See individual entries)
RLIN	Research Libraries Information Network
Robbins-Gioia	Robbins-Gioia Inc.
Rock Ridge Group	—
Rockwell	Rockwell International
Rohlf, Kishpaugh	—
ROSH Intelligent Sys.	ROSH Intelligent Systems
RTT	Regie des Télégraphes et des Téléphones (French, Telegraph and Telephone Administration) (National carrier of Belgium)
RTT/Alcatel-Bell	— (See individual entries)
Sadr, Ramin, JPL	Sadr, Ramin, Jet Propulsion Laboratory
SAE	Society of Automotive Engineers
Sage Systems	Sage Systems
Samtec	—
Sanders Associates	Sanders Associates
SAS	SAS Institute, Inc.
SCAT Conference	Smart Card Applications & Technology Conference
SCC	Systems Compatability Corporation
Schiesser, W.E.	Schiesser, W.E.
Schlumberger	Schlumberger Technologies
Schneider & Koch	—
SCO	The Santa Cruz Operation, Inc.
SCOPE	Scientific Committee on Problems of the Environment
SCS	Society for Computer Simulation
SCT	Systems and Computer Technology
SDIO	Strategic Defense Initiative Organization
SDIO/Ball	— (See individual entries)
SDSC	San Diego Supercomputer Center
Seagate	Seagate Technology
SEC	Securities and Exchange Commission
Sequel Data Systems	Sequel Data Systems
SETA	South Eastern Telecommunications Association

Sherpa	Sherpa Corp.
SIA	Semiconductor Industry Association
Siemens	Siemens Corp.
Siemens Med. Sys.	Siemens Medical Systems
Siemens/Gandalf	— (See individual entries)
Sigma Systems	Sigma Systems, Inc.
Signetics	Signetics Corp.
Sikorsky Aircraft	Sikorsky Aircraft
Silicon Systems	—
SiScan Systems	—
SL	SL Corp.
Smith	Smith, — (Individual)
Smith, Boyle, et al.	— (See individual entries)
SMPTE	Society for Motion Picture and Television Engineering
SMS	System Management Software
SMTCON	Surface Mount Technology Conference
SNA	Software Associates of North America
SNA	Software Associates of North America
SNL	Sandia National Laboratory
Softw. Div. Srvcs.	Software Diversified Services
Softw. Sys.	Software Systems, Inc.
Software A&E	Software Architecture & Engineering
Software AG	Software AG
Software Publishing	Software Publishing Corp.
Sonotek	Sonotek
Sony	Sony Corp.
Soterem	—
SPAG	Standards Promotion and Applications Group
SPC	Software Productivity Consortium
Spectra-Physics	Spectra-Physics, Inc.
Spectron	Spectron Microsystems, Inc.
Sperry	Sperry Computer
SPIE	Society of Photo-Optical Instrumentation Engineers
SPSS	SPSS, Inc.
SQE	Software Quality Engineering
SSS	Systems Support Software, Inc.
Stanford University	Stanford University
Stardent	Stardent Computer, Inc.
StatSoft	StatSoft, Inc.
STC	Science & Technology Center
Stephenson, Brad	Stephensen, Brad (Individual)
Sterling Software	Sterling Software, Inc.
Storage Concepts	Storage Concepts, Inc.
StorageTek	StorageTek
Stratigakis	Stratigakis, — (Individual)

Stratus	Stratus Computer, Inc.
Strohl Systems	Stroll Systems
STScI	Space Telescope Science Institute
Sudbury Systems	Sudbury Systems
Sun Microsystems	Sun Microsystems
SUNET	Swedish University Network
SUPER!	Supercomputing by University People for Education and Research
SURA	Southeastern Universities Research Association
Sweden	Sweden (country)
SWIFT	Society for Worldwide Interbank Financial Telecommunication
Sybase	Sybase, Inc.
Sylvania	GTE Sylvania, Inc.
Symplex	—
Synergy	Synergy, Inc.
SynOptics	SynOptics
Syracuse Univ.	Syracuse University
Systems Center	The Systems Center, Inc.
S3	S3, Inc.
TAC	Telecommunications Association Council
Tandem Computers	Tandem Computers, Inc.
Tandy/R-S	Tandy Corp. (Radio Shack)
Tanzer, H.	Tanzer, H., Langley Research Center (Individual)
Tavaglione, D.	Tavaglione, David, West Virginia Network for Educational Telecomputing (Individual)
Taylor, S.A.	Taylor, S.A. (Individual)
TCA	Telecommunications Association Council
Tecelec	Tecelec
Technoexan	—
TechView	—
Tekelec	Tekelec
Tektronix	Tektronix, Inc.
Tel Plus Comm.	Tel Plus Communications
Telcom	Telcom Technologies
Telebit	Telebit Corp.
Telenex	—
Teleos	Teleos Communications, Inc.
Telesystems SLW	Telesystems SLW, Inc.
Teletype	Teletype Corp.
Telex	Telex Communications, Inc.
Teller	Teller, — (Individual)
Temco	—
Temple Univ.	Temple University
Ten X Technology	Ten X Technology, Inc.
Teradyne	Teradyne, Inc.

TeraPlex	TeraPlex Inc.
TERN Participants	TERN Participants:
	Ball State University
	Barry College
	California State University
	Carnegie-Mellon University
	Christian Brothers College
	City University of New York
	De Paul University
	George Washington University
	Georgia Institute of Technology
	Golden Gate University
	Illinois State University
	Michigan State University
	New York Institute of Technology
	Northwestern University
	Ohio University
	Polytechnic Institute of New York
	Rochester Institute of Technology
	Stanford University
	Texas A&M University
	The University of Colorado
	The University of Houston
	The University of Kansas
	The University of Maryland
	The University of Mississippi
	The University of Missouri
	The University of Pittsburgh
	The University of San Francisco
	The University of Southwestern Louisana
	The University of Texas
TI	Texas Instruments, Inc.
TIA	Telecommunications Industry Association
Time Share	Time Share, Inc.
Time-Life	Time-Life, Inc.
Timeline	Timeline Corp.
Timeplex	Timeplex, Inc. —
Timeview	—
TMA	Telecommunications Managers Association
Tollgrade	Tollgrade Communications
Toshiba	Toshiba Electronics
TPA	Telephone Pioneers of America
Trident Technologies	Trident Technologies, Inc.
TRW	TRW, Inc. (Formerly Thompson-Ramo-Wooldridge)
TSI-Horsham	—
Tukey, John W.	Tukey, John W. (Individual)

TX Dept. of Higher Ed.	Texas Department of Higher Education
UC-Berkeley	Univ. of California at Berkeley
UCC	University Computing Co.
UCLA	Univ. of California at Los Angeles
UI	Unix International
UL	Underwriters Laboratories
UNISYS	UNISYS Corp.
United Kingdom	United Kingdom
Univ. of Cambridge	University of Cambridge, UK
Univ. of Central Fla.	University of Central Florida
Univ. of Delaware	University of Delaware
Univ. of Illinois	University of Illinois
Univ. of Karlsruhe	University of Karlsruhe
Univ. of Lowell	University of Lowell
Univ. of MD	University of Maryland
Univ. of MO	University of Missouri
Univ. of Okla.	University of Oklahoma
Univ. of SF	University of San Francisco
Univ. of So. Fla.	University of Southern Florida
Univ. of Texas	University of Texas
Univ. of Waterloo	University of Waterloo
Univ. of Wisconsin	University of Wisconsin
UPS	United Parcel Service, Inc.
US	United States
US Air Force	United States Air Force
US Air Force (SAC)	United States Air Force, Strategic Air Command
US Armed Forces	United States Armed Forces
US Army	United States Army
US Census Bureau	United States Census Bureau
US Coast Guard	United States Coast Guard
US Congress	United States Congress
US Customs	United States Customs Department
US Dept. of Commerce	United States Department of Commerce
US Dept. of H & HS	United States Department of Health and Human Services
US Dept. of Interior	United States Department of the Interior
US Dept. of Justice	United States Department of Justice
US Dept. of State	United States Department of State
US Government	United States Government (general)
US Marine Corps	United States Marine Corps
US Navy	United States Navy
US Navy/Raytheon	— (See individual entries)
US Postal Service	United States Postal Service
US Sprint	US Sprint
US West Comm	US West Communications Group Inc.
US White House	United States White House

US/Canada	— See individual entries
US/CCITT	— See individual entries
USA	United States of America
USA, USSR et al	— (See individual entries)
USC	University of Southern California
USFS	United States Forest Service
USI	Universal Software, Inc.
UTMC	United Technologies Microelectronics Center
VA	Veterans Administration (US)
Varian	Varian Associates
Varian/H-P	— (See individual entries)
Verdix	—
VESA	Video Electronics Standards Association
VIA Technologies	—
Vidicom	—
Virginia Tech	Virginia Institute of Technology
VISA	Video Electronic Standards Association
Vitalink	Vitalink Communications Corp.
VITec	Visual Information Technologies, Inc.
Vizard, Michael	Vizard, Michael (Individual)
VME Int'l. Trade Assoc.	VME International Trade Association
VOA	Voice of America
VTC	VTC, Inc.
VXM Technologies	VXM Technologies, Inc.
Walker Richer & Quinn	Walker Richer & Quinn, Inc.
Wang	Wang Data Systems. Inc.
WARC	World Administrative Radio Conference
Welch	Welch, — (Individual)
Wells, D.	Wells, D., Johnson Space Center (Individual)
Western Union	Western Union Corp.
Westinghouse	Westinghouse Corp.
Westnet	Westnet (regional network)
Williams Telecomm	Williams Telecommunications Group
WITS	Washington Interagency Telecommunications System
Wollongong Group	Wollongong Group
WordPerfect	WordPerfect Corp.
World Bank	World Bank
WSTA	Wall Street Telecommunications Agency
WU	Western Union Corp.
WVNET	West Virginia Network for Educational Telecomputing
WVU	West Virginia University
X/Open	X/Open Company, Ltd.
Xerox	Xerox Corp.

Xyplex	Xyplex, Inc.
Young, W.	Young, Warren (Individual)
Ziatech	Ziatech Corp.
Zilog	Zilog, Inc.
Ziv	Ziv (Individual)
Ztel	Ztel
3-D Systems	3-D Systems
3Com	3Com Corp.
3M	3M Corp.

Appendix B:
Recommended References

The following works are recommended as additional sources of acronyms, abbreviations, contractions, and their meanings.

1. Robert C. Weast, Editor (1987). *Handbook of Chemistry and Physics*, 68th edition, Chemical Rubber Publishing Company.

   The perennial standard of chemistry and physics. This text contains a wealth of information on all aspects of chemistry and physics, and the mathematics required in both disciplines. Also included are numerous tables and lists of definitions. The most recently adopted standards in symbols and abbreviations are clearly detailed.

2. L. E. C. Hughes, R. W. B. Stephens, L. D. Brown, editors (1970). *Chambers Dictionary of Electronics and Nucleonics*, Barnes and Noble, New York.

    Numerous lists, charts, and tables add to the understanding of a large variety of electronic and nucleonic terms. A table of abbreviations, acronyms and symbols is included at the beginning of the book. The main body of the text contains clear and concise definitions and explanations of the terms.

3. Frank Jay, editor in chief (1984). *IEEE Standard Dictionary of Electrical and Electronics Terms*, third edition, The Institute of Electrical and Electronic Engineers, with Wiley-Interscience, New York.

    The obvious standard for electrical and electronic engineers. A table of some 10,000 acronyms is included. The text will clarify many questions and aid understanding of terms associated with this field.

4. Martin H. Weik, editor (1983). *Communications Standard Dictionary*, Van Nostrand Reinhold Company, New York.

    No separate tables appear in this text. Acronyms are included in the definitions of the terms. Thus, the expansion of an acronym must be known before the definition or explanation can be looked up. Nevertheless, this text provides an excellent source for understanding communications terms.

5. Milton Abramowitz and Irene A. Stegun, editors (1972). *Handbook of Mathematical Functions with Formulas, Graphs, and Mathematical Tables*, U.S. Department of Commerce, National Bureau of Standards.

    There are no lists of acronyms as such, but all the major physical and mathematical constants (such as e, pi, Planck's constant, h, etc.,) are listed to many decimal places.

6. Robert C. James and Edwin F. Beckenbach (1976). *Mathematics Dictionary*, fourth edition, D. Van Nostrand Company, Inc.

    A good source for understanding mathematecal terms, this book includes tables of symbols, which are not covered in this directory.

7. IBM Corporation (1981). *Vocabulary for Data Processing, Telecommunications, and Office Systems*, seventh edition, IBM Corp.

    This publication not only expands IBM's acronyms, but also explains their meanings. Some non-IBM terms are included. Also included are words (as opposed to acronyms or abbreviations) and phrases along with their meaning.

8. IBM Corporation (1987). *Dictionary of Computing*, eighth edition, IBM Corp.

    A compendium of more than 12,000 terms used in information processing, telecommunications, and office systems. Abbreviations are cross-referenced, making it easier to look up unfamiliar terms. This is a revised, updated, and illustrated version of the text listed above and includes many non-IBM-specific terms and expressions. This book is highly rccommended as a valuable addition to any data processing or telecommunications professional's library.

9. F. Mazda, editor (1985). *Electronic Engineer's Reference Book*, fifth edition: Butterworth and Company.

    A well-organized reference work, with extensive tables, lists, and charts on numerous physical and mathematical constants. Included are an abundance of symbols not included as a part of this directory. The book also includes an expansive listing of references.

10. Harold C. Folts, editor (1986). *Data Communications Standards*, third edition, McGraw-Hill Information Systems Company.

    For a detailed description of all communications standards in this directory, plus many others, this is the official reference.

11. Julie Towell and Helen E. Sheppard, editors (1987). *Acronyms, Initialisms and Abbreviations Dictionary*, tenth edition, Gale Research Company.

    A huge compilation (over 340,000 entries) in three large volumes, this collection includes abbreviations of groups, clubs, businesses, organizations, etc., as well as many acronyms and abbreviations of technical origin.

12. Charles J. Sippl and Charles P. Sippl (1972). *Computer Dictionary and Handbook*, Howard W. Sams and Company, Incorporated, The Bobbs-Merrill Company, Inc., New York.

    Typical of Howard Sams publications—clear, yet thorough (778 pages).

13. Jack Belzer, Albert G. Holzmann, Allen Kent, Executive Editors (1975). *Encyclopedia of Computer Science and Technology*, Marcel Dekker, Inc., New York.

    An excellent multi-volume source of "how it works" type of information, complete with diagrams, drawings, and clear text. Recommended for a clear understanding of the intricacies of computer science, communications, and technology in general.

14. Allen G. Debus, Editor (1968). *World Who's Who in Science*, Marquis-Who's Who, Inc., Chicago, Illinois.

    Claimed as "A biographical dictionary of notable scientists from antiquity to the present," this is where to find the complete works of the world's famous scientists, past and present.

15. Isaac Asimov (1972). *Asimov's Biographical Encyclopedia of Science and Technology*, Doubleday and Company, Inc., Garden City, New York.

    A concise, yet rich source of biographical information.

16. Charles Coulston Gillispie, Editor in Chief (1970). *Dictionary of Scientific Biography*, Charles Scribner's Sons, New York.

    This work contains detailed accounts of the major discoveries, inventions, and developments of history.

17. Jennifer Mossman (1992). *Acronyms, Initialisms and Abbreviations Dictionary*, 16th Edition, Gale Research, Inc., Detroit, Michigan

    A monumental work with very broad coverage, this is not a "desk reference," but certainly a valuable addition to any library.

18. Ralph de Sola (1992). *Abbreviations Dictionary*, 8th edition, CRC Press, Boca Raton, Florida

    This is another general coverage book, with 1300 pages and over 60,000 entries.

19. William R. Evinger (1989). *Guide to Federal Government Acronyms*, Oryx Press, Phoenix, Arizona.

    This is a specialized and very complete collection. 279 pages.